AMERICAN SCREENWRITERS

AMERICAN SCREENWRITERS

KARL SCHANZER &
THOMAS LEE WRIGHT

AVON BOOKS ▲ NEW YORK

AMERICAN SCREENWRITERS is an original publication of Avon Books. This work has never before appeared in book form.

AVON BOOKS
A division of
The Hearst Corporation
1350 Avenue of the Americas
New York, New York 10019

Copyright © 1993 by Thomas Lee Wright and Karl Schanzer
Published by arrangement with the authors
Library of Congress Catalog Card Number: 93-439
ISBN: 0–380–76727–9

Library of Congress Cataloging in Publication Data:

American screenwriters / [introduction and commentary by] Karl
   Schanzer and Thomas Lee Wright.
      p.   cm.
      Contains contributions by and about a diverse sampling of American screenwriters.
      1. Motion   picture   authorship.   2. Screenwriters—United   States—Interviews.
   I. Schanzer, Karl.   II. Wright, Thomas Lee, 1953-
   PN1996.A635 1993   93-439
   808.2'3—dc20   CIP

First Avon Books Trade Printing: August 1993

AVON TRADEMARK REG. U.S. PAT. OFF. AND IN OTHER COUNTRIES, MARCA REGISTRADA, HECHO EN U.S.A.

Printed in the U.S.A.

OPM   10   9   8   7   6   5   4   3   2   1

A great many people have contributed to this effort either directly or through their support behind-the-scenes. We'd like to single out just a few here . . .

We owe Eric Ashworth, our indefatigable agent, a debt of thanks for finding a home for this tome with a top-flight publisher, Mark Gompertz, and editor, David Highfill. Helping to find the right interviewees was an often daunting task made easier by friends like Lindsay Doran, Riley Kathryn Ellis, David Friendly, Gale Anne Hurd, Laurence Mark, Casey Silver, and Paul Yamamoto.

Finally, those screenwriters who graciously consented to be part of this project deserve the greatest of thanks for opening up their minds and hearts to us. Without their courage and candor, this book would not exist . . .

CONTENTS

INTRODUCTION

In the beginning, there were no screenwriters. Those who made films found it easy to invent simplistic plots as they went along, with only the barest outline from which to work. But as the audience for movies grew, this situation couldn't last. Although the moguls raged against the necessity of hiring writers, a more discerning public dictated the change.

Fledgling studio heads kept their writers anonymous and undervalued. At a point when stars and directors were coming into their own, most moviegoers still thought the actors were making up their own lines.

But in reality, even then, screenwriting was becoming a singular calling, with conventions and rules unlike those of any other form of writing.

A novelist can tell a reader in great detail what the characters in a story are thinking, define motives and illuminate past lives in whole chapters. A poet can create for a particular audience, which will be moved by a specific image or emotion. A playwright, dealing with the strictures of the stage, sets each scene with spoken words.

Only those who write for film must think in terms of the mechanical eye, which sees only where it is pointed. And while dialogue is important, the screenwriter must create a world at once vast and personal—and must never write anything that cannot be understood by the camera.

When the old studio system was in full flower, novelists and playwrights were lured to Hollywood for their seal of legitimacy. The pay was good, but studio heads were amazed and furious at the independence of writers in general. It is said that Louis B. Mayer referred to writers as "schmucks with Underwoods."

More substantiated is the story that Harry Cohn would walk through the halls outside his writers' offices at Columbia, listening for the sound of busy typewriters. If he didn't hear anything, he would complain violently—he saw no reason why writers should be paid to sit and think.

Major studios no longer give multi-picture writing contracts as a matter of course. Generally, it's more economical to hire screenwriters, like directors and actors, as they're needed. As a result, the profession has become a good deal more competitive.

Today, the complex nature of the movie business dictates that success can be very much a matter of degree. There are writers living well from the sale of screenplays that haven't been filmed and, for reasons that have nothing to do with their degree of excellence, may never be filmed. While one could hardly say these men and women are unsuccessful, they've been denied the validation of seeing their work on the screen.

By the nature of the beast they serve, screenwriters are apt to lead lives of inert calm alternating with frenzy.

As one of our interviewees remarked, "The only time your screenplay is your own is when you're writing it for the first time. After that, you may have to rewrite it for the studio, the producer, the director, or the star."

Another of our subjects offered, "Everyone says film is a collaborative business, but you only hear that in terms of the writing. No one tells the director that he ought to let someone else handle the comedy scenes because he's not so good with comedy."

Of all the vocations associated with the movies, few are as maddening—and rewarding—as screenwriting.

The year 1990 was a banner one for American screenwriters in the motion-picture industry. No sooner was a screenplay sold for a record-setting amount—Shane Black (*Lethal Weapon*) received 1.75 million dollars for his *Last Boy Scout*—then it was nearly doubled when Joe Eszterhas (*Flashdance, Jagged Edge*) collected three million dollars for a psychological thriller called *Basic Instinct*, and Academy Award–winner Ronald Bass (*Rain Man*) was promised two million dollars merely for describing how he planned to adapt a novel.

The buying craze was not confined to screenwriters with impressive credentials. Even young unknowns received astronomical sums for novice efforts. By year's end, more than a dozen screenplays had been sold for amounts approaching or exceeding one million dollars.

There were many theories that attempted to explain this sudden upsurge in the marketplace. Some suggested that a Writers Guild strike in 1988 had paralyzed the development process at the major studios, eventually creating a vacuum for quality material in the production pipeline. Others pointed to the increase in new blood and foreign investment in Hollywood. Still others felt that writers were finally being recognized for the full measure of their contribution to a filmmaking process in which hundreds of actors, producers, and directors are routinely paid in the million-dollar range.

No matter what the reasons for the escalating pay scale, economics alone have not dictated the prosperous start of a new decade—and of a new era—for writers of movies.

As you will see in the following pages, there seems to be a newfound respect for the importance of the screenplay in the moviemaking process, and this is directly related to a burgeoning self-awareness on the part of its writers.

It is certainly reflected in the comments of some of the most prominent people in the industry. At the 1989 Academy Awards, Steven Spielberg talked about the absolute necessity of having a quality script in order to make a successful movie. In a recent interview, Oscar-winning writer/director Oliver Stone asserted that a well-written screenplay could rightly be compared with great literature. And Disney's top executive, Michael Eisner, has often said that every hit movie begins with a well-told story and that "without a good screenplay, you have nothing."

Throughout this book, we will explore the process of writing for movies from the screenwriter's point of view. Truck drivers, actors and actresses, migrant workers, playwrights, film buffs, waitresses, critics, journalists, technicians, aspiring directors, teachers, advertising executives, and many others have written successful motion pictures. Screenwriters are as varied in background and temperament as the infinite variety of movies that have been written, produced, and appreciated by an insatiable moviegoing audience over the past hundred years.

Most working screenwriters have a love of movies and the ability to tell a good story by creating characters we can relate to; they speak a language we can all understand. The best communicate their own vision of the world through the movies they write.

Traditionally, even the best have disappeared into the work as the more visible participants in the filmmaking process build upon the writer's foundation, guiding the movie into production and, eventually, into your local theater.

All of the interviewees in this book have had scripts produced, but many of them have worked hard on stories that they may never sell. After all, there is no standardized way to write a successful screenplay any more than there is a royal road to screenwriting.

What the writers in this book have most in common are endurance and faith. In the long run, achieving success in the screenwriting profession may require luck, stamina, and talent in equal percentages.

We have chosen a diverse sampling of screenwriters who have worked as major studio writers. Some have written only a screenplay or two while others have an impressive body of work. They include hyphenates—novelists, directors, producers. In the aggregate, they present an outline of modern screenwriting.

It is the primary purpose of this book to afford them an opportunity to step out from behind the scenes, to speak for themselves about what they do and how they do it.

LUIS VALDEZ

Luis Valdez is hard to reach, not only because he's always on the move but because the people around him are very protective. He was a founder of the Teatro Campesino, the theater on wheels that reached out to California's migrant farmworkers, supporting them in their fight against exploitation. There have been dangerous times for him; even meeting in the dining room of a good hotel, one feels a trace of the revolutionary.

However, Valdez is dapper, relaxed, a slim brown man in his forties with an easy laugh. The once-indigent farmworker is now sophisticated; he quotes Latin to illustrate a point. The fact is, in spite of childhood wandering he read The Iliad and The Odyssey at an early age, getting them from a library. And he earned a scholarship to San Jose State College—in math and physics. He says he loved numbers because, like drama, they break through so-called reality to a more basic truth.

In his second year of college, however, drama prevailed. He changed his major and began to write. While four years of Latin and a classical education broadened his horizons, he continued to write about the kind of people he'd known in his childhood.

1

But he seems to have retained what was functional from all his experiences. Behind the disarming graciousness is a sense of purpose. The perception of social injustice burned in Zoot Suit, *which dramatized a true 1940s incident in which Los Angeles police framed a group of young Mexicans for murder.* La Bamba *told the story of Ritchie Valens, the Latino singer, and his difficult "crossover" into mainstream success. And his stage play,* I Don't Need No Stinking Badges, *opened up Latino family life to the general public. These issues are still elements of his life, part of his presence.*

To Valdez, his is the theater of alienation. He is a crusading writer and he knows the value of the mythic figure in reaching out to his audience. To that extent, although he may write about the people with whom he grew up, his stories are always universal in concept; there will always be the downtrodden.

He insists that he doesn't always write from his own experience, enthusiastically telling how he wrote a screenplay of the Carmina Burana, *an impressionistic rendering of a medieval chorale which inveighed against the church. Ray Manzarek, the keyboardist for the Doors, adapted the music and Mick Jagger was to play the lead. But inevitably, Valdez adds enthusiastically, "This is medieval Europe we're talking about—renegade monks!" Always the revolutionary . . .*

To Valdez, images are the instruments of his craft, more than words. He thinks it may be because he's been bilingual all his life, but he says, "There are some things I can only express in pictures. Let the pictures speak for me, or let the color and the sound and the movement of the thing speak for me."

He would rather not talk about the mechanics of his craft, preferring to speak of dynamics and thrust. But in trying to analyze his writing, he says, "To me, myth is a tool. It's not something with which you escape reality; it's something with which to get into reality, to deal with it."

Valdez himself is something of a mythic figure. He projects a feeling of manifest destiny. And although he talks about a time when he'll retire to a quiet life with his family and students, that future doesn't seem quite real. He'll always be an activist, always the voice in the wilderness. That's how he likes it.

You know, we all analyze our lives in terms of the events that have led us to our present opinions, but I've had a very clear sort of development in terms of motivations. I was born in Delano, California, in 1940, into a family of farm workers with ten kids. I'm number two; there are five brothers and five sisters.

Although it was June, my family didn't go out to work that year because my mother had just given birth to me. But the next year we went out to pick, and I was severely scalded in a labor camp. I was playing with a cousin of mine on the floor near an old-fashioned wood-burning stove. She accidentally tipped over a pot of boiling water on me, so I lost all the skin on my back and part of my face.

My skin just sloughed off and I was in shock. My dad wrapped me in a blanket and they rushed me to the local hospital. But for one reason or another they wouldn't admit me. I've tried to trace that one down. This was not a hospital that dealt with farm workers, it was for the local white folk—so I didn't make it in.

This was my introduction to life on the road as a migrant farm worker. It was one of the first things that happened to me. Even though I don't remember anything about that experience, I think this kind of physical trauma, this near-death thing, can last for the rest of your life. I think it turned on my motor in some way.

Then, after Pearl Harbor, all the Japanese were evacuated from the West Coast. Suddenly there were all of these prosperous little farms in the hands of the U.S. Army, which needed someone to run them for the war effort. They turned to longtime farm workers who had been working on these ranches, and my father happened to be one of them. Essentially he was offered a ranch—and loans to run it—by the U.S. Army. So he took it; he was no fool.

My first real memories come from that prosperous time, from '41 to '46. World War Two was great, we were landowners. My dad bought three hundred acres with his proceeds and was leasing another thousand. We would tour the ranch in our new car, looking at the workers. We even had German prisoners of war working on our ranch; it was an amazing kind of reality, but I remember they had big *W*'s on their backs.

Then suddenly the war was over and it all came to a crashing halt. There was no more money coming from the army and all these Mexican–ex–farm workers turned farmers started to lose their little ranches. The end came very quickly. By the summer of

'46 we'd lost the ranch and we were impoverished, back on the road again as migrant farm workers.

If my folks hadn't lost the farm, I'd probably be a farm labor contractor now, I don't know. I was always intrigued by artistic stuff, but I don't know where it would have gone. I would certainly have developed a very different attitude toward myself. But we're all faced with the life that we're given; you've got to make sense of the negative shit as much as the positive stuff, right? I mean it's just part of the road and there's a reason for it, or at least it has some kind of use.

At that time I was six, loving the adventure of going out on the road but feeling the tremendous sense of loss because our ranch—and our status—had been lost. That year we picked cotton, grapes, plums, all up and down California. In the fall we were back in the San Joaquin Valley, in a huge camp for cotton pickers. They don't have camps like that anymore, with two hundred tents and a lot of cabins and a couple of thousand farm workers.

If you're a kid it's great fun; you get to run around the tents and make friends from all over. But the season ended and we couldn't leave the ranch because our pickup had broken down. My dad had it up on blocks, trying to fix it. We went into the fall, into October, waiting to get the truck fixed and fishing in the San Joaquin River for food, just sort of surviving.

INFLUENCES

The school bus from a little town called Stratford used to come into the camp. And my cousins were all there also, so we all went to school. This was '46 and there were still shortages—like brown paper bags, just the right size for your lunch. I took care of my bag very carefully and I used to take it home every day after school.

Then one day my bag was gone. The teacher had taken it and ripped it up in a pan of water. I was in a panic until she showed me she was making a mask, a papier-mâché mask on a clay mold. I discovered one of the secrets of the universe at that moment—that you could take paper, flat paper, and convert it into a different shape.

I knew about puppets. I had a cousin who had already started to make them and I recognized that what she was making was what the puppets were made of, although my cousin had never told me because he was eight or nine and it was his secret. But when my teacher told me the masks were for a play, I had to ask, "What's a play?"

It was a Christmas play but it took place in the jungle, and the masks were for magic monkeys. So I tried out for one of the roles and I got it. I got a mask and a green and red costume and little slippers. I mean, the costume was better than my clothes. And I saw the set coming together. My memories of it probably don't match the reality at all, but to me it was magic. And a week before the play was to be performed, my dad got the truck fixed and we moved away.

I cried, but it was economic conditions. They were forcing everybody out of the camp. That's what used to happen. At the end of the picking season the owners would close up, take down the tents and lock up the cabins. So I never got to be in the play.

But I took it with me, man, and it was a gap. I've been trying to fill that gap for forty fucking years, and it'll never be filled.

The next place we lived, I started to stage plays in an abandoned house with my friends, taking branches from small trees and putting them up like a jungle. I wanted to perform that play. So I got hooked on drama by the time I was six. By the time I was seven or eight I was fooling around with masks, and at twelve I was a puppeteer. We'd put up a blanket for a curtain and our stage would be a cardboard box with one side cut out. We did a lot of fanciful stuff. Characters would come in and speak in Spanish or English, it didn't matter. There was lots of action, fights between good and evil. It was fanciful—fairy-tale stuff.

You know, the study of that mythical level is to me the study of reality. It's an equivalent to reality, like mathematics. I love numbers—I got my scholarship to college in physics and math—and I think math has the same importance that myth does, except that one is numbers and the other is what human beings can understand in terms of story. But both have that underlayer of reality—almost a Platonic truth, you know, in the sense that it's the real, original model underneath.

But for me, myth is a tool. It's not something with which you escape reality; it's something with which you get into reality, to deal with it. I need it when I try to understand about America—not just the surface stuff but the mythical level that's at work here.

THE VALLEY OF THE MOON

Most people go through the San Joaquin Valley as quickly as possible. Peter Brook and his group came and lived with us for two months in '73; when we took them into the valley, he said, "What is this place? It looks like the moon." Those are the alkali flats, and there wouldn't be anything growing there if it weren't for the California Water Project. Delano's out there, and it's divided by more than the railroad tracks. I mean, all the white people lived on the east side and everyone else lived in Chinatown, except the black people and they lived outside of town entirely. It was that bad back then.

If you're born in Delano, which I was, you deal on the west side with a landscape that's not productive at all. And then suddenly on the other side of the freeway there's this green hothouse. It's a paradox. We used to go hunting for birds and coyotes on the west side, and on the other side was where we worked. I got the sense that life was reduced to basic elements. There's just the land, mountains in the distance, and a lot of sky.

I've had this conversation with George Lucas—who was born down the freeway in Modesto—about the San Joaquin Valley and the sky. And another guy who was born or maybe just raised in Delano was Gene Roddenberry. When my dad was a farmer we used to take the produce to the local packer and I remember vividly the sign, RODDENBERRY AND SONS, and one turned out to be Gene Roddenberry, creator of *Star Trek*. Now, I have a theory that in the valley all you have are the stars, so you end up dreaming about the stars.

THEATER

This mythical juxtaposition of earth and sky was one of my earliest impressions, along with others that evolved into more political thoughts. I remember my brother and I seeing the workers lined up outside a tent where a couple of prostitutes were doing landslide business, and I wasn't comfortable with that. Then as I grew up, I saw what seemed to be injustices in the fields, or some labor contractor would obviously shortchange us. There were other incidents which gradually came together in my mind.

So in my second year of college, when I dropped out of the sciences and moved into playwriting, my first expressions were political. I mean, they had to be. Also, I had discovered Bertolt Brecht.

To an extent, the theater of alienation is still part of my work. I used it in *Zoot Suit*, although not as heavy-handedly as in the theater. I used it in *I Don't Need No Stinking Badges*, that thing of ripping through not only the fourth wall but the theater wall, of saying, "Listen, there's a reality here that's bigger than this play and bigger than the theater."

I used to get a kick out of doing that to an audience. As I've grown older, I've learned to respect their need for a certain completion and I prefer to tell stories to the end. The other was mischievous.

In college I wrote my first full-length play. It was called *The Shrunken Head of Pancho Villa*. And I had the wonderful experience of having both William Saroyan and John Howard Lawson attend a performance at a drama conference. They loved it from entirely different points of view, Saroyan the humanist and Lawson the social activist, one of the Hollywood Ten. They saw the play for what it was.

It gave me a huge push. I felt, "Hey, I got a crack at it, do something!" I was thinking New York at the time. So I get this offer from Brandeis to get my M.A. there and take my play off-Broadway, and I threw the *I Ching* to help me choose an option. I got an answer that seemed very clear—so I chose to stay, to join Cesar Chavez and go to the farm workers. I had no money. I had no scripts that I could give; all I had was the fact that I'd been born in Delano and I'd known Cesar as a pachuco when I was six.

But there were blood lines connecting me to that place. It was my life that was drawing me back. And I figured that if I could invest in that, I could go anywhere. When I was eighteen I'd been kicked out of the house, my brother and I. My brother got into a fight with my dad and I jumped in to save his ass, so my dad mopped up the floor with both of us and said, "You're out."

I tried living with my brother, but that was impossible—I knew then why my daddy kicked him out—so I got my own room, my own habitation. I felt a sense of arrival, of control over my own destiny. That's when I became a success to myself. There have been many ups and downs since then, but I've never doubted that I could do much of what I wanted to do.

Coming to this point in my life, to Hollywood, was not a straight line. Because of that kind of mischief, I went sometimes in the opposite direction. But I never thought about not making my living as a writer, I just assumed I would.

FROM STAGE TO FILM

When *Zoot Suit* was successful as a play, bidding from movie people got hot and heavy in New York. Peter Guber wanted it, and some other people. I was offered more money than I had ever seen, but essentially they wanted to buy the rights from me, with only a possibility that they would give me a crack at writing the screenplay. Everyone was envisioning this large film and how they were going to open up the play. So when I asked about directing it, they didn't take me seriously. Ray Stark was willing to make me a second assistant director.

But to the chagrin of my lawyers, I wasn't interested in selling the rights. So we got involved with an independent producer, and after six months it turned out he didn't have all the Arab money he said he had. We sent out the word that we were shopping it around again, and Ned Tanen picked up on it. But he wanted to videotape it and blow it up to 35 mm. He said they were doing great things on videotape, so we saw *The Gong Show Movie*, which had been made that way, and I said no. We ended up shooting in 35 mm and having a great deal of fun.

I'd had the idea of going straight out into the reality of Los Angeles and picking out all that art deco and 1940s stuff. I wrote the pachuco, the leading character, as a mythical figure, up on the edge of buildings in downtown Los Angeles, you know, towering over the city itself. Knowing a little bit more about the logistics now, I realize we were talking twenty million dollars. We were talking an enormous undertaking. I had images of recreating the *Zoot Suit* riots.

What we finally got was two and a half million, and thirteen days to shoot it. It was impossible. So I set the limits very close to the limits of the play but allowed some cinematic resonance; it's highly stylized. Translating it to film was relatively easy in the sense that the images and pictures in the film are things that rose directly out of the play, although they would have been impossible on the stage. But suddenly I saw them in different proportions and I began to integrate the movement of the camera with the movement of the pachuco. That sort of gives the film its style.

I'd had experience with documentary filmmaking that went back to 1965. When I started working with Chavez and the union, I was in charge of the propaganda department and I dealt with many film crews. So the visual aspect of *Zoot Suit* was there for me. Some of it has to do with the fact that, being bilingual all my life, there are some things I can only express in pictures. Let the pictures speak for me, or let the color and the sound and the movement of the thing speak for me. The Teatro Campesino was always heavily visual. It was a success in Europe because of the visual aspect, because it was easy to follow, because people could tell the meaning from the pictures.

* * *

You know, there have really been few changes in the role of Hispanics in film. But so far, one of the biggest changes is that all Hispanics are seen as Mexicans. All of them. I mean, what characterizes a Puerto Rican? Maybe a New York accent now, maybe something from the Bronx. But in appearance, how about a Colombian or Ecuadorean? Maybe we can recognize some extremes—Incan Indians maybe, but Peruvians I don't know. It's Mexicans, that's what Hollywood has known.

One of the complaints I hear from old-time extras and people who have been in the business a long time is that the change for Hispanic actors came at about 1965. Before that they had a secure place in Hollywood. Not in terms of leading roles; I'm talking in terms of playing gardeners, shopkeepers, workers of different kinds. But in 1965, Watts blew, and that hit the consciousness of Los Angeles very hard. Hollywood started to do something about black images. And it was as if they had a quota—"We have so many minority roles, so now we're going to give black people more to them, which means that Hispanics are going to get fewer roles, and also Asians."

It's a common complaint in the minority community that jobs fell off because of the civil rights movement. Well, you know, you can't blame the black people. But the fact is, if you look at Hollywood films since 1965, as limited as opportunities have been for black people, they've had more of an opportunity to play lawyers and lawmen than Hispanics.

But what black people have to say about Hispanics is also true, there are a lot of Hispanics who can pass for white. There are many working in Hollywood today that no one knows are Hispanics. Because Hispanics are viewed through a very stereotypical lens. I mean, I'm supposed to look Hispanic but in fact I look Yaqui Indian, which is what my background is. I'm an Indian, you know what I mean?

Hispanics come as Indian-looking as I am, or they look black, or they're blond and blue-eyed, or there's a lot of sandy-haired European types. And so they've managed to work. But the Hispanics who *look* like Hispanics have been relegated to the drug addicts and the gangs and the prostitutes, and maybe about five or six types that repeat themselves endlessly and are forever marginal.

Still, there's a great deal of hope now that the situation will get better. There is hope that we'll produce actors of the stature of a Robert De Niro, an Al Pacino or Dustin Hoffman, or other ethnic types who aren't necessarily considered ethnic types now, they're just accepted.

That has to work hand in hand with changes in the outside world, outside Hollywood—I mean in reality. And inside Hollywood in terms of who is doing the writing. That becomes the crucial question; where's the writing come from? And how sensitive are writers to the fact that if you have a story about a private eye, you could as easily have a Martinez as a McGillicuddy?

It's more a question, for me, of changing attitudes than anything else. And you can change attitudes very dramatically by making something happen, something huge. In some way, I have no alternative but to make something huge happen. Every time I try to make a movie or a play, it has to be a big splash because there's so much riding on it. In a sense, I don't have the privilege of making a small, sensitive, quiet little movie off to the side.

WORKING WITHIN THE SYSTEM

I cooperate with people. I don't necessarily consider it to be a compromise. It's not like I fill so much space and if I have to shave off a corner, then somehow I'm less; I'm open at the edges. I do believe that making films is a question of collaboration. Because it's not an individual talking to another individual, as in a novel; it's really a group of people talking to this mass audience. So multiple opinions can sometimes get you there, be very helpful. You do need to pour a film through a sieve of different opinions. On the other hand, there has to be enough cohesion there, enough of a vision, so that your film doesn't go in twelve different directions. That's the way I see the function of a screenplay, to provide a structure that you can work within. It can only be fucked with to a point or you'll destroy it, but I'm willing to negotiate. That's me, the old union organizer. That doesn't mean that I don't believe in taking strong stands, sometimes you do have to hold the line, but everyone knows where his limit is.

The closest I've ever come to an adversary position is in a creative relationship that I had with Carlos Fuentes and Jane Fonda over *The Old Gringo*. She invited me into the process—which I appreciate—to adapt Carlos's novel for her. We had differing opinions to such an extent that eventually I withdrew. It's always hard to have your work rejected, but then you have to come to terms with yourself. But I haven't yet had to fight a studio over a script.

There are personal levels and desires and there is the mythic level. I not only believe in that level, I live there. What's motivating me, as egomaniacal as it may seem, is that what I'm doing with my life has been a question of social service, a service to a certain historical condition, expressed through the arts. My function is to be what I am, to tell stories, to write plays and screenplays, and to make films. But I'm still serving a cause much larger than I am, even though I'm working here. So if I run up against obstacles, I draw my strength to fight those obstacles from this belief that I'm serving. I see the impact that my work can have on people and that makes me very aware of how many compromises I can make or not make, in terms of the work. If I were involved in a fight with a studio, I don't know what the outcome would be. But most important, for me, is not protecting my own future in the studios, particularly with the way things come and go. A regime in the studio is only here for a little while. Social change is dynamic, particularly in American life. There's a great deal of dynamism here that propels us all into what's coming up, into the next turn in the road. So you shouldn't feel hopeless because you've run into a brick wall.

I don't believe in burning bridges because I don't believe in insulting people unnecessarily. When you can be cooperative, that's the best way to get it done. On the other hand, when you water down your principles and what you believe, you're on the sure road to self-destruction.

CREATING

Getting started on anything is a real pain, right? And getting started on the writing process is the hardest piece of the puzzle for me. Where I like it best is when the momentum just feeds itself. You know, the characters are talking to you and it's a marvelous experience to sit there and see the pieces come together. Because you sort of discover a screenplay. You don't write it, you don't create it, you don't impose anything on it, you evoke it out of these materials. At the same time you realize that you're in there, that you're evoking this out of yourself.

For me, writing the screenplay is a much more satisfying process. Because it's you and the story, you and the computer or the typewriter or whatever. It's a real privilege to be allowed to go off somewhere and write a story. I've entertained the notion many times that maybe I should just concentrate on my writing and that I'm wasting a kind of opportunity here by delving into directing quite so much. I love directing but I know for a fact that going through the process, even if you're Stanley Kubrick or David Lean or Francis Ford Coppola, any of those well-established directors, you don't really get the opportunity to put that personal stamp on it. Not really, because you're always passing the film on to someone else who has to do something else to it. Your film is in the position of a woman patient who goes to see a gynecologist— your film is out there and it's open, with its legs up on straps, and a lot of people are coming in and looking and saying, "Well, I think it needs . . . " But when you're a writer, it's your screenplay and you can hold it to yourself, clutch it to your breast, and it's yours and no one else can see it until you're ready.

Still, I'm in the midst of a love affair with a medium, film, and it is rapidly becoming one of the profound loves of my life. What's haunted me about the theater is the power of visual images. But in film . . . you just go into it, right? This is why the pettiness, the business of film and the pettiness, is so debilitating. Because we all want to penetrate the womb, the dreams, but unfortunately we have to do it in this mundane way. Yeah, you have to floss your teeth before you dream.

THE WRITING PROCESS

I approach the subject from a number of different angles; anything and everything is conserved for research. I figure that getting into a film is enveloping myself with ideas, with sensations, feelings, travel, anything. Once I've set my course, everything that I see and feel begins to feed that. Some of these things are co-incidental, happenings that come together. On the other hand, there is stuff that's very deliberate, the necessary kind of research where you need facts and figures. I do an awful lot of reading, and I enjoy that period too; it evokes the researcher, the student. I love to devour books during this process, and I'm able to read very quickly when I'm in this state of mind. It's different from the other, more recreational kind of reading.

And you're just swallowing. Seeing films, you see what you need to see, hear what you need to hear. And so I enter this period of research. If it involves writing, very often it's followed by a period of gestation, where the stuff has to be absorbed and digested.

I give myself about a month of open research. This is quite apart from thinking about a project for years and just kind of rolling the ball. When I finally decide, "Okay, this is what I want to do," I have to get all the stuff together and begin to digest it. Then follows another month, sometimes, of just note taking.

What I do is, I talk to myself. But I realize that since I'm going to be writing, it's important to do just that, to write. Fingers on the keys, one word after the other, sentences, paragraphs, images. And I lay no restrictions on myself whatever. I don't say, "Okay, now you got to start writing dialogue, not plot lines." And I don't set a certain number of pages I have to write. It's none of that at all, it's totally free-form. So I write poetry, I write letters, I write notes to myself, I doodle. It's totally open. And the openness eventually begins to kick me in. Eventually you say, "Oh, here's a little piece of something," and plot lines start to emerge out of this, descriptions of character. And it's the story outline. I mean I've got to have that, we all have to have that.

I don't work from index cards or an outline, I work up pages. And I keep everything from scraps and I put them all together into a binder, two binders, three binders, whatever it takes. Usually there's a binder of research stuff, apart from books; a fat book of notes; another binder of notes I've written with respect to character; finally there's the binder from which I begin to write scenes.

Then I get to a point where I know I'm ready to take it on. And I go for it then; I go for the overview. The dramatic lines first, the tension. For me, it's a little bit like taking a rubber band and finding a way to stretch it with all these little twists and turns; then I can feel the taut quality of the structure. If it's tight, if it's got power in it, then I know I've got something. If it's limp, then forget it; where's the drama going to come from? So in analyzing the screenplay, I want to know where the drama is and how these points connect, and so forth. It's not automatic, it's gradual, it's organic.

BACK-BURNER PROJECTS

I have a story that I want to write, about this family that was half-Japanese and half-Chicano. I have very vivid memories of that family, and of my friend and his brother who were Japanese and Mexican; their mother was Japanese. It's about how his parents came together in an American concentration camp, and what happened to his father's family. Tremendously powerful, one of those untold stories of World War Two, which I intend to tell one of these days.

Some time ago I wrote an adaptation of the *Carmina Burana* by Carl Orff, and the music had been done by Ray Manzarek, the keyboardist for the Doors. It was through the video division of the Mark Taper Forum; they wanted to do this piece both on video and on stage. So I got Ray's interpretation, it was rock and roll and yet it had the cantata and everything—in Old German and Latin.

I had four years of Latin, so I managed that with a little dictionary. The high German, the low German, that was a new experience. In any case, I really got into this. This is medieval Europe, we're talking about renegade monks, they're the ones who wrote the poems that served as a basis for the *Carmina Burana.* And you know, there's a part of me that was there, I was able to connect with it. When I read *The Iliad* I recognized it also. I read *The Illiad,* then *The Odyssey,* when I was twelve, thirteen, I got them out of the library, and I said, "There's something here that's very familiar to me." I got into Greek mythology like a pig into shit. I mean, I got into it, right? And I loved it; the experience was tremendous. It was the same thing with the Carmina, in the Middle Ages; I got into it. You know, Hieronymus Bosch is the one that's most associated with Orff, so I got into Bosch too, utilizing some of his images.

Well, it hasn't been done. We almost had it. Mick Jagger was going to do the lead monk and it would have been a very interesting piece of work.

My first film, aside from the Hollywood films we've all grown up with, the first film that opened things up for me when I was in college and showed me a whole new world, was *Un Chien Andalou,* Luis Buñuel's film with Salvadore Dali. That opening shot, where they cut the eye, opened up a dimension for me. Now this guy's a Spaniard, he worked in Mexico for many years. And there were a lot of things that were characteristically Spanish about him perhaps, but that movie was speaking to a fundamental level; it had nothing to do with superficial aspects.

So I believe in that level.

There's a good friend of mine, now dead, who wrote a book that I'd like to turn into a film one of these days—his biography. Dr. Ernesto Galarsa, who was a very rare individual in the sense that he was born and raised in a little village in Mexico and came out of there with his mother in various conveyances, stagecoaches and stuff, to escape the revolution. But he eventually made it to Columbia U.; he got his Ph.D. And we're talking about the late twenties, early thirties. So he was a Hispanic turned Mexican-American, if you will, perfectly bilingual.

A very congenial man, brilliant scholar, union organizer. Anyway, he wrote a number of books, some of them in sociology, particularly dealing with farm workers because he was a farm-worker organizer.

He said that the growth of migrant labor at the turn of the century, the growth of the system, has impacted completely on the shape of labor patterns—that the prototype was created in agriculture but has spread to every industry throughout American life. It's the idea of the modular work force, that you can unplug a group of workers from one place and plug them into another, you see? Plug them out and plug them in.

I'm still trying to get Cesar to let me do his story. It's an amazing fucking story; there are already three movies in it. He just doesn't want it at this point. Maybe because he's still living there; it's like saying, "Don't take my plate away, I'm still eating it." Or maybe it's not good. Maybe if somebody does his story, it might end it for him, who knows? Maybe that's his Samson's hair and all that.

CHANGES BROUGHT BY SUCCESS

I'm traveling a hell of a lot more now. Some of this is a function of age really, you get into your forties and one hopes you enter your maturity, right? But I find that I'm on the road a hell of a lot, and I sometimes feel that I'm still a migrant; I work here, I work there, and it's like following the crops. And we kid a lot about it . . . "The crop is waiting, the leaves are heavy with fruit . . ." But this is the pervading experience that has come with success, this is what it means.

For me, ultimate success has always translated to the ability to really stay put. That doesn't mean I want to die, it means to be able to control elements in my life having to do with employment, with family, with friendships, with the creative aspect and all of that—to contain all these elements in one area.

Right now, where my life is taking me is all over the place, and so I'm sort of living in the wind, and able to do that because I've grown wings to do it. But what I'm really driving for is to dig in. And I don't know if that's ever going to be really possible, to settle in.

I have San Juan Bautista, that's my home. That's the place that I've lived in the longest. We moved there in '71 and my home is still there; we own property and all that. But like everyone else, I've lived a year or two here, a year or two there.

Still, I love to travel, see, that's the other side of it. Why not? I love to go into new horizons, visit new countries. There's still a vast section of the world that I don't know, that I want to know. I want to know Asia a lot better. So how is all this going to happen? Well, make a movie in Asia maybe . . .

REFLECTIONS

If it all came to a dead stop tomorrow, I wouldn't consider it a life wasted. I've invested a lot of energy in everything I have done, all through the different stages. Because of the puppets, I went into ventriloquism as a teenager and started making my own dummies. As a sophomore in high school, I became a regular on a local television show in San Jose. I was on for maybe a dozen weeks on Sundays. Live television. I used to write my own stuff, got to work with the cameras. You know, it was great to be sixteen and to be in that position, to be on the air.

Yeah, I'm basically an actor. I'm the kid with the monkey mask; I'm still there, right? I love to act. Although now I tend to expand that a little bit, in the sense that acting for the stage is one kind of satisfaction, acting on the greater stage of the political/social/cultural scene is another one. In Acapulco, I was given an award by Miguel Alleman, on a stage. I had the microphone, there were three thousand people sitting in the theater—mostly Mexicans, of course. And I felt I had to speak from the heart, I had to speak from the gut—I had to speak from my act. And I'm very aware that what they're seeing is an act—but a reality.

I addressed the California Legislature recently. So there they are, all the legislators. And I'm the special guest, I'm up at the podium. That, for me, is acting, right? And I'm very conscious of the fact that I'm acting within the political/social process. I love to do that. At the same time, I see that's my arena also in terms of the work that I do, whether it's a play or a film. The whole social experience enriches everything I write, but it adds something, it gives it a connection.

I'm not embarrassed to say that I'm involved in social subject matter. I haven't done anything, with the possible exception of *Zoot Suit*, that approaches *Matewan*, for instance, but I have a *Matewan* that I want to do, about the United Farm Workers.

A lot of people have said, "Well, where are your politics now?" and I'm saying, "My politics are still intact, I'm still the same person. I'm older now, and you've got to realize what I'm up against."

THE FUTURE

I have a plan for the future, and it began to kick in for me in the past ten years, okay? And that's working more directly with youth. I have people in San Juan now, who are working. We have interns, we have people who are working with the Teatro Campesino. I'm the artistic director there, the mentor. I have to touch base with that because I started it and I'm teaching the teachers.

I can see, some years down the road, just dedicating myself to that. Because I believe that there are two different axes to human activity. One is horizontal, that's broadcasting and making films, the mass media—and certainly this is self-evidently important. But there's a vertical axis, which means when you take on life one-to-one. It's working with twelve kids, working with a handful of people and trying to impact in that way.

Now, I don't know if I'll be ready to do this at fifty-seven. It may be sixty-seven. But I do know that the last big stage of my life involves that, being a maestro. That, to me, is also an extension of everything that I've been doing, you know; it's social service. And I look forward to it.

See, I've been very careful to allow myself an image of myself as an old man, and I enjoy it. So aging for me is not nearly as frightening as it might be for someone who doesn't have a self-image at that age. I think it's important to be able to perceive the trajectory of your life, from beginning to end, so that you know where you are at any point. Inevitably we're all going to be dead, so you have to have that one too, you have to be able to see yourself as a dead person—which means, whatever your legacy is.

One of the fine things about film and video, as opposed to live theater, is that something is left. Something remains. And I've done enough plays now of which no trace remains, except maybe a photograph or an old program, that it's given me an appreciation for the lasting impact of film. And it's great to look back at your old stuff and say, "There it is." There's something deeply satisfying about that.

Even so, the idea of working with a very perishable commodity, which is youth, is quite essential to me. And I have kids that are seventeen, fifteen, and ten years old. Three boys. My wife and I wanted a daughter, but the fourth one would probably have been a boy, who knows?

Anyway, ten years from now they won't be boys. I'm enjoying their youth now, but I wish I could enjoy it more, I wish I could get even deeper into them. But you know, there are other kids coming along and so I see myself doing that. I see myself continuing to extend my own family life, being a grandfather, being an uncle—I mean, the things that we all can be within our family structures. I enjoy it.

Ultimately I think that what I've appreciated about life itself is that each particular period brings new maturities, new sensibilities. I'm doing more now, at this age, than I've ever done—because I've discovered the fundamental principle of simultaneity; I've learned to do things simultaneously. It's like learning to hold your orgasm, you know what I'm saying? You couldn't do that when you were nineteen.

RON BASS

Ron Bass lives in Bel Air—but on a quiet street lined with comfortable, unpretentious homes. Everything about his house speaks of both peace and purpose. His attractive, friendly wife is a little hurried as she gets the kids off to school. A nearby piano holds a sheaf of child's piano lessons.

The back patio, where we talk, is filled with greenery. A small waterfall loops into the swimming pool, which is carefully fenced off because of the children. One could hardly imagine an atmosphere more conducive to thought, to creativity.

Bass is a quiet man in his forties with some gray in his brown hair. He is good-natured but cautious, probably a residue of the years he served as an entertainment lawyer. All in all, he seems the quintessential family man, perhaps lacking the drive demanded by the movie industry—until one remembers that, for a long time, he got up at three every morning so he could write until he had to leave for the office.

Also, one gets the impression that his tranquillity is at least partially self-imposed. He was a top Hollywood lawyer, duking it out with top Hollywood executives; no one arrives at that position

19

without stamina and a strong sense of self. Anyone in Hollywood will tell you Ron Bass is a nice guy, but a former legal associate remembers his breaking one of his office phones in anger. He had several, because he liked to keep more than one conversation going; now he likes to work on several screenplays at the same time.

For Bass, the writing process is methodical. To him it's important that whether it's a murder mystery like Black Widow *or a saga of brotherly love like* Rain Man, *his stories are "simple and about people and their need for human contact, the difficulty of making contact and how important that is."*

ORIGINS

I always wanted to write, even when I was very young. I was ill as a child, bedridden for a long time. I did a lot of reading and my heroes were novelists. Writing was something I always dreamed of doing as a kid, like being center fielder for the Yankees or a rock star. But I never thought an ordinary person like me could be a professional writer—it had to be an extraordinary person.

My dad owned a small business and my mom was what you used to call a housewife. So I went through a very conventional education, trying to learn something that an ordinary person could do to earn a good living. I considered teaching for a while, and the diplomatic service—and politics. But the more I learned about those fields, the more I knew they weren't what I really wanted to do.

By the time I went to law school I was a little interested in international law because it seemed like something that would give me a lot of options. But I never wanted to be a trial lawyer, or had a grand passion for the law. When firms came to interview me for a summer job after my second year at Harvard, I was attracted to the entertainment industry because I was so interested in films and writing. If I couldn't do it myself, I could be close to it, and it would be more exciting than oil or gas leases. So I went with a firm that had an entertainment practice and began to specialize—and I was an entertainment lawyer for seventeen years.

Negotiating is interesting work, very good background for

someone who wants to write fiction. It teaches you how people work, what motivates them, and it makes you think about strategy and psychology.

But as I became more successful, I was still unfulfilled. I didn't think of writing screenplays, that was just a dream. But I began working on something, an idea I'd had when I was nineteen, and wrote it as my first novel. I wrote it really just for myself. I didn't think anybody was going to read it except my wife and some close friends.

At the time, I was negotiating with an editor at St. Martin's publishing house in New York, for a client and a book he was writing. I told the editor I was writing a novel and he wanted to read it since he was leaving his post and becoming a literary agent. He gave me a lot of guidance and eventually got it published, although he had to try a million places. He and I became close friends and he's one of my best friends to this day.

I decided I was going to write books. And after that first novel, which was very abstract and philosophical, I met a publisher who said that espionage fiction was a healthy genre for which there was a market, while writing something that fell between the stools was a good way not to get published. So I wrote a novel called *Lime's Prize*, which is now being developed as a screenplay. It was my first espionage novel and I did it very slowly, over a couple of years in my spare time.

William Morrow published it. I still never thought of writing screenplays. I wrote one just for fun, just to see if I could do it, but never thought of it as a career. I was practicing law very hard—it's very hard work.

Then a woman who worked for Reader's Digest Condensed Books came to me with an idea for a novel about World War Two. My publisher at William Morrow said, "Look, Ron, if you'd really like to earn some money at this, here's a story that Reader's Digest wants to help finance."

I didn't know anything about World War Two. I knew it would take a lot of research and I wasn't particularly interested in the idea when she first gave it to me. But the publisher said, "If you can figure out a way to make it exciting for you, here's something we can really get behind."

At this point I realized that if I wanted to be a real writer, I couldn't take two or three years to do each book. So I began getting up at three in the morning, seven days a week, and writing from three until six, when my daughter, who was then two, would wake up. I'd play with her and then go to the office and practice law all day long.

That novel, which was called *The Emerald Illusion*, ended up with a producer who was looking for his first film to direct. He loved it and was kind enough to let me write the screenplay. I wrote it between three and six in the morning, during the end of '82 and the beginning of '83. People kind of liked it and began to give me assignments and I began to take them, still writing in that early morning time, and I finally saw there was a market for what I was doing.

But about a year and a half of this became tiring, and wasn't really fair to my law partners. Eventually I had so many scripts backlogged from people who wanted me to write for them, I realized that if I wanted to remain a lawyer, I would have to start turning away stories I really wanted to write. I had to make a decision, and this was what I'd always wanted to do with my life.

I went to my senior partner, who said, "This is what you should be doing. If you ever need to come back to the practice of law, you'll always have a home here." That's when I began writing full time, in June of '84, and I've been writing full time ever since.

One of the things I hadn't really figured on, one of the negatives of this kind of life, is that it's a lonely way to live. You work alone, and although there are collaborative moments with directors and producers and executives, you do what you do by yourself. You have freedom to make your own schedule and your own day, work where and when you want, travel when you want. It's wonderful to be able to go to my children's events in school, which other fathers can't see because they have schedules. But I'm a gregarious person who loved the fact that every morning I went someplace where I had twenty buddies and we interacted.

But the work makes it worthwhile. When you're doing the work you always wanted to do, it compensates for everything.

GENRES

I've gotten away from espionage stories, although a lot of the stuff that goes into espionage fits into other genres. Manipulation and strategy and being able to control other people; it all fits very well. But there's not much call for it.

Also, I don't much call on my legal background. There were some legal components in *Black Widow*, and down the line I'll be writing a courtroom drama. But it isn't something that attracts me over any other subject. I really like to write things that are each different from the other, and the more diversity the better.

I do have favorite themes. I love stories that are simple and about people and their need for each other, the difficulty of making contact and how important that is. But I also love things that are tense, closely plotted adventures, although I'm not a guy who writes a lot of action-adventure. My things are about mystery and suspense, but they aren't about car chases and major perils every thirty seconds. Action-adventure is a very successful film genre, but it's not my favorite.

However, I'd love to write all kinds of things I've never written. I'd love to write science fiction someday, or a Gothic horror. But the running thread is relationship. I don't know how I could ever write a screenplay like *Never Cry Wolf*, a movie I admired quite a bit, where there's only one character and you've got nobody to bounce it off of—something it's extremely hard to do. Not so hard in novels; you can be more internal. But on the screen it's all about what people do to each other.

Also, screenwriting is a collaborative medium. The storyteller in film is not the screenwriter, it's the director, and that's an adjustment a novelist has to make if he wants to enjoy a career in screenwriting. You can't do everything by committee, and one person's vision has to tell the story. When you write novels, it's you. I had wonderful editors at William Morrow, and they gave me a lot of intelligent advice, but the final decision was mine. Every word in the book was exactly what I wanted it to be, and that's marvelous; you feel very fulfilled that way.

But you have a different role when you're writing for screen, and you're always going to be disappointed if you can't accept that. Unless you find a director who's your identical twin, his vision will be personal and it will always be different from yours.

THE LURE OF DIRECTING

Of course, everybody says one should be a director because it'll be your vision on the screen, and that's where the authority is. They believe that everybody who creates wants to have his creation reach the public in his own way. And that is an attractive thing.

Also, I do enjoy working with actors. An actor and a writer are natural allies, with similar problems. They're both concerned with bringing a character to life. A director has a broader, more administrative responsibility for the film, but for me the chance to work with actors would actually be the most exciting part of getting to be a director.

There are some negatives. A director can only work on one story for a year, a year and a half. I work on seven, eight, or ten in a year. I'm very prolific. And then, as a director, there'd be a lot of technical aspects to learn—and you're not being creative. As a writer you get to be more purely creative, I think, with your time.

Also, it's very tough on your family and your personal life. I have incredible freedom now. We travel, go abroad, do exactly what we want to do. Directors have to be slaves to their projects. So yeah, directing is attractive and it's also a thing I would only want to do carefully, at the right time and in a way that would be of benefit to my family. I'm not in a hurry.

THE WORK ENVIRONMENT

I really enjoy writing anywhere, although I have an office that I rarely use because it's distracting to hear other people. I like to write in the early morning when it's dark and nobody's up and I'm alone. I work very frequently now in a park. I take a little chair and I have my stuff with me, because my productivity depends on the amount of time I can make myself sit with the notebook in my lap and a pencil in my hand. The more I can do that, the more it comes. And the more I'm around other people, the more I'll distract myself by doing something other than working.

So I can write on the beach, I write on planes, I can write in a car when my wife is driving—anywhere, any time, as long as people aren't pulling my attention away to something else.

METHODS

I don't work from index cards. I write screenplays—and novels as well—from a story outline. I don't like to write any scene until I think I know where everything is going, because everything I do is informed by that. Of course, the outline may change radically as I go. But to just kick off and say, here's an interesting first scene, now where do I want to go from there . . . ? Some people are very successful at that, but it's not my style.

Usually I write on three yellow sheets of paper, in longhand and pencil, in a loose-leaf notebook. My assistant, who is my story editor and very valuable to me creatively, also types up my stuff. But I just start with a pencil and my three little sheets of paper— acts one, two, and three.

My scenes are broken down on these sheets before I start writing, and I have lots of notes in my notebook keyed to the numbers of those scenes, with different ideas I may get about what's going to go into them. Then, when I begin to write scene twenty-three, for example, I look back at this voluminous notebook and find all the ideas numbered "twenty-three," get back into what those ideas were, and use them for what I do with that scene.

My assistant is very helpful in designing the scene. She has great ideas, and also I frequently work best talking to someone. But I have to design every scene before I start to write it.

She also does a lot of the research. The degree of depth depends on what you're doing. Obviously your research for a novel is astronomically greater than what you would do "normally." But for some pieces, you just have to go out and talk to people in those walks of life. It takes up a great deal of time, which becomes a rare commodity.

My workday usually begins around three or four o'clock in the morning and ends at about five o'clock at night. I like to be home to have dinner with my children at five thirty. And a lot of days have meetings in them, so I don't get to write.

I don't set myself a specific goal of pages to write each day. But if I've predesigned the scenes and don't run into snags, and I'm working in the park where nobody bothers me, starting at three in the morning and working until five, I've had days when I've written eight or nine or ten pages that were keepers. I'd be disappointed if I wrote less than four pages, but you can't aim for it. You can't say, "Well, I'm not going fast enough today." That's the road to bad work.

NOVELS VS. SCREENPLAYS

As I write more, differences in storytelling fade away between novels and screenplays. It's all really just about the essentials of writing. Of course, an obvious difference is that a screenplay is very limited in terms of its form. You only have 120 pages, basically. There are far fewer words on the page; you have to do things with great economy. You also can't be internal in the way that you can in a novel. And you don't have the opportunity—or the burden—of expressing yourself with flowing literary description, which helps create an image in the minds of your readers. Instead, the image in the mind of your audience is going to be visual and you have to think what it's going to look like. You have to see it in your mind more.

I create the characters inside me. They're people I can talk to.

I know how they would respond in any situation and I write by watching them do what they do. That's what the process feels like, and it's the same in a novel as in a screenplay.

But actually I haven't been writing the two things at the same time. When you write screenplays the way I do, with so many projects, there isn't any room in your life for writing novels. Since I love small stories—love stories and intimate stories about people—it's easy to think of them as screenplays.

SPEC VS. ASSIGNMENTS

Businesswise, a lot of people write things on spec because they have to, because they aren't employed enough. I've been lucky. And obviously there's an advantage in knowing you're going to be paid for something in terms of making a living, rather than to write it without knowing if you'll be able to sell it.

People say that if you write something on a speculative basis and it sells, you can make far more money because you've taken the risk and the buyers know what they're getting. I'm not always sure, having been a lawyer in this business for a long time, that it necessarily works out that way.

When you write something on spec, you're writing solely for yourself, and I have to do my spec things at odd hours of the morning because I'm writing on assignment all the time. So it's something that goes along for me very gently.

Sure, you're writing it to your own taste, writing it just the way you want, without being restricted by other people and their visions. In that sense it's a beautiful creative experience. But you're always aware that the day will come when it goes to a buyer or a director and the rewrite process will begin.

Actually, it isn't so difficult for me because I feel that all my first drafts are spec scripts. I'll go over the outline with my buyer, the director, the actress, whoever I'm working with at that time, and make sure they feel good about the outline. But once that's done, I'm writing it for myself. I'm really pleasing myself and I know there'll be plenty of time, in five hundred rewrites, to please everybody else.

I write everything that I want to write. Sometimes I'll have an idea and a buyer will tell me, "It's too small for a theatrical movie, it's either a television movie or a novel." But I'll find someone else who wants to develop it with me, or I may write it on spec. Someday I'll be sitting with a director or an actress who's powerful and I'll strike a spark with them on this story and we'll get it made.

But there's nothing that has made me say, "Boy, I'll never get to write that till someday when I retire," and I don't think of things that way. Any story that would appeal to me should appeal to other people too, and there's a way to get it done somewhere, I just haven't found it.

THE ADVERSARIAL CONDITION

The first draft is always a delight, the purest creative process. Every writer dreads and abhors the rewrite. The only way to enjoy it is to remember that it's a different procedure, that it's not completely an adversarial condition but a collaborative process that finds you working with good people whose opinions you respect.

A certain amount of adversarial approach is necessary to the rewrite. People are passionate about their ideas and no two people are ever going to see everything alike. You have to keep an open mind to have your thing improved. And where you think somebody is disimproving your thing, you have to stand up and fight like a tiger.

But you get to a point, after working with the executives and producers, when there's a director on the project. Then you have to realize that this is the storyteller. If you can't surrender your perspective to his, you're going to be miserable.

It isn't about ego at all. It's about the script. You've created something that you love, and you want it to be as good as it can be. You feel that you're protecting the script—or at least your vision, which is the only thing you have to go on. The guy who comes in and does something that I think makes my project worse is going to get a big fight out of me because I want it to get better. But that's what the other guy wants also, and that's what the collaborative process is all about.

It's not always a collaboration among equals, though it should be. But I don't feel that a studio executive's idea or a producer's idea is better than it is, just because they're employing me. I feel that what I owe them is the best that I've got. Their idea is as good as it is, no better and no worse.

I feel a little different about the director because, once it's in his hands, he's the ultimate storyteller. Even where we really disagree and I therefore think he's "wrong" because he doesn't see it my way, my job is to make it as good as I can for him. It's tough because you're still your own person too, but it's a necessary thing. And when you're working with directors who are really bright and good, that makes it easier.

WHEN WRITERS ARE SHUFFLED
LIKE CARDS

Yes, I've been replaced on scripts. Although it hasn't happened a lot, it's painful even when you may know it's absolutely necessary. The director or the studio executive has replaced you in order to go on with their vision of the movie; if you're not giving them what they feel they need, they gotta do what they gotta do. I've never felt it was aimed at me personally, but it hurts because you love the story, and not being able to go forward is distressing.

I don't know if it hurts your ego as much as your feelings. I would say that the purest kind of selfish ego-hurt is where a film gets made and your name is on it—but so much is different from what you created, it's really the work of other people. Then a reviewer or a friend doesn't like the way the film looked, and they think you wrote what they didn't like.

Of course, maybe you're also getting credit for good stuff that wasn't yours. But human nature is such that you don't feel it's unfair when that happens; you focus on the unfairness of being criticized for what you didn't write.

The other thing that's hard on your ego, for me at least, is when you really contributed to something and didn't get credit for it. And you're proud of it and you wish your name were on it. But the way the Writers Guild worked or the way the situation worked, your name isn't there.

In fairness, I've worked on films that wound up with very little of what I did on the screen, and I wouldn't have conceived of accepting credit. I came in to do a certain thing, but the original writer was responsible for at least ninety-nine percent of the film. That's not an occasion of the kind I was speaking of.

But I've also done rewrites in which I felt I contributed significantly and didn't get credit. That's when your ego isn't a part of yourself you're particularly proud of. You don't want to think of yourself as someone who has that kind of vanity. The irony is, the better the movie turns out, the more you wish your name were on it.

ACTORS AND ACTRESSES

On assignment I do a lot of writing for male characters. *Gardens of Stone* is a piece that's almost exclusively male, very small space given to the women. But in *Black Widow*, the relationship between the women was very important.

I write primarily, when I'm writing from choice, about women, and whenever I'm developing spec things you'll find there's a female lead. If there are five characters in the piece, probably three or four of them are women.

What I'm looking for in all my leads is the journey of self-discovery and the changes that happen to them, and more men than women are heavily defended in that domain. They don't want to get into that area of their own feelings; it's less accessible to them, less part of the story.

A second thing that attracts me to writing for women is that it's fresher. People have seen men in the same damn kind of stories over and over again. But when you put women in the same situation it's commercially fresher, so it may be smart business also. I've seen a dedicated cop chase a psycho killer—when they were both men—five hundred times. But somehow, when they're women, it's different. I'm writing a piece now about two women who are high line investigators. I've seen male partner investigators all my life, but the fact that they're women makes it interesting for me.

Also, actresses are more accessible. There are hundreds of scripts chasing the same ten actors, but there are so many terrific young actresses who are hungry for material that you know you have a better chance of placing the script.

I don't often write with a particular actor or actress in mind. What I've done sometimes is to actually partner with a particular performer and then create the story and the character together with him or her. Also, sometimes you come onto a project that's already cast, or it becomes cast by the time you're in rewrites, and then you're writing for somebody specific. Or you may pitch a story using the names of actors because it helps people see who you're visualizing in your mind. You could ask me who I would cast in this, and I would know of an actor who most closely fits the personality of that character—but they're all really me; I'm just making them up.

PITCHING

I used to love pitching stories. I would work out what I wanted to say very carefully in my mind, and I was very good at it. I never pitched anything I wasn't excited about, so it was just a chance to tell someone a great story, and people always responded with enthusiasm, although they didn't always buy it. But the pitch meeting was a pleasant experience.

I haven't pitched an idea to studio execs in a long time. What we call a pitch now mostly happens when I get to meet with actors or directors and we talk about the kind of ideas we have; that's sort of a half-assed pitch. And, of course, your character is being represented on the screen by this particular person and you want to make it as right as you can.

CHANGING PARTNERS

Being a studio executive could be extremely interesting. I know a lot of people I respect who do it. It's a killer job, like being the director of a film when you're shooting. It'll consume all of your time, and whenever you're taking a moment away from it, you could be doing something productive.

That's true of writing, too. But the difference is, as a writer you only have to answer to yourself, As a studio executive, you're answering to other people for things you aren't getting done, and so the temptation is always to do one more and one more—and it's rough. I do know studio executives who have good marriages and personal lives and love their kids. It's not impossible, it's just hard.

But there are certain directors and actors and actresses, creative people whose work I really admire and with whom I would love to be creating stories. I would say that's the thing that attracts me the most. When I've had the chance to work with actors or directors whom I really respected, that's been the greatest excitement.

SUMMING UP

I've had an advantage in being a lawyer for all those years because all my clients were film people. I saw how all-engrossing this business is, and watched what it did to people's relationships. You learn a lot of lessons about what you have to do to protect the personal side of your life, which I believe is the most important.

It comes down to caring enough about that side of your life to honor it. There's no such thing as quality time. Time is time. If you don't give something time, you're ignoring it. Every sixty seconds is the same; you just decide how you use it. People you meet who are so consumed by their careers that their personal lives are irrelevant to them—I think that's sad.

However, that's not me. If I'm not happy, it sure isn't the fault of my career or my family. It may be the fault of my own neuroses. But, yeah, I'm Lou Gehrig, I'm the luckiest guy on the face of the earth. I'm getting paid an enormous amount of money. I'm getting wonderful treatment from people I respect and admire—for doing my favorite thing in the world, the thing I used to get up at three in the morning to do for free. Now I get to do it all day and call it a job. I don't deserve to be that lucky, but I'm not turning it down and I'm going to keep doing it.

SHANE BLACK

Shane Black is an intense, serious man. Good-looking and apparently self-confident, he's also insecure and a bit suspicious. He speaks the way he writes, with a kind of ferocity. Alternately brash and self-effacing, he is frankly searching for a professional and personal security which seem to be denied him by the turbulence of his own nature.

Black doesn't care much about his surroundings. His office is a dilapidated trailer in a corner of the Universal lot. As he says, he can work anywhere. He's a driven man, but he doesn't seem sure of what he wants. He worries that he's going to dry up, that every script will be his last. But at twenty-two he wrote Lethal Weapon, then made motion-picture history in May of 1990 by receiving the highest price ever paid for a screenplay, 1.75 million dollars for The Last Boy Scout.

Black's challenging attitude and raw edge are a protective veneer. He's too wary to make friends easily, but he maintains close ties with the small group of comrades he met while studying film in college; it's as if he can trust them more than anyone else. But even so, he's constantly testing everyone.

33

However, he's as tough on himself as anyone else, and he's certainly not vain about his ability. As he puts it, if his family hadn't moved from Pittsburgh he'd probably be working as a printer for his father. In fact, one gets the impression that he just wandered into filmwriting and stayed because he liked the obstacles.

While Black *calls himself a genre writer in action/adventure, his inventions are dark, laden with the quirks and vulnerabilities of the people he creates.* Lethal Weapon, *which made him a name to reckon with, featured a leading character balanced on the edge of suicide. And while* The Last Boy Scout *has plenty of action and adventure, much of the energy comes from his tough, pessimistic characters, people who have lost their innocence along the way. It's his view of the world.*

Black says he's guided by intuition. But he also says he's not very good at writing. Yet, when his pieces are analyzed, it's obvious that he brings technique as well as instinct to the job.

Shane Black's stories sound simple when the plots are described in a couple of sentences—and it's also a Hollywood dictum that this should be the case. But on examination, they prove to be made up of complicated parts—rather like the man himself.

BEGINNINGS

I think it's very important for anyone who pursues writing professionally to read books—comic books, any type of reading—at an early age. I don't think I'm a born writer, or that anyone is a born writer. I think people have certain predispositions. For instance, till the age of fifteen, I was a math whiz. At about fifteen, I lost it. As soon as I got into trigonometry, I couldn't do math anymore. It was almost an overnight thing, which I associated with puberty and chemical changes in my brain. Anyway, I couldn't do math, so I started writing more and gradually came to enjoy it.

But if my family had never left Pittsburgh, I'd probably be working for my father as a printer or a forms consultant. Which is why I say I'm only a writer insofar as I've written something that's been sold; I can claim that degree of professionalism.

But I might have done something, anything, completely different, just depending on where I grew up, whom I met—pure chance. So I don't think anyone is really born to it. I certainly didn't pursue it; I didn't attack writing from an early age saying, "This is what I'm going to do, I'm going to be a big writer. I have this soul in me, I can feel all the stuff that I need to get out, so I'm going to really hit it hard and make sure everyone knows I'm the next Hemingway."

I never did any of that. I was never convinced—and I'm still not—that I'm anywhere close to being the new Hemingway. If anything, I'm the new—I don't know, the guy who made *Blood Feast,*—because that's the sort of thing that I was raised on. So I don't consider myself anything except sort of a well-paid hack with aspirations to grandeur.

Well, "hack" depends on your definition. I have a solid theory from which I work, which is simply that it doesn't matter what genre you're writing as long as you're telling a story. Storytelling is the most important thing. That's why I don't like something like *Commando;* there's no story. It's literally writing on the most commercial level, which is simply, "Don't even write it, we'll just fill it in later, we'll get the actors together and we'll think of something, we'll think of some action to put here."

Whereas a movie like *The Terminator,* even though it's in the same genre of action and adventure, has a very firm story. You want to find out what happens next, you want to turn the page. There are twists and turns, and the characters have to make choices, hard choices. There are discoveries throughout the script, and reversals. So, you know, as long as it tells a story, you want to find out what happens next and turn the page.

But when I was reading *Commando,* I really didn't care if I turned the page and found out what happened next, because it would probably be another chase or another boat crash.

THE WRITER AS ACTOR

I went into theater arts at UCLA because at the time I wanted to pursue acting. I'm very self-conscious now about the fact that I wanted to be a professional actor. It's really sort of an embarrassment to me because I think it's an embarrassing profession to choose; it's the most nonsensical of all the things you could do. Not only is it silly and self-congratulatory and self-aggrandizing, but it's also virtually impossible to get into. It places a financial burden on your parents and your friends.

I think people who want to be actors and don't have connections into the business, or something to fall back on, are silly. I admire some of them, I think they're good actors, but I think it's a real mistake to try to be an actor.

It's embarrassing because when someone in L.A. asks what you do and you say, "Well, I'm an actor," there's a real stigma attached to that, but in this case not an unwarranted one. I think that if you say you're an actor, then everybody thinks, "Oh, yeah, there's another one. Not really any talent but thinks he's interesting."

When you want to be an actor there's an unspoken assumption, "I think I'm really interesting. I think I'm interesting enough so that everyone's going to want to see me and hear what I have to say." And I just never really thought that, so I just don't think it's a good idea. Anyway, I can still do it as a lark, but not as a career.

That's how I got into theater arts, where I met people like Fred [Dekker]. We'd just hang out in theater arts looking for girls, basically. We both did, because all the actresses would come there to be in plays. And from that came this group of people I hang out with, all of them writers or directors or actors. For the most part all of us graduated from UCLA, and all in the same year. We all support each other. That's how I got my agent, through Fred, and that's how I got my first job and now we're working together.

FIRST SCRIPT

I always enjoyed writing as a hobby, and at UCLA I'd taken some short story classes but I'd never written a screenplay. I didn't really know how to try it. I think a problem most people have, who don't come from L.A. originally, is not even knowing there's a market for screenplays. They don't know how to write them or that they even exist.

I was working with Fred at UCLA on small student projects, or we'd make our own little movies. He got a job working for Steve Miner, director of *House,* and he wrote a script for an American version of Godzilla, which I read and thought "Wow, this is incredible." It was pure pulp, but in the sense that *The Terminator* was, and it took Godzilla and made it American and made it great.

It had adventure, it had kids—it had a secret agent with an obsession. And Godzilla represented more than just a monster, he was a myth. It was an allegorical story, with levels to it, and I thought, "This is terrific, this is what Godzilla should be, this is like *Alien,* this is like *Jaws,* it's everything." And I realized then that I was reading something a friend of mine had written. All of a sudden it seemed somehow less intimidating, because it seemed that if he could do it, then I could do it. I decided at that point that I would at least try it, and I did. When I gave it to Fred, he said it was a good script. And I realized then that it's not a tough nut to crack.

That was "Shadow Company," my first script. It was kind of a mess, but it had a spark of whatever it is that I would eventually do, mostly with descriptive writing, and a weird style that I don't see in many scripts I read. It was not really a conscious choice, it was just something I did that seemed to work for me and I think it still works, so I continue to work in that style. It's—call it stream of consciousness—very short slug lines.

I've seen scripts where the first page looks like huge blocks of paragraphic text, which no one's even going to read. But on my favorite pages, the action is continuous and has a lot of short slug lines. The attention goes down rather than across. It flows, it reads as if you're following the action. I enjoy doing it that way, as a series of statements that build to a capper, which you then give added weight by separating it from the rest. So I like to play around like that. And I found that people responded to the work, so I kept doing it.

Fred was a client of David Greenblatt's at CAA, who's a very nice man and very good agent. And he liked Fred enough to trust his judgment when recommending a new client. But when David read "Shadow Company," he didn't want to rush out and sell it. He did not say, "This is a terrific script." But he said, "You know, I think you can get a job based on what's here."

Most assignments are engendered by people sort of liking the writing. You know, "We like the writing a lot but we don't like the script." Well, that's the kind of thing I did for about eight months, just met people all the time. And after all those meetings, which may have numbered close to a hundred, I realized that I really did not enjoy meetings with all these people.

The first meeting I ever took was with a development person, a sort of get-to-know-you meeting—you know, "If you have anything, will you bring it to us, because we like the writing a lot." Never, "We want to make your movie," but always, "We love the writing." And in the meeting I was offered something to drink. They brought me a Coke with ice, and there were even some cookies laid out. And I thought, "My God, this is the big time."

I was so pleased because I had talked to this development person and I really tried to make an impression. And I described my idea and the person said, "Wow, that's good," and I thought, "Oh my God, I impressed this person."

At the time I was happy my tie wasn't spotted and my hair was combed. But I learned very quickly that development people for low-level producers are not the people in the business that you really want to impress. And for the most part I was very unimpressed with the intelligence of the people that I continued to meet. And I realized also that most of what was said to you was not so much the truth as it was bullshit.

So I retreated from all those meetings. I called my agent and I said, "I don't want to take any more meetings. I'm not going to take an assignment from these people, I know that's not what I want. I want to continue writing spec scripts, and working with my good friends whom I already know, so why should I go out and meet all these people?"

It was about that time that I sold *Lethal Weapon,* which was about eight months after I'd gotten an agent. That gave me the freedom to pursue what I'd really wanted all along, to write speculatively and not to have to take an assignment.

STUDIOS

I don't really like studios. I don't like the idea that there are people in offices who feel, unjustifiably, that the decisions they reach over lunch regarding your script are valuable. You come to a meeting and they tell you, "Oh, oh, wait, Bill has an idea, Bill tell him your idea. I think this is good, Bill, come on, tell him." And they all sit there smugly while he says, "Well, my idea is . . ."

And they think the idea they came up with in twenty minutes is as good as the one it took you three weeks to come up with. I have sat up nights, thinking, "Blah, blah, blah, no, doesn't work, start over. Okay, he goes to A, then he sees B, now he sees B already knew A. Okay. Was C first? Maybe C, no not C because C implies B," and I've done this over and over. And then I walk into a meeting and they give me this stupid idea that they thought of in ten minutes, and I say, "No, no, no, you don't understand. I threw that away two weeks ago. I've been through all this for three weeks and you're assuming that these piddley-shit ideas you're giving me are better than the ones it took me three weeks to reason out."

* * *

I've found two things about pitching. Number one is that it's bad for writers because if you've ever had a great idea that you want to put on paper, one of the best ways to fuck yourself up is to tell somebody about it and blow all the energy that you have stored up, especially in pitching, where you have to do it three or four times; by the time you get to the paper all your energy's gone. Number two is that it's the antithesis of good storytelling because, before you show your story to somebody, you tell them the ending. You go in and you say, "Here's what happens, these guys do this and here's how it ends." Then you go and write it and now they're expected to be excited reading it. I mean, it's just a bad idea.

DISILLUSIONMENT

There was a time, shortly after I'd begun screenwriting—I was very poor, placing a drain on my parents' resources, not wishing to do so. My parents are very wonderful people, but they were not rich. We're not poor, but my parents certainly would fall into what you would term middle-class. So I had to find a way to make some money.

I was offered a project by a studio. And at the time I had *Lethal Weapon* just sort of sitting out there in my agent's office; he was going to send it out over the weekend. And I told him, "Dave, if *Lethal Weapon* sells, I want to make sure I can get out of whatever project I take just for the money." And he seemed to feel that studios were amenable to that sort of thing. Well, it turns out they weren't.

Over coffee one afternoon at a studio, someone said, "Will you do our project, 'Spacemen from Venus,' or whatever," and I said, "Well, I'll give it a shot." And I called up David and said, "I didn't sign a thing. I told them I'd give it a shot." Well, I called him back the next day and said, "I can't do it, I can't do it just for the money. Please tell them no, tell them no." And he said, "Don't worry about it, we can get you out of this."

Lethal Weapon sold the very next day. I came skipping into the office, "Hey, how you doing? Okay, let's go. Make a call, can that 'Spacemen from Venus' shit and let's just go do *Lethal Weapon*."

And the studio would not let me drop "Spacemen from Venus," they said, "You gave us a commitment." I said, "Fuck you, I didn't sign a thing," and they said, "What are you talking about?" I said, "We just had a nice conversation, you gave me coffee, I was nice to you," and they said, "You told us you'd try it." And I said, "Wait a minute, what are they talking about? I've changed my mind." They said, "That's a verbal contract, buddy."

I had no inkling of a verbal commitment or what it engendered. I had no idea what they were talking about. I panicked and ran to my agent, saying, "What are they doing?" He told me, "I've never seen this before. I don't know why they're demanding that you write a script that you say you don't want to write."

But they did. They threatened me with lawsuits. They threatened with verbal abuse. And I was—I just was so angry. I even sat down at my typewriter and started, I remember just this feeling of rage and I hated those fuckers so much, and I was typing and finally I just threw it across the room and said, "No, I'm not going to write for them. I don't care that I'm offending these people, I don't care if I never work again. I'm not going to bite the bullet."

I was just a kid, I was twenty-two years old, had no idea what I was doing, and was so scared that someone would actually consider suing me for money I didn't have that I quite nearly dropped it and said, "Fuck *Lethal Weapon,* I don't even want to sell it."

I had visions of people taking my furniture. And at this point I thought, "I have no business being here; these guys are big wheels, I'm way out of my league, I got to get out of here." I wanted to run back to Pittsburgh, Pennsylvania, and just live there. But my agent calmed me down and said, "Look, they're just blowing smoke, don't worry about it," and then he took care of it.

But it was frightening. I didn't think I deserved abuse. If anything, I'd been ignorant.

LETHAL WEAPON

So I've had conflicts along the way, but I consider myself very lucky in terms of a final product. I like the way *Lethal Weapon* came out. There are a couple of things I disagree with, which are hardly worth mentioning. The director was right as many times as I was. I was wrong a couple of times, and so was he. But what's the point in quibbling if the movie's good? Because ultimately, we got most of it; he got most of it. It think it really works as a movie. And some of the things he thought of, I never would have thought of.

So if I think he screwed up a scene or two, or left something out or put in a little too much, the movie is terrific, I think, a good action picture. It's not Hemingway, but it's good.

I did have a lot on conflicts on *Lethal Weapon* initially, just regarding the studio's refusal to make a commitment or a decision. First they said, "We love the movie, we want to do it."

I said, "Okay, I'll go rewrite it."

Then *Cobra* came out, and even though it was eventually a big hit overseas and proved to be a money machine, the studio began getting that mail saying, in effect, "We don't like your making this kind of movie; you're hurting our children."

So they came to me and just said, "Okay, no violence in *Lethal Weapon*. We want an outrageous, farcical, over-the-top action thriller, but no violence," and I said, "Well, I can't do that." All of a sudden the wind went right out of my sails.

They were ready to make it because *Dirty Harry* was a big hit, *Rambo* was a big hit—now we have *Lethal Weapon;* it's *Rambo* and *Dirty Harry*. Then *Cobra* comes out and immediately, boom. Courage and convictions—where did they go? Nobody knew, but they couldn't make that movie anymore. So it was kind of sad for me at that point.

But I argued and argued. And Richard Donner, to his credit, was able to somehow convince the studio—I don't know how—that this was not a violent picture, it was an adventure picture. And that while people were being shot, they weren't dying violently, they were dying the way they did in westerns. We managed to convince them of that and we made the movie pretty much as we had originally intended.

ON DIRECTING

At some point, given the proper training, I'd like to direct. But I think I'm wary because so many people do direct, not because they have a knack for it, but simply because they get the chance. Either they've written a script that is so wonderful that someone gives them a chance to direct their own material or they know somebody.

I think that's how most people come to direct. They're previously writers or actors or people who don't specifically come to direct movies but end up directing because of clout that they achieve through other fields. And I don't want to be that; I don't want to be an untalented director who just stumbles into it because I can. I want to do it because I've got a talent for it. And that will only be discovered through schooling and study, which I have yet to enter into.

I think it can be a big mistake to direct your own material, because you miss the sort of second perspective that someone else can bring to it. You're so limited by what you've see in your head, as you prepare the material, that you don't really take into account all those other possibilities. I certainly hope that before I would direct my own material, I'd sit down with the director of photography and say, "What do you think? Is there a way that you could just change this totally and make it better?" and then incorporate both visions.

I don't really think that knowing what you want and getting it on film are the same thing. I think it doesn't always happen that way, because there are other factors such as filmic technique and editing and actors. If you don't do it right, it won't work. It won't cut together, the acting will be bad, and it just won't work. And if I directed now, that's what I would do, I'd make a film that didn't work. I'd have noble intentions, you'd see maybe a glimmer of some very high-reaching sort of philosophy, and then it would fall flat for sheer lack of technique. But maybe in five years.

JUMPING IN

I almost never do any research until after I've started writing. I think its important to jump in with both feet. Take the case of a movie like *Lethal Weapon,* where you're dealing with (a) police procedure and (b) weaponry. So you're dealing with regulations and ballistics. Well, those are things that, if you're at all competent at bullshitting you can just make up something off the top of your head that looks good for the read. Later you can go back and actually have the specific details that make it real.

I think people waste a lot of time sitting in research before they actually get to writing a script. For some people that's okay, but I have never had within me the conviction that I will ever finish another script. I always feel that my last script was the last one, literally. "That's it, I'm burned out, I'll never finish another script." And so for me to do all this research beforehand . . .

I'm not very good at writing. If I succeed, it's by a fluke. It's amazing, as much to me as anybody, that I ever finish a script, because I just sit there and I type and I agonize until finally it looks like an elephant. And then I carve it away. And pretty soon I have something that, surprisingly to me, has a beginning, a middle, and an end, and I don't even know how I did it.

I don't work from an outline on paper. I used to say I never would outline. The truth is that I do, but it's just all in my head. But I found that I can keep things pretty well up there.

Probably I'll go on writing originals instead of adapting from another medium. Because the problem with adapting what I would choose is that invariably it's big-budget material. And so we're talking about doing a movie for a major studio, writing it on assignment, getting the rights, doing twelve drafts of it.

I'd much rather make up my own character and do it on spec. And I don't have to deal with the input, as I'm writing, of the people who have hired me. And also, deadlines kill me. Just the knowledge that I have to turn in a script and can't throw it away is enough to totally freeze up any ideas that might otherwise occur.

Left to myself, I usually get to my office around eleven, and I'll pace around. I used to smoke cigarettes. I quit smoking, but we'll see how that goes. But I pace for about an hour and a half. Start around noon. Write till seven. Hardly ever work at night. Night is when I relax and I just want to go out with my friends. I don't drink, because I can't drink while I'm writing. I find that it fuzzes up my head, even if I just drink a little bit, for the next three or four days. I'm just slower, I'm not as quick on my feet. And by extension, ideas don't come while I'm writing.

Ideally, when I'm in my most creative flow of writing, about three weeks in, I've established this "norm level" of caffeine, nicotine, all these intakes, coupled with high-protein foods that I've been eating, and my body assumes a level of hum that proceeds from then until the end of the script. I don't sleep very well, but I do think very fast. And toward the end of the script, I will lie in bed all night just running possibilities in my head. Just the *ABC* game of "Okay, if he goes here and then meets this person, could he then see this? No, because if he saw that, that would mean that he wouldn't need to meet that person. We need to meet the person because otherwise how will we know who he is when we see him here?" And I can do that all night and I just won't sleep, I'll just sit there, literally hum. Yeah, I know just how it feels.

I write whenever it feels appropriate. The least pages I've done in a day is three. And the most I've done is twenty-seven. And toward the end of a process, the end of a script, it speeds up. Once you reach that magic point—for me it's sixty pages in—a little light goes on, and I think, "Oh my God, I'm going to finish the script. It's not going to go back in my closet or in the trash can, I'm actually going to finish the script," and your whole body just relaxes, knowing that. And then it's just on to the end. What's tough is starting when you don't know if you're ever going to get to that finish line.

* * *

I can work anywhere. I used to be very picky and superstitious about the places I'd work—until I found I could work anywhere. I wrote *The Monster Squad* at my house, at home. "Shadow Company" I wrote at my parent's house. *Lethal Weapon* I wrote at a friend's apartment, and then did all the rewriting in an office. And I wrote *Lethal Weapon 2* at Joel Silver's office. So wherever.

What I don't need is to have people coming in and out all day long, talking to me, bringing in coffee or doughnuts, discussing the ball game. I just need to be alone. I need my typewriter, a cup of coffee, a bathroom, and a radio maybe, and just leave me alone so that I can adapt to the environment.

SUCCESS

For me, success doesn't come from financial things or professional things. Success is a personal goal. When I feel successful is when I'm not as shy as I used to be. Or when I do something that's important to me, like writing a script was important to me—not to sell it, but because I didn't think I could write it and I did. That makes me successful. I used to stutter. I don't anymore. That makes me successful.

I'm driven toward feeling like I'm a good person, feeling like I have a set of standards that I live up to. My own standards are, of course, the most stringent and the hardest. At the same time, I only work in spurts. If I've made enough money to live the way I want, and I've met a girl, and I'm going out and having a nice time, then I relax for six months. And it's only after six months have passed that I even consider getting back to work.

I worry that being financially successful has an effect. It's unfair in a way. I find that, for instance, people who wouldn't even listen to me before now want to know what I think. No one gave a shit what I thought about movies three years ago. Girls at parties weren't interested in anything I had to say. Now they happen to be interested, or they want to know what it was like to work with Mel Gibson. Well, in a way that's sad because—why weren't they that interested before?

I guess financial success really means a great deal. But it seems sad to me that you have to do that before you can be afforded any level of attention. For instance, if you sell a script for a lot of money, it has to be good. And people will actually read it differently. Even if they have a problem with it, they'll say, "Well, it must be me, it can't be the piece. The piece is, you know, worth a lot of money."

It's truly the emperor's new clothes. I mean, so many scripts are just dreadful and sell for half a million dollars because everyone in town is afraid to be the first one to say, "Guys, this is really not worth half a million dollars." And so they go ahead and pay the money because everyone acknowledges tacitly, "Well, they were smart to pay that much, I guess," when the truth is that the movie is dreadful.

FLAVOR OF THE WEEK

The thing that people in Hollywood don't realize is that the pendulum swings so easily. If you say that what's popular now is not going to be popular next year, they say, "Oh yeah, you're right, you're right." And yet, a movie comes out and is successful, and for the next two months the things that sell are exactly like that movie. Whatever is hot or topical in that two-week period continues to generate money and have people interested.

People say they understand it, but they keep doing this flavor-of-the-week bullshit.

"Oh, it's popular now so this is what people want, they want *Rambo*."

"Well, no they don't because *Cobra* is a bomb."

"Well, they don't want that, that's what people don't want."

"But then, *Raiders of the Lost Ark* . . . "

"Well, now they want it again."

They always just change their minds and equivocate. And it seems to me that what they want is a good story, which knows no pendulum. It knows no season, because a good story is a good story.

CRITICS

I enjoy listening to critics. But really, I mean, considering these are people who are paid to have careers doing this, I think it's very silly. At the most, what they're doing is saving you five dollars on a given night by having you avoid seeing a bad movie. That's the critics' function. That's the upside. The downside is that these people are paid every week to decide in two hours whether the last two years of your life are worth giving a look.

People spend years making these movies that the critics see in two hours, then come out and say, "Ehhh, thumbs down." And I think we could do just as well without them. I think the best critics are the more entertaining or flamboyant ones, just because they're fun to watch, or funny. But these television critics don't address a movie filmically at all. They say, "Oh, I liked it, it was suspenseful," or "It was sexy."

Well, if I want to know that, I can ask the guy in the street, he could tell me it's sexy. I want to know what the filmmaker intended, is that what he achieved, is it well shot, is it well staged, is it exciting and paced well? But instead we get, "Sexy, woo wee. William Hurt, oh my God, my heart stopped." If I want to listen to an elderly homosexual discuss how much he likes watching William Hurt, then I can find better places than on television, watching movie critics do it.

In fact, very recently on one of the morning network shows, a critic was talking about the movie *Some Kind of Wonderful.* And he talked about how John Hughes is really improving as a director, he's become wonderful, and went on and on about John Hughes directing the film when in fact Howard Deutch directed the film. Joel Silver called me into the office, and said, "Come here, you've got to see this!"—and there this guy's just making an idiot out of himself. Didn't bother to take the time to find out who directed the movie.

IMAGES

I write the things that I read and enjoy. I have a vast repertoire of imaginary characters in my head, based solely upon books I read when I was a kid. When I was writing *Lethal Weapon,* I had a very vivid picture of the Mel Gibson character in my mind. He was not a star, he was not Gibson, he was not Harrison Ford, he was just somebody, and I thought, "Well, who is that guy?"

And I figured out he's from my childhood. He's a cross between the guy on the cover of the paperback series "The Executioner" and a hero in a really low-budget British spy thriller I'd seen when I was a kid, and I can't even remember the title. But I realized he was these two guys just melted together as a sort of face that I carried around in my head.

And there was the face I had for the other cop in the original script; he was not necessarily black, he was just this older plodder of a cop who's sort of a grumpy man. And I took him from when I read *The First Deadly Sin,* which was a pretty effective picture of an older cop. But more than just this, I think it was a piece of art

I saw, when I was a kid, of an old man. Or a picture of a cop in New York City, I must have read in the newspaper sometime.

I just picked up these heads and sort of carried them around. When I'm writing this script, "Shadow Company," the hero appears to me in my head as I'm writing—the same way that Riggs in *Lethal Weapon* appeared to me—it's the same face with a slightly different voice. This guy's more crazy and less hip. He's actually more crazy.

As I go through my day I feel little character bits. I'm sort of attuned to a certain time of day or a certain situation. I'll just say something and suddenly I'll click into a character. Not that I'm acting, but I'll feel the way a character would feel in a situation.

Or I'll recognize something as an emotion that would play in a script. And I'll catalog these little emotions I have throughout the day, or these feelings I have, and say, "Yeah, there's a way of talking or a way of acting or gesturing." Or even the way that I just felt, leaning against this wall and staring out there, would suggest to me an idea or a character.

I really do like to live in the shoes of my characters, or try to. And I hope the effect is that when I do eventually write the character, he casts a shadow. So that it's not just a cardboard figure, but he feels like a part of me that I've taken away and put on the paper. And different sides of me reflect different characters, each one being a different aspect of myself.

That's how I start, but also images will occur to me. Mostly, I'll be writing and I'll have an image so strong and so striking that it just sticks in my head. And before I sit down to write a screenplay, usually I'll have four of them, sometimes fewer, sometimes more, anywhere up to ten images that are there very strongly.

Sometimes I don't know where they'll fit in the script. In *Lethal Weapon*, I had an image of a man alone on a ledge, just deciding whether he's going to go or not. And he's a cop, so I threw that in. And then I got the bit with the handcuffs, he was handcuffed to a jumper and they were standing on a ledge up on a building, and it was nighttime in the original script.

They're both looking, and one's suicidal and one's a cop, but you don't know that the cop wouldn't like to go too. And I started giving them little things to say in my head. I just had this sort of neolithic cop character who was crazy enough to go and stand with the jumper and say, "Listen, I'd really like to join you."

That's the kind of thing that will occur to me, but then I have no idea where to put it for a while. The ending of that movie, not the very ending but the scene where there's a freeway, the image didn't quite work out in the script either.

The image hit me while I was driving in downtown L.A. and there was an overpass with one of those big green signs, all latticework and chrome, right over those zipping cars, and I thought, "You know, this would be a perfect place to put someone."

In the script it was an actual freeway and there were cars moving very fast. The guy was on foot in the middle of these cars on the freeway and he was like a scared rabbit, and he was insane. And he had a gun, that was all he had.

In the script I have him hanging from that green sign with a gun in one hand, waiting for a particular car, just swinging above the freeway. And when the car comes, he drops, and cars around him just swerve and crash and he doesn't even look at them because he's so obsessed with getting the one car that he wants. So I had that for the ending. Okay, that's the end, the jumper scene's somewhere in the middle. Also there's a guy who falls into a swimming pool and the pool cover sucks him in, surrounds him and drowns him; I had that image. The other image, of course, was the girl jumping off the building, naked, and hitting the top of the car and lying there sort of spread-eagle. Okay, now I've got four images, and from there who knows how they connect? I mean it could be a western—well, not really with a freeway—but it could be anything. It seemed to me, a cop story worked best, given those images. And so then I just went from there and connected the dots.

These moments help make a movie. For instance, I feel that's one of the reasons *Aliens* was such a huge hit. It's a wonderful movie up to the point where the planet blows up and Sigourney Weaver gets away with the little girl. But they capped it on the ship by having the Alien come back—and then, even after you're ready to leave the theater, they have three moments in quick succession: guy ripped in two, Sigourney Weaver saying, "Get away from her, you bitch," and that thing falling into the airlock. Within thirty seconds of each other, these great moments, right after you've already thought the movie had ended. And that's what made that movie a hit, it pushed it right over the top, I think.

Ultimately I hope to combine emotional realism and action in one genre. For instance, I've always been a big fan of pulp. Good pulp, like the original Doc Savage stories; there was a certain raw energy to them. Or the original Tarzan novels by Edgar Rice

Burroughs, who was not a great writer but knew how to tell a good story. I've always been a fan of that kind of thing. My goal is to do genre pictures with real, solid, psychologically sound characters.

REFLECTIONS

You know, my biggest disappointment so far is that having a career has not made me happy. I've made more money. But—and this is something that people usually don't believe—aside from the fact that I'm able to stay at home during the day now and don't have to type letters for a loan company anymore, I'm not really happy. I'm just as frustrated by my lack of ability to come up with a piece of writing I like, just as frustrated that my last script was truly my last and that I seem to have lost it or have nothing important to say. Certainly in my personal life, I'm not suddenly the toast of the town, nor do beautiful girls follow me around trying to get dates.

Some people are interested in me now. I always feel a little like I'm ripping them off. I feel like the garish paperback novel with the guy and the girl and the blood on the cover, but you open it up and it's some Italian translation of a twenties whaling text.

I feel like that's what it is, they're interested in me purely because I seem to have a touch of what they would consider Hollywood or magic, until they get close enough to realize, "Oh, he's just a guy," and then, "Oh, fuck him," and off they go. Smoke clouds with their shapes just sort of hovering in air.

It would make me happy to finally feel secure in my writing, to know that I'm going to continue to do it. That it's not agony every time I try. To have a life-style that's still adventuresome but not quite as paranoid or agonizing as the one that I currently enjoy. More money wouldn't do it. More travel might, I think I'm going to try that, I'm going to travel some more.

I have absolutely no idea what I'll be doing in a few years. I find it very hard to believe that I'll be doing this, writing I mean, because it's so hard. If I can make it through this year, I'll be very surprised. Also, I've always had a problem thinking even six months in advance. If it's January and I hear we're going on vacation in October, I think, "Ah, shit." Because I think, lurking in the back of my head, is the hidden and secret belief that somehow between now and then—"then" being anywhere longer than six months—we're all going to be dead.

So I really don't even bother to think years ahead. One of the reasons I had so much trouble quitting smoking is because people said, "You have to quit, what about when you're sixty and your lungs—" Sixty, I mean who can think that far? So I always assume that somehow, between now and then, I'm going to buy it and it won't matter. But—assuming I'm still around—I would hope that I'm happy.

JAMES CAMERON

James Cameron, whose name has become synonymous with gripping, hi-tech science fiction films, came to Hollywood by a fluke. If his family hadn't moved from Canada to southern California during his teens, his affinity for film would not have been supported—and we wouldn't have Terminator or Aliens— or even Rambo as we know it; he wrote the first four drafts of Sylvester Stallone's prototypical adventure.

The Abyss characterized Cameron as well as anything he had done to that date, but Terminator II topped it. No one had made a movie quite like this before; no one had married technical expertise with art in such a telling manner. Actually, it's possible that no one else would have tried. But despite the enormous problems inherent in these stories and the tremendous complications of production, he succeeded with his epic technological fantasy.

Cameron, a tall, lean man whose manner is guarded except for bursts of enthusiasm, originally set out to be a scientist. His association with Roger Corman, master of low-budget special-effects films, started him on the road to his present success—and it came about because he could inexpensively devise the effects demanded *by Corman. He thinks in technical terms; his ability as a writer is tied inextricably to his vision as a director.*

Cameron says he doesn't consider himself a good writer, but his screenwriting affirms his ability. However, even here he tends to think in terms like the "Recency effect," an expression he coined to describe how the audience remembers best the last thing it saw on-screen.

When Cameron was faced with near-impossible deadlines in which to finish two scripts, he carefully divided the allotted time into pages and set himself a certain number of pages per day. At that point, having solved the problem mathematically, he followed the formula. Few screenwriters would have been as methodical, but Cameron likes to have everything laid out before he goes into what he calls his "juggernaut" mode. Then, however, he produces scripts that are both technically and artistically solid in an amazingly short time.

Although Cameron sees himself doing westerns, historical dramas, even comedies, no one knows better than he that he will always return to science fiction. It's the genre that best fulfills his nature—and his "hybrid vigor," a term he's used to describe a film but that also characterizes him as a writer/director.

BEGINNINGS

I wanted to be a filmmaker when I was in high school, and I had done some little super 8 films. I was intensely interested in special effects and how a lot of the images were created photographically. But I never really put it together with reality. I was living in Ontario, Canada, and I had never known anyone personally who had ever worked on a film. I was so removed from the environment where it was actually possible to work in film that I never really thought anything would come of it.

I recall very distinctly that my father, who at least wanted to give the surface appearance of being democratic, asked the individual members of the family whether we wanted to move to California or not when he was offered a transfer within his corporation, to move to Orange County. But he generically called it Los Angeles.

And I said, "Isn't Hollywood near there somewhere?" He said it was actually in Los Angeles County and I said, "Let's go!"

That's all I needed to know. I didn't mind rolling over all my high school chums for a shot at the title. I was thinking of it in a very abstract way, but then the realities hit home once I got down here. I was seventeen, I'd just finished high school and hadn't made any applications to college; I was kind of in limbo. I really wanted to go to film school but didn't have enough money. So I never really thought I would get into it.

I wound up going to a junior college where I majored in physics for, I think, three or four semesters. Then I switched to English for two semesters. At a certain point I was forced to confront the fact that my math wasn't strong enough. I wanted to be a scientist, I wanted to be a physicist. But I like to be able to think—whether I'm going to be the best or not, I like to think that I at least have the potential to be in the front-runners, and my math just wasn't good enough.

But I actually don't think the framework of a scientist is a lot different from that of a filmmaker in one sense—you have to be able to think abstractly. And I tended to take all the principles of physics and relate them in some visual way, which I hear a lot of physicists do.

I don't know, life takes you down so many interesting paths if you're willing to make a clean break at a certain point and take a turn. I always had a strong sense of trying to tell a story—what I call the narrative drive. If I couldn't entertain someone through a film, tell a story that way, I'd probably have opted for writing novels.

GETTING STARTED

Before I really became involved professionally in film at any level, I had a close friend, still one of my closest friends, whose great ambition in life was to be a screenwriter. And he had made a great science of studying other scripts. We lived in Orange County at the time and he would make the trek down to Hollywood and buy manuscripts at a Hollywood book and poster store. He made a study of screenplay form and format. And I knew nothing of all this. I was writing a number of stories for myself in a strictly prose style. I just talked to him one day about screenplays and he kind of showed me how they were written, and nothing really came of it.

Then he managed to get in touch with this group of dentists

in Tustin who wanted to make a film as a tax shelter. He called me up and asked if I had any thoughts, and we put our heads together and came up with a list of ten ideas. *Star Wars* had just been released a couple of months earlier and was going through the roof in a history-making way.

Of the ten, nine were low-budget commercial concepts—very commercial and very low-budget. The tenth was a science-fiction epic that was, of course, the one thing the group of dentists wanted to do because of the success of *Star Wars*. It didn't occur to any of us that there was no way we had the resources to create that kind of imagery. We just sat down to write the screenplay. So that was my first brush with it, cowriting the script for that film.

I'd been working as a truck driver for about two years, right after college. I walked into my job and said, "I'm leaving," and they said, "You have to give two weeks' notice," and I said, "No, I don't," and I walked out and started on the film the next day.

Nothing ever came of it, although I did finish that script. There are, I think, some good scenes in it, although it's too big and sprawling and not tightly structured. But I learned a lot about the actual mechanics of it.

My friend is just now getting going. He's had a low-budget script produced by New World and has been asked back to write another, which is always a good sign. So he's getting started. And that two friends start out ten years earlier with a certain goal in mind, and both of them manage to achieve some semblance of that goal in this business, is certainly a statistical anomaly. Even more anomalous is that a third friend of mine from Orange County is also making it as a screenwriter—although neither one of them has pretensions to directing, which will probably keep them sane in the long run.

It was by the thinnest end of the wedge that I got my foot in the door at New World. I'd applied as a special effects cameraman, which they didn't need; their camera unit was full. *Battle Beyond the Stars* needed a miniature builder and that was, even at that point, several steps backward for me. But I thought, take the opportunity, get in, get the lay of the land. So I hired on as a miniature builder and somehow managed to get the job of designing and building the hero's spaceship, which everyone else seemed to have overlooked up to that point because nobody could come up with a concept for it.

I met Roger Corman almost right away because he was asking for all the people involved in the production to submit designs.

He had a very democratic way of working. It didn't occur to him that he *had* a production designer; he would take input from anybody, which I think is a good lesson. So I got it. And, as I was working on the miniature, I just got more and more involved in other aspects of the production. I had a very extensive theoretical knowledge of process projection, even though I had never done any in my life, just experimented with it on a small scale.

I convinced Roger that over here he had this really great miniature unit, and over there he had this big live-action unit—which was filming George Peppard and Robert Vaughn and all the other actors—but he had no way of merging the two and having the actors ever look like they were involved in the miniature imagery that was being generated. I said what he really needed was someone to do matte paintings and process photography, both of which I professed to know—at least on a level that was satisfactory for a New World picture.

So I generated my own department, got an office, and put a little sign over the door, then scrambled around for a week or two and generated a front-screen projection system. I believe it's still in use down there, at least the last time I checked. We used it again on *Escape from New York*, for which we converted it to work in 70 mm.

It was kind of fun because we were reinventing the wheel. Nobody there was an expert; everybody was taking a bit of native cunning and putting it together with some book learning and going out and doing effects. The Skotak brothers, who won an Academy Award for the effects on *Aliens,* started there, and a number of other people who have gone on to work for different effects houses.

Previously Roger had been spawning cameramen, directors, writers, people who were taking a bit of navel lint and baling wire and going out and shooting a picture on location someplace, and learning basic filmmaking skills. But here, for a very brief window, he was actually spawning a kind of second level of film technical craftsmen.

Shortly after the little interlude with process projection, I'd replaced the art director and now had to build umpteen sets—I think twenty-two spacecraft interiors and planetary surfaces—in as many days. And only about two of them had been designed at that point. I don't know how we did it. We had three crews, I remember that, we had a day crew, a swing crew, and a night crew—and I worked all three shifts.

The interesting thing is that I never wrote for Roger, even though that would have been a good way for me to insinuate myself into his thinking as a possible future director for the Corman assault force. But I always came in contact with him by showing him designs when I was working as an art director or production designer, and I managed to insinuate myself anyway. Roger doesn't seem to have any strong predilection for where people come from.

I think he said once—this is possibly apocryphal and I want to give a disclaimer because there are so many apocryphal quotes from Roger—"Anyone who can operate a turret lathe could direct a motion picture."

I told him, "I've operated a turret lathe, I used to work as a machinist."

He looked at me and said, "I'll think about it."

Within a couple of pictures, I convinced Roger I should be directing second unit. He put me on a picture called *Galaxy of Terror*, and I worked a couple of weeks. Then I was plucked out of second unit on *Galaxy of Terror* to direct my first film—but not for Roger, for an associate of his. A guy who was involved in the first *Piranha* had gotten with this Italian producer and they'd cooked up *Piranha II* on a negative pickup for Warner Brothers. They were looking for a first-time director who knew special effects.

They'd had another director for some time, but they decided to switch just three or four weeks before the film was scheduled to start shooting in Jamaica, and they asked me if I would do it. I hadn't read the script or anything. I just said, "Yeah, as long as there's not going to be any borderline pornography in it, I'll go for it; I don't care if it's a cheap horror film."

I'd been weaned on cheap horror films working for Roger, so it was not a moral distinction I was willing to make at that point. I signed on, and that's how I got my first directing assignment.

So far my writing had consisted of that one piece that never went anywhere, the science-fiction thing. I did do a quick polish on the *Piranha II* script, trying to punch it up a little bit, which was really difficult to do because no matter how good it got, it was still about flying piranhas—one of those things you just can't do much with.

My only regret now is that I didn't just say, "The only hope for this film is to make it really funny." That's what I should have done. I should have done it as more of a horror/comedy. They might not have accepted it, but at least I could have pushed it in that direction. I think that's why the first director got fired, actually, so I was probably taking my cue off that. But if I had it to do over again, that would have been the smarter thing to do.

But I took it too seriously. It's easier to deal with actors if you as the director are taking the dramatics very seriously. That infuses the actors with a certain desire to create a good performance on a scene-by-scene basis, and a cohesive performance throughout the arc of the film. So I don't regret that aspect of it. But I think in a lot of these horror/comedies where the director knows that it's just a kind of a camp exercise, the acting tends to be more superficial because the actors sense that. They're smart, they work at a very instinctive level in their work and they pick up things.

SUCCESS AND FRUSTRATION

My first success as a writer was *The Terminator*. And it was successful, in a way, before the film was ever made. I wrote the script entirely on spec, for myself, and it was sent out by my agent as a writing sample. It was only sent out, to my knowledge, to a few people, and I managed to land jobs with two of them. One was on *Rambo* and the other was on *Aliens*.

Terminator had already been sold, but it took us about two and a half years from the time the script was done to get it into production. First it was all about casting. Orion and Hemdale and HBO had gotten together and formed a production deal around the project, and John Daly had his output deal with Orion, but nobody could agree on the casting.

In my hubris as a fledgling director, I took the position that it didn't have to be a great cast because it was a concept movie, a visual film. I was ready to take three unknowns and run out and start making a film. But of course they didn't see it that way.

Our casting strategy for some time was to cast a star as Reese, the freedom fighter from the future, and possibly a second-level name for the girl, Sarah Connor. And I saw the Terminator as possibly an unknown because of the fact that from a story standpoint he had to be kind of anonymous. That was his function, to be an agent of infiltration, to penetrate the human security systems by appearing to be a very innocuous human being.

Of course, Arnold Schwarzenegger is the antithesis of that; nobody stands out in a crowd like he does. I think I put Arnold's name down on a very early list of Terminators because I just liked his face. I really didn't know much about him. I hadn't seen any of the things that he was in, but I'd seen pictures of him and I liked his kind of chiseled bone structure; there's a lot of strength and a sense of latent power in his face.

But nothing happened with that, and then somebody at Orion came up with the brilliant casting idea that O. J. Simpson should play the Terminator and Arnold Schwarzenegger should play Reese. This apparently generated a tremendous amount of excitement over there, so we were called upon to meet with Arnold. I thought, my God, this is terrible, this is horrendous, this is never going to work. I thought, I've got to go have lunch with "Conan" and pick a fight with him.

But I wound up finding out that Arnold is a wonderful person, very funny, intelligent, articulate, and—more to the point from my perspective—extremely gung ho about the script. Interestingly, the scenes that he liked best weren't the ones that involved the Reese character; he liked the Terminator. He didn't say so, he knew he was there to talk about a certain character, but between the lines I saw that he actually liked the other guy better. So I went back to meet with Gale Hurd and John Daly and said, "Well, he's not Reese, but he'd make a great Terminator."

John Daly picked up the phone and called his agent and said, "I know he's never played a villain before, but it is the title character." And Arnold took it that afternoon and then we were off and running.

I'm kind of digressing a bit, because it took us a year to get to that point. But once we had Arnold cast, we were off to the races until there was another little fly in the ointment, which was that Dino De Laurentis wouldn't release Arnold from his contract to do *Conan II*. He wouldn't let us shoot *Terminator* first, even though there was time to do it before he started *Conan II*, because he didn't want two Schwarzenegger films on the market at the same time. He knew they had a longer postproduction period than we did and they'd come out at the same time. So he didn't allow Arnold to be preempted.

We were on hold for about seven months, I think, and during that time I wanted another writing assignment. So I had my agent send out the *Terminator* screenplay as a sample. That's a roundabout way of explaining how I had some downtime after *Terminator* was already a go picture.

That's when I got involved in *Aliens* and *Rambo*. I actually got both of the jobs offered on the same day and I didn't know which one to turn down. But the producers all knew each other, so I got them on a conference call. Writers are supposed to be very secretive and not tell anyone anything, but I was sort of stupid and idealistic and I told them I didn't want to get anyone angry, so I got them on a call together. And, confronted with having to tell their friends that I shouldn't write for them, they all backed down and said, "Well, we think you should do both projects." So I did.

With *Rambo,* which was rewritten after I finished it, the final result was very different from what I wrote. It was not so different structurally or in terms of the action—say, in the last third or whatever—but it was very different in tone and in the psychological portrait of the character himself, which was the most important aspect to me dramatically. I think a lot of that was lost.

I'd really tried to get into the psychology of a returned Vietnam vet, very specifically a guy who'd been in the Special Forces and had been an unquestioning exerciser of American foreign policy in a covert way, and how he was kind of rethinking all of that.

They decided to clean it up and make it much more straight-line. That's the simplest way to put it. Mine was a much more convoluted way of getting to the same end result. Another important difference was that I tried to create genuine characters for the POWs, the guys that he actually rescues. I wanted them to be real people, and he interacted with them more in my script. I really got the feeling in *Rambo*—the finished film—that they were symbolic. And to me, that wasn't good enough. I mean, what's the point of rescuing them if they're just a symbol? For me, dramatically, there had to be some payoff.

Maybe the script was a bit big and unwieldy, but sometimes a couple less explosions and a couple more lines of dialogue is the proper solution. I felt that it was devoid of good characterization. It was all simple solutions. It was almost like parachuting into 'Nam to pick up a six-pack of beer.

But it's very easy to be critical when you're external to the process of actually making the film. I'm sure they went through the budget and what they could do, and they knew they were going to be shooting in the jungle and that sort of thing.

Another thing that was different was that my script was a buddy movie. At the request of the producers, it was about Rambo and another guy who go in, and their misadventures on the way. They saw it as something, maybe, like John Travolta and Sylvester Stallone, I don't know who they had in mind exactly. So my four drafts of the script were a buddy film. And I think that at some point—after four drafts—they realized that something wasn't working. Sly wasn't getting the funny lines, because he plays better as a kind of stolid figure. He's not a wisecracking guy. I was giving too many of the good lines to the other guy. So the other guy was cut out.

That changed it substantially right there. The other guy just ceased to exist and few of the funny lines were kept. Although, interestingly enough, in the novelization of *Rambo,* a lot of the lines were folded back in and given to him or distributed to secondary characters around him, so that all those drafts didn't go one hundred percent to waste. All the good dialogue showed up in David Morell's novelization, which was amusing to read. It was a bit hallucinogenic for me, seeing all this stuff coming back in very strangely refracted ways.

Arnold had some funny lines in *Terminator,* but they weren't necessarily intended to be funny before he was cast. The larger-than-life quality that he brought to it was the result of his casting, not the writing. It was written more on the nose, as a realistic film. But I knew that the style of the film had to support what he brought to it. So as a director, without changing a line of dialogue, I was able to shift the emphasis; I was fortunate to be on both sides of the fence.

I always knew the line "I'll be back" would play ironic. When the film first opened and an audience saw it cold, they didn't get the joke because they didn't know what was going to happen next. They got a sense that it was a threat because of the way he played it, and there was kind of a titter. And then he came crashing through, and that's when they laughed, when the car came in. That was opening night. But about two weeks later, it had changed around and the audience fell about when he said the line because they knew what was coming.

It's an interesting thing to see the learning curve for an audience that gets into a film as a multiple-viewing type of experience. I've been lucky in that both *Terminator* and *Aliens* have been that type of picture, where people will bring their friends back and they'll sit and watch for their friends' reaction.

I hate to feel manipulated when I'm watching a film, so I try not to manipulate an audience in an obvious way. I think you can do it in such a way that they know they're being manipulated but they like it anyway. Or you can do it in a way that just upsets them—and usually it's because they can see the girder work behind the construction.

For me, success is making an audience react, getting a uniform response. Obviously people respond to films differently, but if you can get a universal response to a film, then you're reaching for a majority. I think when I saw *Terminator* in a big house and saw the crowd responding to the film, I felt successful at that moment; I had accomplished what I set out to do.

There wasn't nearly as strong a sense of satisfaction from *Rambo*, because from a directing standpoint I hadn't made *Rambo*. A few times, people would laugh or respond to one of my lines of dialogue, and then I had the satisfaction of knowing it was good writing that had survived through other hands which could have interpreted it, refracted it, in a different way. I think the test of good writing is that it works on the page and it works at the end result—in the film—almost regardless of what happens in between.

THE BUSINESS OF WRITING

I like the end result of the writing process very much. The actual physical business of sitting and writing, I despise for about the first four-fifths of any project. Then when I get into what I think of as the home stretch, where I've solved eighty percent of the problems and I've picked up a lot of momentum, I'll have the time of my life because at that point the characters are alive, the story is sort of a juggernaut—you know, it's a living, breathing entity. That's the only part that I enjoy. The blank page—I'll circle around that sucker for weeks.

The day I start writing on a screenplay, every cupboard in my house has been cleaned out, all my files have been neatly filed in alphabetical order, all my books are on the shelves according to author. I mean, I've done everything else that I can conceivably do to put it off.

I don't really have a lot of screenwriters for friends. I have a few that I know well, and they don't work the way I do. I have a process where I'll just sit in an armchair and drink a lot of coffee and think for eight or ten hours or whatever it takes, and try to start generating story elements.

It's like a juggling act trying to keep them all airborne at the same time, because I know the second I commit to something I'm locked down. I try to find the place where they all seem to fit together the best and then do a quick outline, usually stringing together dramatic or visual set pieces with lots of space in between, and come up with a real bare-bones skeleton of a story. I know that somewhere around the middle of the second act, I want this visual set piece to happen, and somewhere about the latter half of the third act, I want this conjunction of dramatic lines— that sort of thing. It's a process of sitting down and thinking rather than putting it on cards or writing a lot of notes to myself.

But once I get started, I go into juggernaut mode. It's the only way I can work. I'm not the kind of person who can write and talk on the phone and take meetings or whatever, so I intentionally set up my workday to be out of phase with the rest of humanity. I start at about six o'clock at night and I will have returned phone calls or whatever for an hour. I sit down about six-thirty, maybe even seven o'clock, to start writing. Because no one will phone after that, in normal business courtesy. And I'll write all night, and about seven o'clock in the morning I'll go to bed.

And I do that for about three or four weeks and the script's done. I try to work in a very compressed period of time very intensely. For me, it's an all-or-nothing thing. If I do less than that, I just stop. So I have to do it to the exclusion of all other influences. That's why I don't think I could ever be a writer who's working on three or four things at the same time for different producers.

I've actually done a number of scripts at the same time. At least it appeared that way to the people I was working for, because I would say, okay, it's going to take me three months to do your script. And I would tell the other guy, it's going to take me three months to do your script. But in reality it was a month and a half on one and a month and a half on the other.

Specifically, that was when I was writing *Rambo* and *Aliens*. In order to achieve both of those within a certain period of time, a deadline imposed more by me than by anyone else, because I had to begin *Terminator*. There was no way that I could be even a few days late because at a certain point I had a cutoff. Beyond that, I was working on *Terminator* and we were actually going to be filming the movie.

So I sat down and I said, okay, I've got X number of days, that translates into X number of working hours. I figured how long it takes me to write the average page and divided into the amount of time I had. The mathematics worked on paper, so I called back the people and said I could do both scripts. But then I had to meet my target, so it was X number of pages per day and per week. I could always tell if I was falling behind or really ahead.

You can do that only if you have a very good map. One thing that's very important that I didn't mention is that I always write a very, *very* extensive treatment before I start on the script, usually fifty to sixty pages, single-spaced. It has all the scenes, it has the characters. So I work in a novelistic style first, but in stream of consciousness. I don't have to worry about indenting or creating dialogue. If I feel like I want to flesh a scene out, I can. If I don't, I just write, "They have an argument."

I can dilate or contract, a little faster or slower. I don't get blocked, because I can jump over it. Sometime I may only know what I want to achieve with a certain scene, so I'll just write a couple of lines. Other times, I'll have the whole scene so clearly in my mind that I'll expand it out. So I write it in that form first, and it's a bit uneven for that reason but generally it hits all the bases.

At that point I can read it like a movie. Then I'm basically translating it from the treatment to the script form, into a different computer language essentially, from Fortran to Basic. I've found that with my treatments running in that range, sixty pages single-spaced, I usually end up with too much, having to cut it back. Usually my first draft from that treatment will run from a hundred and forty to a hundred and fifty, and then I'll have to cut further at the script stage.

But as long as you keep cutting what's not so good and leaving what's good, it just improves—up to a point—unless you've made a story so convoluted that the pieces start getting dropped. What I found on *Aliens,* which ran very long, was that it's a lot easier to cut at the script stage than it is after the fact. There was a lot of pressure from the studio on *Aliens* to make the picture shorter. The first cut I showed them was about a hundred and fifty minutes, and the release cut was a hundred and thirty-seven minutes. That's pushing the outside of the envelope for a commercial picture, in terms of length.

But curiously enough, *Return of the Jedi* was exactly the same length, so I used that as a precedent and I said, "You guys made a hundred and thirty million from that one." Well, they bought that argument but they weren't happy about it.

I had actually trapped myself in a story that was very convoluted, and I would have been able to cut more later if I'd simplified it at the script stage, but I'd reached a point where I was up against a wall of story logic. If I had cut too much at that stage, the audience would have felt lost. You can't do that, that's the worst thing. All your production value up on the screen means nothing if the audience doesn't understand what's going on.

I don't pay attention to structure in the sense that I studied screenwriting and a professor showed me the classic structure and I've internalized that. When I was writing *Terminator* and *Aliens,* I never thought about act breaks. Later I was able to go back and find where the act breaks were, but I didn't think in those terms. I think that maybe at some point, back in college or something, I learned that sense of structure osmotically and apply it now, but it certainly isn't a considered thing where I write down three acts and this happens here and that happens there.

I've tried using index cards and it just doesn't work very well for me. But now that I'm working on a word processor, I find that you can move information around so quickly, it's probably almost doing the same thing.

PUTTING IT TOGETHER

Film is a fantastic medium but very limited when it comes to complex ideas of internal motivation. You can have the most eloquent actor in the world, but a reaction shot is still just a reaction shot; it's a shot of the outside of his face. It's probably the biggest challenge in filmmaking, to get behind the eyes and try to relate past events in their lives to what they're doing at that exact moment and how they're feeling emotionally—which you can do very easily in a novel.

There are techniques. You can do flashbacks or you can use a very mannered, repetitive film grammar where you're able to relate film images together because of the way the film has been structured up to a certain point, and the audience is led to know what a character is feeling. Or you can use elliptical dialogue that will relate one scene to another—cross-reference it that way—but it's always a bit clunkier than a novel, where you can just say directly what's on a character's mind.

Of course, I also think that a lot of screenwriters miss the boat. They try not to be obvious, but what's simpler than having the character say what he's thinking? And very often they say, "That's too obvious, we can do it with a reaction shot or have him looking in the mirror thinking about himself," but you have no guarantee that the audience is following you in that ten-second shot of a character thinking, whereas if the character just says what's on his mind . . .

Sometimes the hardest thing to do is to be obvious, because that's not your impulse. Your impulse is to be more artful. You're trying to find a clever, elegant solution to a dramatic problem when probably the best thing to do is just have the guy say what's on his mind.

Sometimes the overall film is better served dramatically by being almost crudely simple in some places so that you don't lose people. And in other places you can finesse it a bit more.

I believe strongly in the third act, and I believe very, very strongly in the finish. A very important thing that I always try to keep in mind is what I call the "recency effect." The most recent thing that you've seen sticks in your mind.

It's been confirmed to me by the films that I've made—and in a curious way. In *Aliens,* Bill Paxton, who played the Marine, Hudson, got almost no critical notices. Yet he's in the first two-thirds of the movie. When you watch the film, he's got the audience in the palm of his hand, they're falling about laughing at practically everything the guy says. Yet that last third, which is almost a solo story with Sigourney—or the last quarter, I guess it is—is so strongly etched in your mind that all the reviewers and all the critics went home and wrote about Sigourney.

They almost forgot about the other characters. In fact, many of them said that the Marines were almost featureless and indistinguishable. And yet, when you watch the film, you know that's not true because the audience is responding very clearly to the individual characters. So what's been reinforced for me is that how you finish is, in a way, the most important thing.

A screenplay can be running along great, and all the dramatics are working very well, and then it has an ambivalent ending, or maybe the studio tacked on a different ending. For me, any ending that could go different ways is the wrong kind of ending. There should be one true and proper ending that's satisfying to the audience.

I feel that in both *Terminator* and *Aliens,* there were false climaxes before the true one, but I always gave the audience enough respect to say to myself, they're gonna know that this isn't really the ending; they know it's not over. The threads haven't all been tied up yet. Anybody who's been paying attention will know that the questions have not been answered yet. And when it's finally over, they know it's over, they know that the questions have been answered.

Sure, there are a few people who have been conditioned for that last knee-jerk shock to come out of nowhere right at the end, and they're braced for that, but I think for the most part the perceptive audience understands when the dramatic cycle is being completed.

Originally I wrote as a stepping-stone to directing, a means to an end. I never saw myself as my close friend Randy Frakes does, a screenwriter and nothing else. To me, writing is a way of conceiving the film before the fact, or directing the film before the fact. That's how I perceive it; I'm directing the film in my mind before I ever go on a soundstage or before I ever talk to a cast member.

So I actually direct the movie twice, once on the page and once in reality.

I feel like I'm a good filmmaker, but I don't feel like I'm a good writer. I feel that my writing serves as a basis, as a guide. When I write dialogue, I do my best to make it ring true. But if an actor comes up with something better I put it in. If my visualization of a scene can be improved by the designer, I put that in. I feel more secure as a director than I do as a writer.

THE PERILS OF SUCCESS

You can become very involved in the concept of success. Having done two hit films, it would be very easy for me to become trapped in the mind-set that if my next film doesn't make eighty million dollars, I'm a failure, I'm washed up. Which is ludicrous because many filmmakers might take ten films to make a movie that makes eighty million dollars, and how many films a year make that kind of money? You can be a very successful filmmaker, successful artistically, successful in terms of your own goals and working with actors and writing and bringing things to the screen, and never have that kind of gross box-office success.

So I have to constantly precondition myself for my upcoming films. If they don't make that kind of money, it can't matter. That was something it was hard for me to get over, in terms of writing. After *Terminator* it was hard for me to write *Aliens,* because of expectation. It took me a couple of months to deal with that, but once I actually started writing, I forgot about it. It didn't matter because the piece has its own internal roles, and you become immersed in the world and the characters you're writing for.

You know, I almost think, as a writer, that I'm serving the characters in a certain way. Once I'm writing for them, all that other stuff goes away because it's external. I found that to be true as well after *Aliens,* but the process of coming back to the page and actually sitting down and writing gets harder. The thing that saved me this time was that I switched to a word processor. Just the process of learning how to operate the thing got me back into writing. Just typing exercises to bring my speed up became little story fragments, which I then filed, and I actually got writing that way.

Another mechanism that I found to work is: never write the thing you're going to film next. In other words, let's say I've got three story ideas and I know that the next film will be one of them. I write the other two first, then I write the one I'm going to do next. That way I'm sitting down knowing that what I'm writing is purely abstract; I may or may not make it. You see what I mean, it does take the heat off it.

Now the amusing thing was, the last thing that I sat down and wrote first, thinking I wasn't going to do it for five years, is now the film that we're making next. But I can make that choice after the fact.

We're not ready to announce it yet, but it's a science-fiction film, quite an epic. I didn't really want to make another epic right after *Aliens,* and for that reason I had slotted it in my mind downstream a bit, but we've moved it up and now that's the one we're doing next. I've had enough time off; I'm ready to get back in the saddle.

I did a tremendous amount of research on this project. I hired a research assistant who wrote to various universities, got actual papers that had been published by various scientists working in that field. I took it very seriously and absorbed as much as I could and then at a certain point said, "None of that matters." You know, write the story, make the story work. If you can give it a patina or a texture of reality and make it resound with scientific accuracy, that's fine. But don't let the technology guide the story—that's the true and proper use of research in a screenplay. You have it there as a kind of reservoir of detail, but you don't let it dominate and guide the characters.

So on the one hand I did three weeks of research, and on the other hand I threw most of it out and used very little. But it's there, it helps flesh out that world. You're creating a big computer simulation of a certain environment in your mind, and that just adds extra texture.

With this one, I came up with certain visual set pieces that I'd wanted to see for some time and then I thought of the most unlikely juxtaposition of characters that I could put with that environment, thinking that it would strike sparks. Then I wrestled for a long time trying to reconcile characters who almost didn't belong with the environment. When I finally created the merge, I thought it was better. I noticed later that I had done the same thing, in certain ways, in the other films. The idea of taking the kind of *Platoon* movie, the classic ground-pounders in a war situation, and making an alloy out of that with the film *Aliens,* which is a very different type of film, gave it a hybrid vigor.

In *Terminator,* there was a combination of elements that didn't necessarily go together. I had a main character who was a waitress in a coffee shop, juxtaposed with this epic, futuristic war that was going on, and that war was resonating back through time and affecting her life. So you have a mixture of very unlike elements, which ultimately came together in a way that was dramatically satisfying; they weren't just thrown together haphazardly. I think sometimes the best drama comes out of that, like a class drama or a class comedy, where you have the poor guy and the rich girl or whatever. Anytime you can create strong polarities like that . . .

I'm convinced, by the way, that many people become writers because of the experience we've all had of being at a party or being in a conversation and thinking of the great line—the total, perfect, drop-dead line—about fifteen seconds after it's too late to say it. Or, as you're walking away, you think of the great line you should have said; the only way to ever have the satisfaction of saying that line is to recreate the scene from scratch and do it in a screenplay.

COLLABORATING

I've been thinking about collaborations. I'm actually going to be writing two scripts with friends of mine, in fact the two that I mentioned to you, just to see how that works out. I've never collaborated with a writer I didn't know well as a person, so it's hard for me. Obviously I have a cowriting credit with Stallone on *Rambo,* but that was a sequential thing; I wrote and then he wrote. And I knew that was a given, so there was certainly no animosity before or after the fact as a result of that—just less satisfaction.

And I've collaborated, as I said, on that first script that I wrote with a friend of mine. It's an interesting process; you have discoveries that are positive things, there are serendipities that come from your being forced to confront what's good and what's bad about a scene or a line of dialogue.

But I also find it very frustrating to try to justify the exact wording of a line of dialogue. I don't think you can do that. The line—sometimes you write it as fast as you can think it or say it, and if it sounds right, it sounds right. And if you change one word, it doesn't sound right anymore. It doesn't work idiomatically or something. That's probably the most difficult thing in collaboration, to try to justify a line of dialogue, which to me is sacrosanct. I hate messing with the dialogue on the page.

Now, when I get with actors. I'm more than happy to throw it all out if they can do it better. I'm not one of these spoon-feeding types who's very autocratic about the words. I don't think you can be. Once they've gotten into character and into a mind-set, good actors can just run. They can create their own dialogue, beyond what's on the page, and it should be in character. That doesn't bother me at all. So I'm going to be exploring the collaborative process.

These next two projects are both science fiction, the one currently in preproduction and the subsequent one, primarily a detective thriller but it takes place thirteen years from now.

I feel I have the capacity to do any type of film, and that any good filmmaker should have that capacity. But when push comes to shove and I sit down to think of a story, I always tend toward the more visual. And most of my original ideas are science-fiction/fantasy oriented, probably because of my design background and the desire to create new worlds.

I'm not satisfied as a designer with just creating a great Manhattan apartment; that doesn't excite me. What excites me is creating something really new, something that you just haven't seen before. I'm always striving to show people things they haven't seen before. So I like to say, "Oh, well, as a competent filmmaker I think I can go in any direction, I can do a contemporary romance or a period piece or whatever," but in reality I keep finding myself coming back to science fiction. I don't know what that means in the long run.

What I'd like to do is to continue to make science-fiction films and oscillate back and forth, do other films that people maybe wouldn't expect me to do, keep them off guard, which is always best, not get pigeonholed.

AMBITION

I've decided not to write on commission anymore. From now on, what I write will be for myself. *Terminator* was written for myself. *Aliens,* at the time that I got it, was something that I just couldn't pass up; I loved *Alien* too much, and I hadn't even directed *Terminator* yet. The opportunity to even be considered to direct *Aliens* was something that I could not have turned down.

But from this point onward, I want to be the spark plug, I want to be the person who generates the idea. It gives me a certain security, working with the actors, when the characters are my own. I don't come from a background of acting workshops or having been an actor myself, so my way of communicating with them is not through the specifics of their individual working style or a general sense of different working styles. It's through the character. I can speak to them about the guy or the woman they're playing, I can talk to them about that person.

So I become their most valuable resource about that character. If I'm interpreting somebody else's character, I don't have that mandate. And I'm very insecure about that. I mean, I'll say it right up front. I'll tell my actors that.

Not that I'm so intimidated that I can't function. I love the process; I love getting in there and seeing it come alive. There's nothing that gives me greater pleasure. Special effects are a nightmare. Even though I started out in that area, that part of it is just a working process.

THE INDEPENDENT ARTIST

I draw a very clear distinction in my mind between writing for myself as a director and writing on assignment. The last assignment writing that I did was on *Alien Nation*, which was for Twentieth Century Fox, but I wasn't directing the film.

So when they had comments, I absorbed the comments. I said, "Fine, I might not have done it that way if I were making the film, but because I'm writing for you I will do as you ask to the best of my ability." That was the mind-set that I used on *Rambo* as well.

Sometimes I might have thought that idea was completely bogus, but there's a challenge inherent in that. And also, the yoke of responsibility is off your back at that point. It's not your decision; it's their decision and you're only a cog in their machine. I make that distinction so it doesn't bother me.

But when my name is on the film as director, when the critic or the average citizen considers me to be the final arbiter of the image or the line of dialogue, I'll fight tooth and nail—unless a studio executive makes that rare comment that is actually valid or an improvement.

Of course—sometimes when you write, you're not one hundred percent happy with it. Maybe you love certain things and there are other things you're not certain about, where you could be very easily persuaded to do it a different way. And sometimes someone, through objectivity, will have a comment that is very incisive and very helpful.

Ultimately that will pay off because you'll have a relationship of mutual respect. Ego still has a lot to do with it, but I don't think anybody who's achieved anything in filmmaking or in any creative realm doesn't have an ego of some sort. It takes an ego to think that my finger painting is better than your finger painting—or that someone else will want to see mine.

People who don't have strong egos, whether they're creative or not, will not think that what they've done will be of interest. So they will never present it—they'll never put it forward—and they'll never achieve anything in this type of business. I don't think ego in and of itself is necessarily a bad thing. Otherwise nothing happens. It's just a matter of its being kept in balance.

THE PITCH

You're never too big to pitch your story, no matter who you are in the business. I suppose if I were Adnan Kashoggi and one morning I decided to be a film director—and could write my own checks—I wouldn't have to pitch to anybody.

Well, maybe Spielberg doesn't have to pitch, he can kinda do what he wants. But I think there's him and then there's everybody else. Everybody pitches. You're asking somebody else to sign on the dotted line, to put up money for a very large project. It's only courteous to be able to show them what you're doing.

If I have to get up on a desk and tap-dance to show them what the scene is all about, I'll do that. Also, I think it's smart to get the enthusiasm level up with the studio, with the distributor. They're being asked to take your finished project; when you're done with it, it goes to them. And how your film is perceived is vital—how well they market it, how well they put it out there. If they're not enthusiastic about it, they're not going to do a good job. It's really that simple.

So it's very important to get people hyped on your project, and the best person to do that is the person that creates it. If it's the producer, then the producer should do that. If it's the writer, then the writer should do it. Part of writing that a lot of writers hate is having to be articulate in a pitch. You have to be able to give your reasons. Why did you do it that way? What's the intent?

Conversely, there are writers who give great pitch and can't write worth a damn. That ultimately sorts itself out, but I think the best are the ones who can communicate on the page and also person to person. That's what it's all about. Filmmaking is communication. A director is communicating with actors, he's communicating via images that maybe don't even have people in them. But it's all intended to create an emotional response in an audience member.

AGENTS

I think agents are great. It's very easy to be an outsider or to be at a very low level and to despise agents; for a long time I thought of them as a necessary evil. But now I think that they're very necessary and—for the most part—they're not evil. They're the necessary buffers between creative people and studio people, who often are not as creative as they think they are. And let's face it, without agents and attorneys, there'd probably be about five hundred homicides within the first two days, with everyone strangling each other.

PLANS

You have to constantly be looking for new challenges. Just recently I shot a kind of glorified rock video; it wound up being about eight minutes long. It was shot on film and it was an hommage to Sergio Leone, done as a western. I managed to recruit all my favorite actors from all the films I've worked on, and a few that I knew peripherally that I hadn't worked with yet. So it's kind of a star-studded cast. But it was a western and I had the time of my life; I never had more fun. I could see myself making that as a theatrical feature. It was a western with a twist. But I don't like to set limitations on what I might be doing five years from now. I can see myself doing what Richard Attenborough is doing, except maybe with a little more lightness. But who can say? I know I love science fiction, so I know I'm always going to return to that periodically, even though I make forays into other genres.

Comedy, as well, is a possibility, although I doubt if I'd ever do the Blake Edwards–type comedy, which has a certain form. But the *Beverly Hills Cop* kind of comedy, which is essentially a dramatic story that's been leavened with comedic touches throughout, is certainly something that I wouldn't be intimidated by.

I might not write it myself; that might be a good situation for a collaboration. I think I can write humor better if I'm working with somebody else to bounce ideas off of. I'm writing a comedy in that general vein—it's not *Beverly Hills Cop* but it has the feeling that it could have been a dramatic film that's been lightened.

SUMMING UP

If someone had told me ten years ago that I would have at my disposal the resources to make a major motion picture like *Aliens* and present it to the world and have it be successfully received, I never would have believed it. That would have been the end goal of my life, that I would have been willing to work toward for forty years.

So now, having accomplished that, I almost feel, well, okay, I can stop now. I'm happy—I'm satisfied! But then, of course, there's that little nagging voice in the back of your mind asking about these other fifteen ideas that you haven't done anything with yet.

The great thing about this, I think, is that basically it makes you feel free to be a little bit more outrageous maybe, because you're not so goal-oriented. I feel I've made my statement to my own satisfaction; now I can experiment.

RICHARD PRICE

There is no screenwriter more streetwise than Ivy League–
educated New Yorker Richard Price. The pulsating
rhythms of the street, the gutsy unadorned dialogue of the
American underclass, disenfranchised youth, loner cops, and their
hood nemeses have characterized Price's distinctively urban voice
since his early days as a much-praised novelist.

Today, he is one of the top-rated—and top-paid—screenwriters
in the business. Just recently, he received 1.7 million dollars for
the film rights to his newest novel, Clockers, which he will personally adapt for the screen. He has worked with director Martin
Scorsese on such films as The Color of Money and New York
Stories, adapted his own The Wanderers and Blood Brothers,
and written Sea of Love, among others. He couples brutal honesty
with a compassion for underdogs, and his fearless depictions of the
struggles of those for whom life is as hard as concrete are without
exception visceral and full of heart.

His vocal disdain for the craft of screenwriting may be because
it seems to come to him so easily. It is as if he has adopted the pose
of a reluctant gang member who has learned to disguise his per-

sonal brilliance with a self-deprecating attitude. Price's gritty re-alism and unfailing ear for authentic dialogue are a natural by-product of his talent.

I was born in the Bronx in 1949, and I grew up there. I started writing seriously after reading books about working-class and lower-middle-class people who reflected my own experience, what I knew personally. Books like *Last Exit to Brooklyn* and *City of Night* and some of the black autobiographies like *Man-Child in the Prom-ised Land* made me feel that I could write about what I knew about.

I don't really know how to write about what I don't know about. One thing you find out with screenwriting—unlike novels, where you basically choose what you want to write and it's your embassy, your autobiography—is that your talent is separate from your sub-ject and your talent is transferrable; it's not tied into writing about variations on your own growth.

That's one of the few good things that came out of screenwrit-ing for me, it made me realize that I don't have to know pool hustlers, I can learn about pool hustlers. I don't have to know cops, I can learn about cops.

As a novelist, I never got away from my autobiography. But when you're given a screenwriting assignment, you're forced to learn about something outside yourself and I found out that I could do it.

People didn't know where my first novels, like *Blood Brothers* and *The Wanderers,* were coming from, so they romanticized them. Since *Last Exit to Brooklyn,* there'd been next to no books written about white working-class kids. Not impoverished, just basically conservative children of cab drivers and mailmen. Yeah, there were gangs, but not like the gangs of *West Side Story* with guns and knives. They were just for posturing. And I was never in a gang, or arrested. I went to the Bronx High School of Science.

A lot of people feel that if I reach for a pen I'm reaching for a switchblade. Well, not so much anymore. But when I was younger, a lot of people took my books literally, the way they look at *Less Than Zero.* They say, "Oh my God, what's happening to

these children?" and I say, "Hey, it's a goof, the book's a goof."
People get very disturbed, but it's a book, a stance. The writer
probably knows some sort of variation of that self-indulgent, rich
life.

The same thing is true of me. Yeah, I knew tough kids. In a
working-class environment, there's a lot of tough kids and gangs,
and there's a lot of kids who go to college, too. But the ones who
write about it are usually the ones who go to college, and that's
what I was.

I'd always wanted to write, ever since I was a little kid. I thought
I wanted to be a journalist. I didn't have much sense of what a
writer was, except a writer. My grandfather wrote some poetry,
and he was a laborer. So that's what I decided I was. There were
kids who decided they were going to be pilots and Indians and
nurses and writers.

Well, I ended up at Cornell and got a degree in labor relations.
One of the problems of growing up in a less than privileged background is that you feel obliged to do things that will bring in
money because your family is so haunted by economic insecurity.
You don't feel you have a right to do anything indulgent, like
becoming a dancer or a poet. So the best minds become engi-
neers and doctors, but very few pursue the arts. There's just nobody in your background to validate you. They think you're crazy,
that it's financial suicide; that gets pushed at you a lot.

So I got a degree in labor relations, simply because I felt that
it would be really sensible. Although I wanted to write, I thought
writing was going to be a hobby when I grew up, something to
do in the den. But when I got out of college, I went to Columbia
for a writing master's.

I really didn't worry about it too much because I was only
twenty-two or twenty-three and I'd graduated from an Ivy League
school. I didn't have any particular job prospects, but with the
combination of my age and my educational background, I
doubted very much that I was going to starve. I didn't know how
far I was going to go, but I took different jobs to make ends meet
and it didn't bother me; I knew that I was young so I could be
anything I wanted.

And I always knew I was going to make it as a writer. I don't
know why I knew; it just never entered my mind that I couldn't.
If I'd thought I wasn't going to be a writer, I wouldn't have had
the nerve to *not* go to law school. But I just knew it.

Also, because I was still in school, I was protected from reality.
I could do anything because I was a student, and that took care

of any anxieties. I thought, at worst, if nothing happened when I finished being a student, I'd be a teacher.

I did a lot of adjunct teaching, stuff like English composition, sort of schmucky jobs, just enough to make the rent. I was living with a bunch of guys, sharing an apartment. It was like there was no such thing as real poverty. It was like play-poverty. It was optional, your white, middle-class play-poverty; you're out of school and you haven't decided what you're going to do to be a success yet.

Then I published *The Wanderers* when I was twenty-four. I'd finished writing it when I was twenty-three and I was living with these other guys in a big Western Avenue apartment. I had no real expenses, I was making no real money, I was doing jobs I didn't particularly hate or like.

But when the book got published, everything changed. I was very lucky, I didn't have to lean on my father, who had a tiny hosiery store in the Bronx and was a cab driver and a window trimmer. I had nothing to fall back on, I could have wound up sleeping in a big box on the street. But it just didn't bother me.

You know, when you start writing, you write about stuff that you think people want to hear, or stuff that you had to read in school. You thought, "Well, this is literature!" And it was invariably like *Return of the Native* or *Silas Marner* and it was intimidating—and so my writing was very self-conscious.

But there I was at Cornell, and there's something about coming from the Bronx, knowing that you're never going back there again, that part of your life is over.

It made me feel insecure. I was surrounded by people who weren't from the Bronx, who couldn't care less about it. Yet that's the only thing I had to keep my head above water in this strange new environment where everybody was either from the Midwest or from wealthy suburban families. So I started acting very Bronx, like, "This is who I am." Then it leaked over into my writing. I began writing as a way of preserving my ego, to say, "Well, this is the thing that makes me special: I'm from the Bronx."

I started writing about it and I realized, for the first time, I was writing what I really felt. I wasn't thinking about, "Well gee, how did Allen Ginsberg do this?" It was like, "This is my experience." I didn't do it for literature, I was trying to make myself special. But then, inadvertently, I discovered that I really felt passion for what I was writing about. It was the subject; the voice has never been a problem for me. But when I found my subject, the voice got better because it came out of a particular place rather than just drifting around all over.

When the book came out, I was involved with a therapy group that had a large emphasis on feeling like it's more important to be a peer than a star. That sort of kept me tied to the earth a little bit, for whatever good or bad reasons. It felt unreal to have the book published, although I was so naive that I took it for granted in some way, because I always knew I was going to get published.

But I was still a college student. I just felt as if it was the best term paper I'd ever handed in, and as a reward it got published. I didn't feel like an adult, or a man. I wasn't out there in the world yet, so it was straight from the cocoon to publishing. It wasn't like, "God, I got two kids and a wife and I'm teaching in this shit-ass one-room schoolhouse in Flotsom Hell, Arkansas." In other words, I didn't have to go down in order to come up. I just started where I'd always been and went up. It felt unreal. And it wasn't a real book to me because I wrote it, so I didn't know what to make of the success. I just felt like stone. It never sank in.

It got terrific reviews, partly because it was sort of the *Bright Lights, Big City* of its day. *Bright Lights, Big City* is the first yuppie cocaine novel, and as such it grabs people's attention because they say, "Yes, that's the way we live now. Somebody's finally nailed it." And there was nothing else like it around, although of course there was a whole flood after that.

But at that time *The Wanderers* got the same reaction. Not that it was the way we live now, but nobody then was writing about working-class kids. And it came in right before the greaser craze, the whole nostalgia-greaser craze that hit about mid-seventies or the Sha Na Na time period. But I didn't do it for that reason, I wasn't even aware of that.

Samuel Goldwyn Jr. picked it up and I got fifteen hundred dollars. I didn't even have a Hollywood agent, I had a New York literary agent. They picked it up for a two-year option and dropped it before the second year of the option. Then it sat around. In fact, *Blood Brothers* got made before *The Wanderers*. It just sat around forever until Phil Kaufman's teenaged kid was reading the book and showed it to his father. That's how it got made.

I was writing in a very cinematic way because I grew up on TV, and I liked movies. Books weren't any more or less important than TV and movies. So I always had a visual writing style that seemed very much like a screenplay. It's like reading a prose script, like somebody wrote a screenplay that was published.

So the book was published, but my life-style didn't change except for the fact that I went from making three thousand dollars a year to making more money than I needed or should have made at that age. But all of a sudden, I felt like, "Oh my God, I've got a career now. I'm not a writer anymore, I'm an author."

There's a big difference between a first book and a second book. You can always become a better writer after the first one, but I don't think you'll ever have as good a time writing again. With the first book, you're completely unself-conscious. You don't even know if it's going to get published. You don't care, you write it because you like to write and there's a joy in it. You're a writer.

With the second book, you've got a track record, you're an author. There's an opinion about your work—or a divided opinion—which all comes down on you when you're trying to write. Even if the books get better (and they should) you never have the innocent lightheartedness that went into the writing of the first book.

LURES AND PITFALLS OF HOLLYWOOD

Screenplays are all shit. You can ask anybody. Scorsese keeps saying, "I don't understand why anybody who can write a book would write a screenplay." I appreciate the honesty because I know the answer, which is twofold.

If you can write a novel, there's absolutely no artistic satisfaction in writing a screenplay. But—and I'm paraphrasing here—S. J. Perelman's quote is, I think, the best quote on screenwriting, "You pour your heart out into this, you take all this abuse, you take all this crap and grief. And for what? For a measly fortune!"

But that's what it's about. All of a sudden you get this big bundle of cash, on a drug-dealer level. And then they say, "Hey, do it again, we got even more, we got plenty." So what happens is, you do it once because you're intrigued by Hollywood. You know, when you're growing up, Hollywood's the most glamorous proper noun you can think of. You say, "Hey, I'm going to work for Hollywood. I'm going to get a check that says "Warner Brothers" on it, that means I'm part of Hollywood. It'll be a goof. Then I'll go right back and teach creative writing at Columbia."

And so you do that once and they drop all this money in your lap and say, "Do you want to do it again?"

You say, "Well, you didn't make the first one."

"Well, we still might, you don't know." It felt good, it's going to happen. But meanwhile, everybody loves your script, everybody, it's close to the audience, it's physical, it's right there.

It's not the way it was with the books all those years. These are producers, they're businessmen. It's just really instant gratification, which you don't get even when you're writing novels for years. The other thing that lures you in is the immediacy of the feedback, and the amount of interaction that just doesn't exist when you're writing books. The process is more fun—phone calls and airplanes and name-dropping and more phone calls and more airplanes and more money. And all of a sudden there's this concrete arena of people who are ruining you by telling you how great you are.

If you're vulnerable to that, which I am, it's very attractive. You get some attention as a novelist by doing your readings at various colleges and stuff. But these are big guys, with lots of money, who want to give you some. And you say, "I'll never do it again, except this one last time."

I mean, I'm not complaining. I'm just saying how things are. But creatively it's a bunch of shit because you put everything you have into the first draft. The rest is chipping away at what you did to make it look like everything else that's ever been done, so they can feel comfortable enough to put their millions of dollars behind it. So after you finish your first draft, you say good-bye, you kiss it, you wrap it up in its bundle, and you just watch it get changed. And if you want to get it done and you want your name on it, you have to do the hacking. But you never care about it as much after that first draft.

There's nothing to it, creative-wise. It's not a finished product; it's just a script, not a movie. Even if every word that you wrote is precious, you're just the first colored gel on the light, you're the orange gel. But then here comes the producer's gel and that's purple, and then comes the director's gel and that's blue, and then comes the actor's gel and that's red.

They're saying your words somewhere in there, and it follows the progress of a plot that you figured out, but it's not yours. It belongs to the director. So there's no real satisfaction except for this name thing. More people know me from writing *The Color of Money* than they did for four books—and *The Color of Money* is a Scorsese, even though they were very faithful to my script. I feel like it's Scorsese's movie, you know, the director's medium.

Oh sure, I came up with it. Just about everything, every progression of events, came out of my head. But it's Scorsese's judgment of how to frame it, how to picture it, what to zero in on. They hear my words but they don't hear my voice—they hear Paul Newman's voice. I think, "I wouldn't say it exactly like that," or, "I didn't envision that scene exactly that way."

It's my work as much as any screenwriter's; I was lucky in those terms. But there's something sobering about that. And I'm not criticizing, I'm just saying that it's not my movie, anywhere near as much as some damn short story that I could publish in some college journal.

Screenwriting—there's no reason to do it except to make money. I would take the crummiest novelist over the best screenwriter as a talent, as a legitimate artist. I mean it's a job, screenwriting is a job. And I enjoyed it, but I enjoyed it up to the point where they got really serious about the movie and then—I don't know, it just crumbled.

THOUGHTS ON SCREENWRITING

I had two books made into movies way before I started writing screenplays. I started writing screenplays in '83, but *Blood Brothers* was '78 and *The Wanderers* was '79. I always had people asking me to do scripts and I never wanted to go near them. I had a feeling that once you go, it's tough to come back. And I was right. After my fourth book, I felt like I wanted to do something different, I wanted a change of scenery.

So I started calling up people who were in touch with me over the years and said, "Let's talk," and I came up with an idea with Scott Rudin, who was working for Edgar Scherick, and Marty Brest was going to be the director. You know, we *potchkeed* around for two years with this thing and it turned out to be a pretty funny script, which—surprise, surprise—became unproduced. But it was a very good calling card because it went around and everybody could see it.

You know the process for a novelist, if you're courted out there. Everybody tells you how wonderful you are. It's like, "God, we think your books are so great, we just want you to do something." But the minute you sign on the dotted line and they're giving you money, it's, "All right, asshole, prove yourself." So the tune changes.

It's really better to be a potential screenwriter, because everybody fantasizes about what you could do, everybody forgets what happens to the best and the worst writers as they become screenwriters. It took a year and a half to write this thing. I didn't know what I was doing. And really, to go from novels to screenplays you have to unlearn so much. With a novel it's like you're walking, you're stopping and sniffing the roses, you take your time and set things up. And you go at a novelist's pace. Nobody says, "Hey, this is too long." Your novel could be a thousand pages long if it's good enough. But no screenplay can be more than a page a minute unless it's *Potemkin,* you know? So I had to learn momentum, and I had to learn to cut out all novelistic impulses.

And I had to unlearn. Plot has never been a strong point with me, and all of a sudden plot became the most important thing. And dialogue, you know, everybody is affected by good dialogue. But dialogue is like the last thing in a screenplay. I mean the most important thing in a screenplay, that I see, is construction—the structure—which was always my worst point. I'm no architect.

I was best at improving scenes with great dialogue. But you can have a hundred and fifty scenes in a hundred and fifty different movies—if you don't have a tight story line, it's all tap dancing. And I had to learn to master—and I still haven't, after about twelve screenplays—how to construct a tight story. I can write page-for-page stuff at least as good as anybody. But I'm just no good in terms of construction.

After a year and a half of banging away at *The Color of Money* with Scorsese and Newman, I learned the difference between a script that you indulge in and a script that becomes a movie. The only scripts that don't get tampered with are scripts that don't get made. It's hard only up to the point where it becomes real; then they start tearing your head off.

So I had a great time as long as we weren't going to make the movie. I did a great first draft. They would say stuff to me like, "Well how did you write this novel?"

"Well," I'd say, "I saw this interaction in the street one day and I just started, I didn't know where it was going to take me. . . ." But you'd better know where a screenplay is going to take you, because you've got to be over and out in 110 pages.

We had to go through all this because my screenplay was so fucked up. They were going to do it in spite of the structure, but I had to rearrange efficiently and take all the slack out. It was just like shuffling cards. I had to have the director and the producer help me with this, I didn't know what the hell I was doing. I mean, I wrote some great stuff but they had to tell me how to put it together.

* * *

I didn't think I could write for Newman because he's so American and I'm so New York. But Pacino, I could write for Pacino in my sleep. And when you first meet them, it's like, "Oh my God, it's Al Pacino." But the second time, it's like, "Oh God, what is this guy going to make me do." You get over the novelty because they become guys who are not writers but who have the power to say, "This is no good." You ask why it's no good. "Because I don't do it this way." And that becomes reason enough.

When you're at their mercy, the excitement wears off and the dread sets in. And you might admire them and think they're terrific, and might like working with them, but there's always a nausea and an anxiety when you see them, or when you hear their name, or you hear that there's a message from Paul Newman or Al Pacino. It's not like, "Al Pacino!" It's like, "Oh my God, oh no, he's probably rethinking the whole thing; oh my God, now what do I have to do?" It's a job. It's just a job.

Then I had another project, a movie with Jagger and Bowie. And man, I had this plot tighter than a crab's ass. And it was supposed to go, it's still at U.A., but, you know, everybody's waffling as usual. The point is, it took me about six weeks to write because I had it so tight. It's called "The Rocket Boys." It's well written and some of the characters are really great, but it doesn't have the heart of a book, where I just let myself go. Because I'm a novelist, I'll always be a novelist. Even if I become a great screenwriter, I'll always be a novelist. And a novelist, has to explore, we have to wander. You know, when I'm a novelist, I'm an artist. When I'm a screenwriter, I'm a craftsman, I'm a shoemaker.

Nobody can mess with you when you're a novelist. Your editors can say, "Will you kindly change this scene?" and you could say "No," and it doesn't mean they're not going to publish you. If you're working with an editor, that means you've got a publishing contract, which means your book is going to go. But if Paul Newman says, "You know, this is just not a Paul Newman character," it might be a great character but it's not a Paul Newman character and therefore it's no good. And it'll tear your heart out.

I had to learn that plot's very important. The dialogue, man— they can hire a dialogue doctor. I've done it on other people's work, they've hired me for five days on various things to make other people sound good. That's an accepted thing, a minor thing. But studio executives get excited about the wrong things, over and over again. They get excited about my ear for dialogue, but they of all people should know that that's the least of it. I would much rather hire somebody who has good ideas and could block out a great story. Then you fire him and you hire somebody else to come in and make the thing sing a little.

The Color of Money was my first produced screenplay, and I wrote thirteen scripts of it. I've got a credit on *Streets of Gold*, but none of my stuff made it to the screen. In fact, they weren't going to give me credit for *Streets of Gold*, because I doctored somebody else's script and then they got somebody in after me. But I threatened to make a stink if they didn't give me the credit, so they gave it to me.

Then when I saw the movie, I realized there was nothing of mine in there; I should have just let it slide. Because I don't want my name on anything that's not mine. And that's the dilemma of screenwriting. What's up there is not yours. Your name is on it—if you're lucky—but maybe your name shouldn't be on it. You're damned if you do, damned if you don't.

A movie will never be yours. You might have been the first writer on something, and at the last minute you refused to make it look like *Fatal Attraction* or whatever everybody's trying to imitate this year. So they hired some whore who was willing to make it look like the other thing, and the studio executives could feel, "Oh, thank God, at least we're not doing anything new." And your name is on it, and it's not you.

Do you want your name on it or not? That's what I'm saying; sure you want your things done, but you want the images to go from your forehead to the screen. There's just too many people in between. No matter how much they love your script, what you see up there is going to be eerie to you, unnerving.

That's why a lot of writers become directors, and I understand that. In fact, I think the only screenwriters worth a shit are the screenwriters who direct, because they're the only ones who have any kind of control over what gets up to the screen.

How do you know if something was a great screenplay or not? It might have been a bravado performance by Steve Martin or Paul Newman or Mel Gibson or whomever. It might have been an awful screenplay, how do you know? All you've got is what's on the screen. It's as if I write a book, but you don't get to read it. What you get is somebody singing operatically a paraphrase of my book. Could you tell if that's a good book or not? What if the guy's voice was shit? What if the guy's voice was great and the book was terrible?

* * *

Scorsese asked me to do a rewrite of a remake of a 1950 Jules Dassin film called *Night and the City*. And I did a really great job. The only problem is every third word is fuck, but you know, that's not insurmountable. But it was good—jewel-like dialogue, airtight plot. I really banged this sucker out, and it was great.

Scorsese decided not to do it because it was too much like his other movies. This made sense to me because I was in awe of him and basically I had given him his own greatest hits in one screenplay, in terms of the mood and the values, your very Scorsese values.

Then it was going to be produced by Scorsese and Tavernier, and then there was an ownership dispute between Fox and MGM, I don't know who had it. And then Island Pictures was going to do it, and Tavernier and Scorsese were going to coproduce it. But Barry Diller apparently just didn't let it go, for some reason I can't get into, but that had nothing to do with the script. It was painful that the movie wasn't made, but it wasn't like the script got shredded. It's still there and hopefully will get made someday.*

I feel like this script, *Night and the City*, is a killer. The fact that it's unproduced has as much to do with the writing of the script as it does with sunspots on the road. That's the heartbreaker with screenplays. You can write the greatest thing in the world and the studio says, "Well, where's the audience for this? We don't know what to do with this."

Or someone will say, "Well, because the guy who represents this script screwed me on a picture four years ago, I'm going to fuck him by putting this on a perpetual back burner and make it die." So my script becomes a weapon between two guys trying to screw each other.

I won't do any more rewriting. The point is, if some other writer's stuck and somebody asks me to rewrite it, the assumption is that I can make it better, not that I can make it more Hollywood. There's just too many guys out there, real journeymen, who can make things more Hollywood if they just want something better than what they've got.

But when I got rewritten on *Streets of Gold*, it was like I never wrote anything. There was not one line of mine. I didn't hate the movie and I didn't love it. I just felt like it was some movie I was never involved in. It was like a nonexperience. I would never do

---

**Night and the City* got made and was released by Twentieth Century Fox in 1992.

that again. I feel like who cares, you know? You put everything you've got into that first draft.

I'm hoping against hope that *Sea of Love* will be mine. The director respects my work. I don't think Pacino can say anything wrong in this script because he's Al Pacino, he's such a great actor. Plus he's got to go nuts to do this wrong. He's got to be on drugs to do this wrong. If this gets done, it might or might not make a lot of money, but it really means something to me emotionally.

I feel wiser and more cynical with each new project. And I understand the pitfalls more and more, through experience. But you know, every story dictates it's own way of getting written. *Sea of Love* wrote like a novel. As a result, it came out sloppy and everybody wanted to do it, I mean *everybody* wanted to do it. But it needs a huge amount of reorganization to make it efficient. Then I write something like the Jagger/Bowie thing, "The Rocket Boys," where I went in there like an architect. But, there's a spark in this that maybe was not in "The Rocket Boys." I think the Jagger/Bowie thing was in the top two percent of anything the studios are going to see. But for me, what I'm looking for, is for things that make me feel fiercely proud of myself.

LABORS OF LOVE

Lady's Man, in a way, was my favorite book. It took me three weeks to write. And it takes you three minutes to read. Well, I was thinking about this thing for maybe a year and a half. I just didn't have time to write it. But it was my favorite book. It's about loneliness and the city, and it's about cops; it's very romantic in that sense. And I got hooked on cops. You know, every writer of our generation grew up thinking when we were little kids, the cop is your friend, if you get lost go to Officer Joe Boulder; it's like the policemen in Norman Rockwell's paintings.

You go from that to the pigs with the bloody nightsticks in Chicago. So you don't know what to think at this point. Nobody's radical anymore, everybody's come back a little bit toward the middle, it seems to me. Nobody that I know of is in SDS anymore. Things are not as black and white as they were when you were nineteen and the whole world was good guys and bad guys.

Then you start hanging out with cops. And you just get overwhelmed because you've had such lifelong extreme associations with them. When you were a kid, they had wings. And when you were in college, they had snouts. And here they are, they're very complicated people and it's a very complicated job. And you get hooked on this stuff because it brings up so many associations in your mind, through the years, that were wrong in both directions. Angels or devils? And the truth is somewhere in between.

I got really hooked on this stuff. Plus, who knows, there's a thing in you—whatever you write about is autobiography. If it's science fiction, it's autobiography. You could write a gardening book and it would be autobiography. And you don't have to write about yourself, but the way you choose to see the world is your autobiography. So I started thinking, "What about me made cops so fascinating? Do I have a thing about physical courage?" Is it, "God, I'm too scared to do this job. I'm not tough enough, I'm scared of violence."

I thought about that, and I thought about uniforms and isolation. You know, cops are so isolated, it's like nobody treats them like human beings. Cops are like black people in the sense that you see something first that has nothing to do with what's inside, and you can't get past that to the humanity. If a middle-class white person sees a black person, the first thing that hits his head is skin. You see a cop, the first thing that hits your head is uniform, gun.

A cop said to me once, "The only thing I ever see, eight hours a day, is assholes. Nobody ever treats me like a person, they're either being more obsequious or more pugnacious than they would be with anybody else. I never see people. The only people I can hang out with is other cops."

And there's something strong there, you know, the isolation of that kind of life, but also the power of being a priest, except that you have a gun instead of a collar. You know, "He's not like us, he's got a gun. He's not like us, he doesn't fuck." There's something strong there, but it's so complicated.

So I took that and then I took the city, which is my thing, and then I took this situation of looking for love in the bowels of the city, and it became a novel.

I want to write more about cops. I want to write about myself, something like, why would I become a cop? Well, I *wouldn't* want to become a cop because I'm terrified of physical violence and I feel like that diminishes me in some childish way—diminishes me as a man—that I'm not willing to be violent. So I might become a cop to constantly prove to myself that I'm not a physical coward. And I'm terrified by the notion that we're going to die someday, me too, and there's no way out of that. So I might become a cop to become friends with death—because death scares me so much that, if I rub my nose in it, maybe the familiarity would make the fear wear off.

I also want to write about children in some way, because I have two kids, two little girls. And I didn't know until I had these girls how much I could be stretched emotionally, how much you could really care about somebody other than yourself.

It's like you never knew that you could be so scared for any-body, and you never knew you had all that love in you that asks for nothing back. It's not like your wife. She's another person who has her own history; she was an independent adult before she met you, and that will continue. But a kid has got its starting point in your arms. It's an entirely different love than the love you would feel for an adult. And it's a love that will always go unrequited, because there's no way kids can love a parent through their lives as much as a parent loves them. I can feel that now.

One of them is going to be a year old soon. Already I feel like her life is going to be a constant drawing away from me. I'm already nostalgic for what she was like when she was six months old. I'm already losing her, losing my memories of her. But any-way, I feel like I want to write something with that feeling, with that sort of overwhelmingness that you feel around children.

It came together in my mind when I went to the forensic mu-seum at the coroner's office, which is closed to the public. I got a connection to go in there. I spent four hours looking at body parts and murder weapons from various crimes, from the twenties up to last year. I mean ghastly stuff—dicks floating in formalde-hyde, people's faces that have been ripped off in airplane crashes, mundane objects that became murder weapons, scissors, a skull with rectangular holes in it from where the scissors went in. And in the middle of all of this stuff, they had a child's cobbler's bench, with a little hammer to bang the pegs in. I said, "What the hell's that doing here?" They told me two little kids had killed their one-month-old brother with it.

It's a parent's worst nightmare. But it's a child's worst night-mare too, killing your sibling. So I started thinking about cops and children, and what if this cop killed his brother when he was two years old? I mean, he's as innocent as the victim, and he became a cop to stop crime—but the big crime was this thing that he did when he didn't know any better. And now he's got a child of his own, but he's surrounded by death, his whole life is sur-rounded by death. And he's got this little life that terrifies him, because the last time he had a little life in his hand, he killed it, willfully.

There's something I want to do with all that. I can't go at it efficiently, like an architect, because I don't know what it is. I have to feel my way, I have to write a novel. I know every scene I want to start off with, but I don't know where it's going to take me. But I need three hundred pages to wander around in with these ideas. I can't write this as a screenplay. Can you imagine, if I wrote this as a screenplay, what they would do to it so it would be acceptable, so they could spend millions of dollars on it?

So that's why I'm sort of thumbing my nose at my own screen work. But when you do your scripts, do the best job you can because your name is on it. Even in a rewrite, I would never do anything but the best I can. But there's always something inside me that's in check when I'm doing it for some other people, because I know what is going to happen.

If I were just doing screenplays, I think I'd go nuts. I couldn't take myself seriously as a writer and live with the reality of the business. And you cannot bump that reality, that's the way it is. You don't like it? Get lost. There's nine million other screenwriters out there, everybody's expendable, every director, every star. The only thing that's precious out there is money. And anything that's going to fuck with the money is history.

You know how many movies had great stars they brought in just because they couldn't get other stars who were equally great? They got Richard Gere for *American Gigolo* because they couldn't get John Travolta. They got so-and-so for *The Godfather* because they couldn't get so-and-so. It's like, "Hey, we can't get this one, let's get that one. We can't get De Niro, give me another Italian— oh, Pacino. No, he's too short. Well, if we're going to do short, let's get Hoffman."

And if that's what they do to the stars, what are they going to do to the writers? "The only thing that counts is that we got twenty million dollars sunk in this motherfucker!"

ADVICE TO THE SCREENWRITER

My advice to the screenwriter is, don't fight. You can't fight it. Understand the reality of the business. Concentrate on structure. If you look at the movies that get made, there's empirical evidence that good writing is not a major criterion. The movies that are out now, the movies that people are seeing, maybe 20 percent of them are even of high entertainment value.

Understand the nature of the screenwriter, that he serves people. You're a service craft. If you want to feel good about yourself, consider yourself a craftsman. The most important thing in getting a job is not how well you write—because if they don't know you, they won't ask for you. For them to want you, you have to go in there with a great story.

You have to pitch to get started. I feel better pitching other people's ideas, I feel a little protected. Better it be their idea, so I feel less torn up and possessive about what's going to happen. But they don't know you can write, so you have to catch them with a great premise and you have to be very organized.

I don't know if reading scripts helps. I don't like to read other people's scripts because I write differently from anybody else. Everybody writes differently from everybody. That's why I was never an English major, because I'd have to read Henry James and then go home and write my own stuff. It would be unbearable. But I think seeing a lot of movies helps, just watching how they develop. To sell a story, look at what's being done, over and over again, and just repeat the essence of what they've been doing. You have to have some stature to go in there and give them something that's odd. You have to have done *The Color of Money* before they'll let you do that.

Basically, the Hollywood system is run by people who are terrified of losing their jobs. The way they lose jobs is by saying "yes" to projects when they should have said "no." They don't lose jobs by saying "no" when they should have said "yes," because the movie never gets made. But the minute a movie gets made and it takes a bath, your ass is on the line. I can't tell you how many My Lai massacres there were in various studios after two or three failures in a row. Everybody is gone.

And of course they pop up to do the same mediocre shit somewhere else. But the point is that nobody wants to say yes to a picture that has any kind of gamble to it because the gamble might result in their personal unemployment. When you tell them whatever you tell them, the man or woman who's sitting there across from you is thinking one thing: "If I say yes, will I lose my job?" That's assuming they have the power to say yes.

I'm just saying I think screenwriting is as much salesmanship as anything else. You have to be able to sell yourself. You have to be able to pitch, or you have to have an agent you can talk to and who can talk for you. But—at least at first—the cops call it GOY-AKOD: Get Off Your Ass and Knock on Doors. And you have to do it. They want you to get them all excited about your picture. One of the things that I'm good at is projecting enthusiasm about my own work, and I can tell the story very well.

Most of the time, you're going to be talking to people who can only say yes up to fifty thousand dollars anyhow; they can't say yes to a movie, but they can commission a launch. Once it's launched, you go off and you write the shit out of it. Then you give it back and keep your fingers crossed. But if that person is only a vice-president, he can't do anything but give it to a higher-up.

ART IN HOLLYWOOD

I write really fast. I can do a script in a month if I know what I'm doing, and my first drafts are usually pretty good. The danger for me, and I think the danger for any writer, would be the endless rewrites, how to keep your bite after you're going over the same ground. And basically you're going over the same ground not to make it a better story, but to make it a better movie. A better movie means you get more people in that theater. The last fifteen minutes of *Fatal Attraction* being rewritten, for instance, just slays me. I mean, they spend all that time creating believable characters and throw it all out for "Halloween VI." Right there in a nutshell is why screenwriting sucks a big hairy one.

I don't give a shit about what's more satisfying, I want to write what makes the most aesthetic sense, the most logical and emotional sense to me. You know, you create a real person, a very complex woman. Why bother to talk to all those shrinks and get a profile of how a woman would act like that if at the end Glenn Close is just going to turn into fucking Jason from the *Halloween* series?

But that's how Hollywood works. I hear the original ending had the woman committing suicide; that makes sense to me. Of course, it's not as "satisfying" an ending. If I were writing that thing, it would have torn me apart for them to change it. And I don't understand the fact that Adrian Lyne himself decided to do that. I don't understand where he's coming from.

Also, people forget what the movie is really about. This movie's really about AIDS. You know, everybody's so uptight about fucking around because of AIDS, let's give them this really cautionary tale. And why are we afraid about AIDS? Not only that we're going to get it, but that we're going to give it to our wives and our kids. We're going to bring the disease, which is our sin, home. A guy fucking around and bringing his sin, in the embodiment of this nightmare woman, down on the heads of his family. And it's so slick and sinister and manipulative that it really pisses me off. But gee, according to the statistics, this is what people want.

FAME AND FORTUNE

Screenwriting didn't change my life-style at all in terms of getting attention. I've got a reputation as a novelist, so it's not like, "Ah, finally, I'm getting attention." But I get more attention as a screenwriter, even though I feel less responsible for the finished product, because people see more movies than they read books.

If I said I was Patrick White, what would that do for you? Do you know who Patrick White is? He won the Nobel Prize a couple of years ago, he's an Australian novelist. If I said, "I'm Patrick White, I wrote *Voss*," it wouldn't mean anything. But I can say, "I'm Richard Price, I wrote *The Color of Money*," or, "My name is so and so, I wrote *Jumping Jack Flash*," it's different. I mean, more people know Bela Lugosi than Bram Stoker, you know? More people buy margarine than butter.

How does screenwriting affect my life? It made me slightly more famous, not because of my writing but because of Paul Newman's acting. And I was doing all right before, but now I'm doing great. But do my kids need three college degrees from Bennington? How many shoes do they need?

It's not as if we were scraping. The fact of the matter is, I think I would be scraping, just as a novelist; I would have to be doing something else to make money. I could be smug about being a novelist when I was by myself, in terms of the money being enough. Since I've been writing screenplays, we've become four as opposed to one, and so I shouldn't be too cavalier about the money thing.

I bought a house in East Hampton, like every other schmuck with money. And I bought a loft. But I created a Frankenstein monster. It's like we're going uphill so we better keep going fast, because the minute we slow up we're going to start rolling backward and everything's going to fall apart and I won't even be able to pay myself my own pension plan and all this shit. So you can wind up being in hock to yourself.

THE WRITERS GUILD

I believe that everybody out there wants to fuck somebody so bad that you'd better have protection; you have to have a union. In my own personal experience with the union, the most important thing has been the arbitration process for credit. I almost got screwed out of a sole credit on *The Color of Money* because there had been another writer hired earlier than me. And even though I hadn't even read his script, let alone taken anything from it—and my story was entirely different, with different characters—he sued for cocredit, so it had to go to arbitration and I had to sweat that out.

If the guild had said, "Look, he was involved in it," he had a right to go look for a credit. But without the guild . . . suppose you get into a situation where you're on a picture and you have a falling out with the director, and you leave the picture while exchanging words and death threats. You know there's a good way to screw you, boy. Hire somebody in there for ten minutes and give them the credit. So how do you protect yourself without the guild?

I'm not really concerned about guild minimum or health and welfare, but I'm just one guy. If I'm talking about the whole business, or if I wasn't as lucky or demanding as I am, yeah, I could say the minimums and benefits would be very important. That's the center of any union, providing for the members, protecting them and their families, getting them the recognition, the credits.

ON BALANCE

Screenwriting has helped me, as a novelist.

It's been liberating to the point of intimidation, because there's a whole world out there for me to learn about now. I'm not obliged to think, "Well, now I'll write about from when I was twenty-two till the time I was twenty-four. And then I think I want to write about the early thirties." It's liberating. Or at least I hope so. I mean this book might not get published. I might not ever write another book, and I'll just bitch and *kvetch* and write three more screenplays.

I would say that, if you want to know whether you're dead or not, the kiss of death is when a producer or studio executive says to you, "Man, this is the best screenplay I ever read." The operational word there is "read," because you can't hold up the pages to the screen. So when they say that, it's a very nice way of saying that it's no good. Because when they say, "It's the best thing I ever read," it's the wrong physical activity.

Now, if they say, "This is going to make a great movie," that's something else.

BRUCE JOEL RUBIN

Bruce Joel Rubin's home is in a quiet section of the San Fernando Valley characterized by its rustic air. It's almost farmland, not at all what one might expect from a man who'd written one of the all-time profitable movies, Ghost, and it's certainly far from the usual haunts of the successful. Our interview is punctuated by the sound of a train going by not far away, which is one of the reasons he stays here; he likes the sound. Also, the neighbors have horses and other animals; it was a good place for his kids to grow up.

He is slight, wiry, with graying hair, a small mustache—but his most arresting attribute is a feeling of repose. The man is very centered. He gives the impression of great inward strength, and one tends to believe him when he says he doesn't measure success by what he's earned. In fact, he has walked away from the entertainment industry a couple of times, which makes him anomalous when measured against his peers.

It may be just this feeling of detachment, even when he's passionate about something, that makes Rubin's stories so different—this and the fact that he spent a couple of years in a Nepalese monastery while trying to find himself.

His films are generally about the interface between life and death—and about how people react when confronted with it. One can see this in Brainstorm, Jacob's Ladder, Ghost. *They all exhibit both a preoccupation and awareness of other states. Whatever the source of his perception, it yields both comedy and drama in quantity.*

I always thought I would be a filmmaker. Always is a long word, but when I was very young I wanted to be an actor and I discovered early on that I wasn't very good at that. Then I wanted to be a director, which remains for me a goal. So I decided I would write as my means of entrée to the directing field, and then I decided, "Look, if you're going to be a writer, be a good one."

One of the great fears I had as a young man was that I had an extraordinary urge to write and nothing to say. It was terrible to be able to sit down and poise my pen on a regular basis and then not be able to come up with any words.

I think I was looking for a teacher, but not just to learn writing. I really wanted someone to teach me the processes by which one can go deeper into oneself, to really enter into the hidden centers of the soul. The whole purpose of living, in my mind, is to make that journey. To me there's a deep significance to our presence in this plane of existence, and so the journey I began was a kind of search without knowing exactly what it was I was searching for.

I was twenty-one, still young enough to be innocent and romantic, and I really felt that this person existed somewhere in the Himalayas or near the source of the Ganges in India. I didn't really know. I began by going to Greece, much as the Alan Bates character in *Zorba the Greek* does. I had so many books that, like that character, I couldn't transport them from the boat to my house up on this island, so I had to get a donkey to carry them with me. I had the *I Ching*, I had books on the Cabala.

I was very hungry for something, but in the end reading about it wasn't enough. Sitting on this Greek island, as wonderful and as magical as it was, I decided what I really needed was to go to India. So I sent all my books back to America to my parents' home and bade them all farewell.

Even when I went to Greece I had bade everyone farewell because I had bought a one-way ticket there. I didn't plan any kind of return until something in me said, "Time to go back," so I was very open-ended in this experience. I just stuck out my thumb and began this year and a half journey that took me around the world, overland, which is a great way to see the world, because it surprises you. If you watch Tom Brokaw or Dan Rather or Peter Jennings, they cut to Cairo, they cut to Afghanistan, they cut to India, and each time you have a sense that this is a discrete place, somehow isolated in its existence from everywhere else in the universe. When you travel overland, around the world, you understand that there is no barrier, there is no line of demarcation even though the maps provide them. Cultures blend across borders and races blend across borders and what you start to see when you travel, at least what I saw, is the ebb and tide of culture, the flow and the blending of cultures, and you don't see any distinct lines separating one from another.

I spent a year and a half, and the centerpiece of it was living in India and Nepal. I lived in a Tibetan monastery in Nepal, which was an extraordinary opportunity to see life from a totally alien perspective. I meditated every morning and just had a wonderful immersion into that culture. They were incredibly accommodating and would have let me stay there until this day, except that the Nepalese government became very suspicious of my presence in Nepal. It was a very tense time with the Chinese, and they asked me to please leave the country and gave me forty-eight hours to get out. Although a lot of the monks came with me to the government buildings to plead my case to let me stay, they refused to hear me.

I had no desire to leave, so I can't say how long I would have stayed, but I know I was enormously comfortable there. They're very much like the depiction of the American Indians in *Dances With Wolves*; they have that kind of attachment to the land in the sense of the spiritual and material. They were isolated for so long in the Himalayas that the Western world didn't touch them, and they kept a kind of purity about themselves.

The West has made a huge mistake, but on the other hand it's the progress of the world. I believe technology is a gift. I believe that technology has within it the seeds of greater spiritual possibility for man. Yet, for instance, birth and death in America are totally mystifying because they're taken away from our normal experience and made technical, taken into the hospitals, done behind closed doors. Up until a hundred years ago, people were born and died mostly at home, and people got to experience the continuum of life. It's been made a mystery, but all our religions tell us that we are spirit, we just happen to be in this body.

All these things became powerfully important to me and I decided that this is what I would write about. It seemed like I wasn't going to have a lot of competition, that there weren't a lot of people in the same arena, but also this was what I needed to talk about. I've never had any skills but writing, other than typing. So I've never had a choice to do something other than write. I tried other things. I left the film business several times. When I went to India I had been working at NBC as an assistant film editor and decided it wasn't what I wanted to do. I was too ambitious for the ten years of apprenticeship. I left that security several times, and every time that I did, I had great results. Leaving NBC for this trip to India sparked creative juices that gave me something to write about.

On my way back, I was lying between the walls of a house that had collapsed in the deserts of Afghanistan, trying to sleep, and I thought, "No matter what happens on this trip, I've gained enough newness in my life experience for a lifetime of writing." And that was great. I had begun to take on the world in some fundamental way. I was no longer simply an observer or someone who is learning through television or film.

We tend to isolate ourselves very much from actual experience, painful or scary or threatening or too wondrous or too big. But in writing you've got to go for it. If you write around emotion, if you don't go to the heart, your audience feels it. I don't want to do flat material, I want something that goes for it, even if it's maudlin. I'd rather have a maudlin emotion than a fake emotion. Or no emotion.

It makes me concerned that when I go to a film I don't come away nourished. So much of it is just hors d'oeuvres, and I don't want that when I go to the movies and I don't want to write it.

I think film is the only thing I want to write. I'm not a playwright. Short stories don't have enough story for me. And although I love poetry, I respect it too much to do it badly. But screenwriting is storytelling, and I love that. And it allows you to do just enough good writing to make you feel like a writer. But not so much that you think of yourself as a novelist, a real writer.

When I first started writing screenplays, I was working as a mail carrier at the Whitney Museum in New York. I had to write and I didn't have days available to me as a writer, so every night I would sit down with the baby, Joshua, who is now my nineteen-year-old son, in the next room, with the telephone ringing and my wife washing dishes, and I would write one scene a night. And she gave me that time to do that. It was never completely comfortable, I was tired from a day's work, I would rather be watching television or anything else, but I would sit down and write my one scene a night. At the end of three months I had written the script that became the movie *Brainstorm*, my first produced film. I don't know that it was a success, but it was a film that got made, and that was in itself a success.

If you're really in flow, it doesn't matter where you are, it's going to come out. The kids can be yelling in the next room, the television can be on, your mother-in-law can be screaming, it doesn't matter. On the other hand, if I'm in a space in my writing where it's yet to be born, I need to be quiet and away from everybody. That's why I have my office separate from the house. It's the first time I've ever done that; my office has always been in the house with me always yelling, "*Shut up!* I'm writing! Turn down the TV!" Now I don't have to bother with any of that.

But I still think a real writer should be able to write under any circumstances. That's a hard thing to say, but ultimately you have to be able to write no matter what's going on around you. If you can afford special circumstances, great, but if you're a writer you're a writer.

Twice, in moments of desperation, I locked myself in a hotel room and said, "You are not coming out of this room unless you have a finished, and I meant *finished,* 120-page screenplay." I had no idea what I would write about, but in both cases I produced finished screenplays. They were very much first drafts, though at the time I thought they were great art, but it was extraordinary because I learned that I could do it, that if the exigencies are strong enough, you can do it. I felt these would buy me out of the doldrums, out of the trap of my normal life. I think that for aspiring writers who don't have the time, there's always your two-week vacation or your one-week vacation. There's always the night. There are options if you really want to be a writer.

I'm told there's branch of science fiction, called "cyberpunk," that is derived from *Brainstorm*, which is about technology as a mode of access to a metaphysical plane. I was intrigued that my screenplay had inspired *anything*. I do hear from people who've seen *Brainstorm* and are touched by its visions and its themes, even though the film was not the finest expression of what it could have been. But I think a writer always suffers that in Hollywood. Even, I suspect, when you make your own movie, you're always translating the written word to the visual medium. It's going to be either heightened or diminished, and normally not heightened. That's just part of the frustration of being a writer.

I maintained the story credit because I love the story of *Brainstorm* and I really think that it does have a certain richness of concept. I really love the idea that technology allows us to perceive the depths of the human experience in ways that Western man seems to have lost in himself.

MAKING IT HAPPEN

I always had a kind of terror of actually coming out to Hollywood and trying to make it here. I had a fantasy that I'd make it from somewhere in the Midwest so that I wouldn't actually have to come out here and be tried by the experience. I wanted a sort of cushion, so I could send my scripts out here from wherever I was living and they would send back all these checks; whenever I would go out to Hollywood, I would just be driven through the gates as the hero. I didn't want to ever be a struggling screenwriter in Los Angeles.

Getting an agent, getting someone to look at my material, was a major trauma.

My first agent was years and years ago back in New York. At NYU I was in a class with extraordinary people. Brian De Palma directed my very first screenplay, Marty Scorsese was in my class, people who were all going to go on and do things. I just took twenty-five years longer than everybody else. But Brian opened the door to the very first agent we got at William Morris, who read my first screenplay, "Quasar," and set it up within a month. Ingo Preminger, who took an option on it, had just won the Academy Award for *M*A*S*H,* so it was an exciting period—but the film never got made.

I ended up moving out of New York after a while and living in the Midwest, and my agent stopped being an agent. He left me with his secretary, who had became an agent and was a bit cool to me. I would send her screenplays, the ones I would write in hotel rooms, and she would read them and say, "Well, I don't know . . ." At one point she stopped answering my phone calls and I didn't know what to do. I kept calling her and finally her secretary said, "Bruce, she is never going to answer your phone calls again, so stop calling." And that was that.

I was in a pretty desperate situation because I was stuck in the Midwest with no contacts and I really figured that my career was over. Then I contacted my lawyer, who had a friend, formerly an agent, who had gone off to get a degree at Heidelberg in Medieval Ecclesiastical Philosophy. She was great for what became *Brainstorm*, which was called "The George Dunlap Tape" then.

A friend who was a producer in New York wanted to see the script, and there was a point at which I was going to make the film on my own in the Midwest. They had gotten money from a shopping mall magnate in Indianapolis and he was putting up lots of money, four hundred thousand dollars, to let me direct *Brainstorm*. We had sets built, and we had casts out of New York and I had film being shipped from Chicago—and the guy got cold feet. We had to abandon everything. I ended up getting the script to a friend who got it to Doug Trumbull. He ultimately got it made. When it opened, I thought, "Now I'll get an agent!" But in truth, an unsuccessful movie in Hollywood is like a child who died. Nobody wants to talk about it. It had no effect on my career.

I'd been living in De Kalb, Illinois, in a little corn tower. My wife was teaching, and I was doing industrial films in Chicago. So I had no idea the impact the film was having. But we came out for the premiere and had lunch with Brian De Palma, and Brian said, "Bruce, if you want your career in Hollywood, you've got to move to Hollywood." My wife heard that, so we went back to Illinois, and she put our house on the market and quit her job and said, "We're going to move to California."

That really was faith. She was willing to invest in me. After we sold our house, we only had enough money to live for four and a half months. But we decided we had to do it. The day we sold the house I got a call from my then agent—I had gotten a new agent who would hardly ever take my phone calls either—and he said, "Bruce, I don't want to represent you anymore. Your work is too metaphysical and nobody wants to make movies about ghosts."

So my wife and I were going out to L.A., and two weeks later I was supposed to be going to pitch meetings, and now I had to find an agent!

We came out to L.A. and I found an agent named Jeff Sanford, who had read *Jacob's Ladder* through a friend and said, "I want to represent you."

I said, "Jeffrey, I have enough money to live in L.A. for four months, and if you don't have work for me within that period, we're gonna be living on a beach and I don't mean in Malibu." But he said he'd take me on, which was an incredible act of faith on his part. So it was a very magical trip because I ended up getting an agent, my wife made a presentation to the J. Paul Getty Trust and they liked it so much they offered her a full-time job. Then we found this house—although it wasn't this house, it was a little tiny house for rent. We've since bought it, torn it down, and rebuilt it. I love this place. We have a good piece of land, we have animals near us. We also have a train going through the backyard, which to some people is a detriment but to me it's wonderful.

Doug Trumbull directed *Brainstorm*. We weren't at loggerheads exactly, but he made a different movie from the one I wrote, and that was very painful. And then I was no longer involved. On the other hand, I was awed by being on the set, just being around and watching all this happen. But Doug and I didn't really have much of a dialogue about the movie after the very beginning. I've been an associate producer on my recent films because at least that gives me contractually more of a dialogue. It doesn't guarantee it, because if you have a hard time with the director you can still be barred from the set. My intent has always been to be collaborative.

THE VOICE

Then there was *Deadly Friend*. I was very embarrassed by that movie. It was a very strange story, with a robot brain and rats and horrible stuff. I was offered a job adapting it from a novel and I thought, "This is not the kind of movie I came to Hollywood to make," so I very politely told the producer no, and felt very smug about having maintained my integrity in Hollywood.

The next morning I was meditating and a voice said to me, "Schmuck! There's more integrity in providing for your family than in turning down jobs!" And it said, "Get up, go to the phone, and call this producer right now and tell him you will take the job. Tell him you found a new way to do it." I hadn't, but I went to the phone. The producer hired me, and I came up with a way to do it. I decided that inherent in this material was a very touching love story, and I wrote the movie that way.

There were many transformations, but I like to think that little tiny bits of it survived. The film gave me enough money to pay for my son's bar mitzvah and it gave me enough money to buy my house. And during the writers' strike, when things were getting pretty dry, I got a residual check, and it was enough to keep me going for months.

So that voice saved me, and I try to tell other writers, "Don't turn down projects for integrity's sake. If it's an opportunity to write, do your best work." I think that's the whole idea. If it gets co-opted by other people, that's not your problem. Your problem is to do the best work you can possibly do under *any* circumstance, and go for it. If you can get paid, get paid.

JACOB'S LADDER

I felt successful when I finished the screenplay of *Jacob's Ladder,* even before anybody else looked at it. I knew I'd gotten very close to what I had set out to do. But then *American Film Magazine* called it one of the Ten Best Unproduced Screenplays in Hollywood, which was a very dubious distinction.

I was pleased by the recognition, because I'd had very little of it up to that point. Recognition is nice, but it really isn't crucial. I was glad when people liked it, but it was a script that I had to write. It was my exorcism. There were a lot of things inside me that wanted to come out and they came out on paper with *Jacob's Ladder.* They were powerful images, images that I felt certain could be put on film, but they needed to have a real filmmaker, someone with an extraordinary visual capacity who also understood the metaphysics of the movie. A director like that is hard to come by. It's also hard for the screenwriter to identify who that director really is, even though you look at other people's work and you say, "Aha, well, that in some way is close to the images I had in mind," or "That person seems to have the kind of talent that would be appropriate for this movie."

Half the time those are the directors who don't want to have anything to do with somebody else's script. They're writing their own movies or they have their own particular vision. I was very lucky with *Jacob's Ladder* to end up with a director who I thought married the capacity for imagery with the very strong storytelling sense—Adrian Lyne.

When Adrian first said he would do this movie, I thought he was the only person in Hollywood at that moment who could capture the kind of images I was talking about. Of course, the film was full of visual effects, and in the early days of our discussion I still believed that Adrian would do them pretty much as written in the script.

But one day he came to me and said that he didn't want to make an effects movie, that he really felt intimidated by the idea of some other company creating images he very likely wouldn't see until a month or two before the actual release of the film. And he said, "I can't do the movie this way. I'm a filmmaker, and I want to make this movie without those images." I couldn't imagine how he could do that. It really frightened me to think that so much of the script was described in ways that could only be blue-screened as far as I was concerned. Although I respected his choice, I was worried about what would happen to the movie. Then I began to understand the kind of visual genius that he brought to the look of the film. But Adrian really felt that he couldn't portray it the way I had done it, and because he had to change the visuals, he also had to change the significance of much of what was taking place.

I was willing to change anything as long as it maintained its integrity, as long as the film was still about what I had wanted it to be about. We had enormous "discussions." But they were polite, always couched in terms of "with all due respect," and then we would launch into our various positions.

We needed to do that in order to maintain our relationship. The writer's association with the director is one of the most fragile relationships in Hollywood, and a director who becomes frustrated in that relationship has recourse to replacing the writer. To his credit, Adrian wasn't willing to do that. He was willing to do battle, and we created a movie that was a blend of Eastern and Western sensibilities.

GHOST

Winning the Oscar for *Ghost* was magical. It's a mythical moment in American culture—the giving and receiving of the Oscars. To be one of the recipients was extraordinary in terms of the feeling it engenders and the sense that you've achieved something archetypal that you can take into your home and say, "Look, this was something I dreamed of when I was ten years old and now it's sitting by my bed.

It's a great achievement. I don't know, in the end, that it makes me a particularly great writer. It means I wrote a movie that a lot of people loved, but there were a lot of detractors for *Ghost*. While it was a popular success, there is a coterie of "intellectuals and critics" who were not kind to it. I don't know if I need their approval to feel myself as a true success.

As a script, *Ghost* was darker than the movie that resulted from it. It was more muted, there were more gray tones. It was a little bit less of an entertainment. When Jerry Zucker and I began working on it, Jerry wanted changes that resulted in a film that was somewhat different from the earlier screenplay. It had a lighter touch.

I'm totally grateful to that lighter touch. I think we made the film into a very popular movie. In the process, I may have lost some of the critics, but in the movie I called the art critics "failed artists with pimples on their asses"—you know, the ones who flunked out of art school.

I don't mean to be totally demeaning to critics, but I found from reading the reviews of *Brainstorm* and again in the reviews of *Jacob's Ladder,* one starts to understand them.

Both films were deeply split; there were people who loved them and people who hated them. What really threw me was people hating *Ghost.* I could see not *liking* it, but there were people who were vitriolic in their hate. One critic said Jerry and I should go to hell for having made this movie. This was in a major publication.

I deal with themes religious, spiritual, whatever. A lot of people don't like me touching those things. They're angry if I get in the way of their particular world view.

Since *Ghost* made so much money, people in Hollywood think I must know something. They pay more heed to me, and they're more respectful, and there's also the sense that I don't have to work so hard. I don't have to pitch the story to executives, I just tell them a one-line idea, and if they like it, there's a willingness to risk with me. The risk seems to be somewhat diminished by the fact that *Ghost* made money. That means a lot in Hollywood. One likes to think that lightning will strike twice, or three times or twenty times.

This has happened in Hollywood with certain creative people. Lightning struck with Preston Sturges, maybe twenty times in a row! He wrote one hit after another after another, and it went on and on—and then he had three in a row that didn't work, and they never let him make another movie after that.

Any successful movie is a product of its time. I think that's how it connects. A lot of good movies aren't successful because of the time they get released.

Ghost was very much the right theme at the right moment. If there was ever an expression of hunger for things of a higher plane or another dimension, I think this is the time. We're in an age of such extraordinary materialism that I think people were hungry for it.

I think the response to *Ghost* is a sign of that hunger, and I think one has to understand that you as a writer are, in a sense, a teacher. You're telling people things that they need, you're providing something. You *can* be doing that, not everybody takes that responsibility when they write. But I believe that you can take that responsibility and use it well. I believe you *are* responsible as a writer. I believe you do pay a price for what you put out there into the universe in a sense that what goes around comes around. What you put out will come back. And if you put out love you'll get love; if you put out violence you'll get violence. I really think that you have to be responsible, not out of fear of what's going to come back, but just out of understanding your fellow man. What do you want to give to people?

RELATIONSHIPS

Your relationship with the studio depends on the studio executive. I've had great luck and some misfortune. I've had studio executives who had worked for the president of the company and became executives by attrition. They could be very nice people, but I question whether their authority was any greater than my grandmother's. They didn't seem to have a much greater sense of script.

On the other hand, I've also had Lindsey Doran on a number of projects. To me she was a teacher. I used to think, when I went into an office with a screenplay, that I had to know everything because I was the writer. I was always embarrassed if my script was wanting at any level. And then I realized that the studio executive, in the ideal sense, was there to help.

Of course, it's always amazing to be sitting in a room with a lot of executives, all trying to ponder over "Should John do this or should Mary do that"—grown-up people dealing with these fantasy characters. I keep thinking, "God, what a way to spend a life, what a way to make a living." But Lindsey had some of the best story sense of anyone I've ever known. She was like a confident gift to me.

A lot of the relationship has to do with how you interact. If your artistic vision must be unassailable, then you're gonna have problems with executives. Be a good listener and respect what they have to say. If you don't agree, be honest. You may not respect them, you may not respect what they have to say, but if you show disrespect, then they're going to be disrespectful to you. So much of Hollywood is about relationships, and people who don't know how to have good relationships are going to have problems in this business.

I've been very lucky with directors. Adrian Lyne and Jerry Zucker were incredibly collaborative directors. Adrian had never before had a writer on the set and was very happy when I would appear. We would always talk about interpretation. "Is this good, is this bad, what should we do here?"

The hard part for me was that *Ghost* and *Jacob's Ladder* shot simultaneously. I would be on the set of *Ghost* in L.A. and get a call from Adrian in New York saying, "What do I do with this?" and I would have to solve that problem, and Jerry would be calling, "Come down to the set, we have to do something with this," and I was back and forth.

When we were shooting *Ghost* and *Jacob's Ladder* in New York in a five-week period, I would take a cab from one set to the other, and then at night I had the incredible experience of going to the lab. Both films were being developed at the same lab, so we would screen *Ghost* from seven to eight. At eight, *Ghost* would leave and I would stay and the whole *Jacob's Ladder* group would come in and we'd sit and watch *Jacob's Ladder* until about ten or eleven at night.

It was a delicious experience. I was a madman for two years, especially in the early rewriting phases, because I had three offices at Paramount. I had my own office, the *Ghost* office, and the *Jacob's Ladder* office when it was still a Paramount film, and I used to run a triangular route from one to the the other, trying to keep the rewrites and everything going. It was totally demanding, and I hardly saw my family for that whole period. But it was an extraordinary time.

WRITERS AS A SPECIES

I don't know a lot of writers, and I think the truth is you only meet them on the picket line, because otherwise you're all home writing! So every five years or whatever it is, when we strike, we get to say hello to each other. The writers I've met in Hollywood have been rather fascinating people. They all have incredible stories to tell. The ones who don't get bitter—and I think it's easy to get bitter out here, and cynical and jaded—the ones who can avoid letting that happen, maintain a connection to something within themselves that's wonderful, and they can remain wonderful people.

I feel very badly for people who get bitter and sour out here. It's so sad to watch it happen to sweet and juicy people. But it does. That's the sad part of Hollywood. It eats people up. And unless you can eat *it* up, you're going to have a problem. There's no guarantee on which way it's going to work. But if you can have something in life that's more important to you than writing movies, chances are you'll survive this better than if movies are your only source of nurturing.

Yet it's the magic of Hollywood to know that you put something out there and millions upon millions of people respond to it—if you're lucky. I've put things out there that nobody responded to, so I know both sides. But when they do respond, it's wonderful.

As a screenwriter, you have an opportunity to talk to the world. You have to decide, given that opportunity, what you want to say. To me, that carries with it an incredible weight and responsibility. If someone were to come up to you right now and give you a microphone that keyed into every television on the planet, what would you tell people?

I think a writer has to consider that element before he starts to write, and if what you're going to tell them is *Deadly Friend,* that's sad. You may have to do it if that's the way it works, but if you have your own options and you have your own choices, what are the stories you really want to tell? If you're just out there to waste people's time or indulge them in destructive experiences, is that the legacy you want to leave behind? Is that how you want to use the mike?

I'd like to think that if you thought in those terms, you might change your mind a little bit. Not that you can't just tell wonderful entertainments, not that you can't tell good frightening and thrilling movies, but I think if you feel there's a higher purpose involved, your film is going to have a greater richness and a greater impact.

MEDITATION AND WRITING

In meditation you pass through a veil to a level of storytelling and creativity. I try to meditate every morning, but when I'm in the middle of a script it's very hard for me to leave it. What I've done—which many people who meditate may think is terrible—is to keep a pad next to me when I meditate. So when an idea comes across, I'll write it down and then I'll just go deeper. I can keep meditating and not have to worry about that idea floating away forever.

Often I just trust that an idea that comes to you once will come again. That's not always true, but so much of the technique of writing is in the moment. If you watched a particular newscast or read a particular article in the paper, had a fight with your wife or a loving moment with your child, all of this is going to impact on what comes through the computer that day, or the typewriter or the pen. And you can't get away from that. For me, if you trust the moment as you write, it will always bring you what you need. Most of the time, the idea that floated away four weeks ago or four years ago will come floating back.

Writing is a flow condition. If you are writing from the top of your head, that's something else altogether, that's just craft. I've had periods where that's all I could do because there was no flow. I would sit there and I couldn't find it for the life of me. But meditation is a technique for doing just that, for getting back to the flow state. A writer has to fight battles with his own deadness. If he isn't willing to do that, then he'll just take the easy route, which is to make it up off the top of your head. The problem with that is that it looks just that superficial.

I have a very simple schedule when I write. I wake up in the morning and I meditate. I swim at the YMCA and I come home, have breakfast, go into the office and read what I wrote the night before. And I rewrite it.

The rewriting phase in the morning sort of gets me in gear, so that after lunch I can start pounding out new pages. If I write less than two pages, I'm unhappy. Five pages a day feels great, but I don't always do that. Depends on the pressure. Contractually in Hollywood, you normally have twelve weeks to finish a screenplay, so often I'll take advantage of that. You kind of write within the time frame. But though five pages a day isn't impossible for me, the writing isn't quite as good as at two pages a day.

One thing I love about computers over typewriters is that you can work it, you can go back and change this line and this word over and over. I'm much more careful about my writing, now that I've become part of the computer generation, than I was when I was typing it. Changing a word used to be too much of an ordeal, and now it's nothing. I love that.

* * *

Theme is often the first thing that comes to me as a writer. Then I try to invest it in character and let the character evolve the plot. When the plot drives itself, I tend to find the script has less truth to it, it's more structured and more—me. What happens to me in my best writing is that I disappear and the characters take over.

I always do a biography of my characters. I write out a biography of who they are, what they've done, all that stuff. And the minute I start writing the screenplay, it disappears. It has nothing to do with who these people are. I don't know why I keep writing them because something always emerges that's different.

I'm a very intuitive writer. I'll often create a treatment for the story to give me a sense of where it's trying to go, but the treatment comes out of a state of flow. I just try to let it happen. Then, as the characters *really* start to come alive, they'll often change the story. I've usually been willing to let them do that because they often know more about where it should go than I do. It's an act of faith because you don't really know where the twists and turns are going to take you.

Jacob's Ladder started like that. I ended up against a wall. The characters had really taken off somewhere and suddenly I didn't understand my own movie. I was in a state of despair for days. Often I go through these despairing periods because you get so lost so often, at least I do. But what happened in *Jacob's Ladder* was a great breakthrough where I suddenly understood my movie. I thought I had understood it, but I wrote myself into a hole. In the depth of that hole I discovered the truth and it became, on paper, at least, profound.

I was knocked out by that moment, when I suddenly realized what this movie was. I couldn't sit still. I had energy coming out of every pore of my body. I literally ran circles around the dining table, just because I didn't know how to contain my excitement about suddenly knowing what I had. The characters finally brought it to me. They didn't bring it in a gentle way, I had to find the light. But that light revealed to me what that movie was about.

Writing to me is like that. It has a kind of ritualistic aspect. As you write, you start to discover the deadwood around what you've written. You have to trim it back and find the living branches, the source that really works. In writing you have to kill a lot of what you've created because it's going in too many directions, it's an unruly plant. You have to cut back until the flower can emerge. What happens for me is that the cutting back is so painful, the bloodletting, that it's like a ritual that brings it life. And I always have to do that. By the time I've bloodied my hands cutting up half my script, it's ready to come alive.

I always think, halfway through the screenplay, that I have the biggest piece of shit that's ever been written. And I always start chopping at that point, until the source energy starts to reemerge again, and takes me in the direction where I'm supposed to go. It's a very extraordinary period for me when it happens, painful but liberating. Sometimes I have to do that several times during the writing. It's a process of destroying the stuff that isn't right. I'm starting to get an ear for that, Hemingway's "shit detector." You have to have that.

SOMETIMES THE RESEARCH WORKS, SOMETIMES IT DOESN'T

Research is a great thing for distraction. It also provides a kind of tangential approach to the material. A lot of it is a delaying tactic, but usually my best ideas come from the side, unexpectedly. Rarely do they come head-on. So while I do my research and reading, I start keeping notes about ideas that percolate through me or the script. It's a process I love. I wouldn't give it up.

But once I was doing a movie with Bob De Niro and Quincy Jones on the music business, about which I knew nothing. Quincy had the keys to every major door in Hollywood and New York that dealt with the music business and got me an opportunity to talk with everybody, on every level of experience. I spent about a month, month and a half, doing the research. And when it was all over, I knew less than when I started. It was very frustrating.

I could not, if I spent ten years, come up with enough knowledge to write the heart and soul of that business. I could get some of the images, but they weren't the truth. Quincy saw through it in a second. He was upset by it, but just immersing yourself in something for a week or two weeks or a month doesn't mean you've perceived the truth of that experience. I felt blind the whole time I was writing it. I just felt frustrated.

So I think research can be valuable—and it can be overrated. I think in the end you have to write the truth of the characters you're dealing with and that's what really counts. And if you put them in a business or an industry you know nothing about, you can run into trouble.

THE WRITER AS ACTOR

To me, pitching is gathering the Cub Scouts around the camp-fire and telling them the story. I like the role of storyteller—when it works. I like the challenge of having to sit with these very jaded executives—not that I don't like them, but they've heard every story there is! And here you are having to capture their attention, and my objective as pitcher is to turn all these people into little children with their mouths open.

If you accomplish that, which I've managed to do on occasion, you know you have the sale, which is great. But also you've achieved something, you've taken people who have heard all the stories, and made them wonder again. You made them express some kind of awe again.

You don't get that feeling very often. Writers hardly ever get feedback except after the fact. One of the great things about a produced movie, especially a movie like *Ghost,* which has a lot of humor in it, is to hear the audience laugh. When you write the line, nobody's sitting there laughing with you. An actor delivers a line and wants applause after every take. Writers never get that applause. All they get is someone saying, "I loved your movie," or "I loved your screenplay." But when you actually sit in a the-ater and get that feedback, it's great.

The only other analogue to that is the pitching process, where you tell your story and get eye contact. Importantly, you also see where they start to drift off. In pitching *Ghost,* which I did over a three-year period, I learned where the story was weak and I kept strengthening it.

When I pitched *Ghost* originally, it was a very serious drama and the character of Oda Mae was not funny at all. But when I pitched to Bruce Evans and Ray Gideon, who did *Stand By Me,* they started laughing. They were laughing hysterically as I was telling the story, and I was looking at them with my eyes crossed thinking, "Why are they laughing at this, this isn't funny." And they said, "This could be the funniest character ever." They're the ones who told me that Oda Mae could be a funny character in this movie. That's a gift!

So pitching is a process of collaboration in a very quiet way. You get feedback from these people and it helps you shape your story before you write it. That's not a bad thing to do.

A lot of writers are really sort of quiet, inward-drawing people, but they have to become outgoing actors to pitch. If you don't have the capacity to do all of these things, you're going to have trouble making it in the business. You have to go from one sort of persona to another to another, and be willing to do that.

A lot of writers are very solitary. You have to be willing to go out there and share with others and draw from others and give back to others. It's really very important.

WHERE IT COMES FROM

I draw on my personal background a lot, but a lot of it is from "inner space," a meditative layer that is my personal experience but also, in Jungian terms, *all* of our experience. It's the primordial unconscious. The level of archetype. I watched *Ghost* play in different countries around the world, and the audience responses were the same. It was universal, because we told the right story. There is an unconscious place in all of us that you can make conscious, that you can enter into and draw from as a storyteller, because it has the stories that the world wants to know. That's a great place to go. It's not just my place, it's everybody's place. I just channel it through my particular limitations, really.

I understood some time ago that a writer gets to tell essentially one idea per movie. My understanding of this is that if I'm lucky enough, my career will be a paragraph. I will have gotten to say one paragraph's worth of things to an audience. I don't think you can say more. And I'd like all of my films to lead in that direction. Obviously I have a message to tell, so I'm not limited by "What do I have to say?" It's just how to let it get through. How to say it entertainingly enough so that audiences will go to it, and at the same time make it significant enough to be worth their time. It's a dilemma. I don't always solve it, and I'm endlessly insecure. Every time I sit down to write a script I'm in a mixture of terror and surrender. I just have to keep working until it comes out right.

WHERE IT'S GOING

If my directing debut works, I hope to do more directing. I would like to be able to write the last draft of my movies, which is what I think the director does. That would be ideal to me. To the extent that I'd like to have a career at all, that's the direction I would like it to go. But there's a part of me that is very capable of walking away from a film career.

I got my Oscar. Whatever symbolic purpose that has, I did that. I've been validated, and to me my life ultimately is *not* about my career. It's about something much more real and much deeper to me. And to the extent that my career satisfies my urge to grow, then I will keep working in that arena. As long as I can do it, it's certainly a wonderfully entertaining, joyous experience. I'd rather do this than almost any other profession. But this is just what I'm going to do until it's time to move on.

I think you only have strength in something based on your ability to leave it behind. The only real strength comes out of detachment. If your happiness is based on material achievement, then you're going to be in trouble because you become addicted to the things they gave you—the pleasure, basically. Happiness and pleasure are two different things.

Happiness is a state of being, it's not a state of attainment. It's not a state that you earn. It's a state you have a right to. Even the Declaration of Independence said that. I believe that you have to find your happiness in being, and if your being is conditioned by what you do or what you own or what you possess, then you're in trouble.

It's always been frightening to me to run into a person in Hollywood and say, "Hi, how are you?" Often they say, "Well, I got this film in production, I've got that going on," and that's not what I asked! But that's how they respond, and if they don't have a film in production or something going on, they seem to not exist. And that's not how it works.

It's very hard to say this from the viewpoint of having gotten something that I wanted, but—it's not what life's about. I think the only reason that I got what I wanted was because I left it behind three times. I walked away from it and it came back to me. *Believe* me, it came back. It was kind of amazing to me that it would do that. But there are just more things going on than Hollywood. I've got a family, I have other wonderful things happening.

Hollywood is great. God knows I'm grateful to have the opportunity to play in this arena, because it's been the most joyous kind of activity that I've ever had. But it's not the end-all and be-all of existence on this planet.

The spiritual life really emerges in countries of great poverty, like India, and countries of great wealth where people have the luxury of time. But anywhere in between, the middle-class experience usually tends not to be spiritual because there's too much to be done just trying to support your own life. I've been given the luxury of having a spiritual life in this lifetime, and I'm going to make the best of it.

In a sense my writing proceeds from all of this, and to whatever degree other people read this and understand what I'm saying, I think the most important thing to know is that life is not just about your art. Life is about more than that. And if you don't have the other, your art's going to suffer.

CALLIE KHOURI

Callie Khouri lives with her husband in a small, old-fashioned house in Santa Monica, California, a few blocks from the beach. The house has generous windows, which fill it with natural light. Surrounding the house is her garden, which includes corn, squash, and other vegetables as well as a profusion of flowers.

The country air is sustained by Khouri herself, who is casual and relaxed, with blond hair and an open face. But she speaks with such passion and intelligence that the easy attitude is quickly forgotten. She brings excitement to everything she says, and her eyes tear up when she speaks about something important to her. She is so open that she seems defenseless, but whatever she feels comes out at once, in words, and there is strength in her openness.

Khouri writes about the concentric circles of human influence, how people interact on each other. Her characters are flawed and very human, sometimes unaware or uncaring of how their behavior affects others. However, she believes in forgiveness—to a point. In Thelma & Louise, one can see the varieties of human behavior, *with all the warts. This film is all the more impressive because it's the first script she has ever written.*

My father did his Army residency in Texas, and he wanted to set up a private medical practice somewhere when he got out. We actually came out here to look at California, but it was in the early sixties. He saw all the beatniks, as he called them at the time, and he was afraid to raise kids out here because we were already wild as March Hares. He thought it was just too seductive an environment for children.

So when I was six, we moved to Paducah, Kentucky, which turned out to be just as wild a place as anywhere. You know, you go to a little town and all the kids are crazy; this certainly was no different. We had a wonderful house there that was built in 1897 or something like that. It was on wooded property, a really idyllic place to grow up. But the town was very small and I never wanted to stay there. Even when I was growing up, I always thought, I gotta get out of here.

Also my entire school experience there from second to ninth grade was absolutely horrendous. I hated it. My teachers just didn't get me at all. I was an eccentric kid, unfocused but extremely active, and I just had a terrible time. But in ninth grade my parents had the wisdom to put me in a Catholic private high school, kind of an advanced environment. It saved my life. It was an open school, you didn't have to go to class; you weren't graded on attendance, in other words. You worked at your own pace.

But the teachers were really interested in the kids. It wasn't the kind of place that you could skate through; people were looking at you. You were a part of something. You weren't just a kid that had to show up, the way you did at other schools. And I absolutely loved it. It instilled in me a sense of self-esteem that I had just never developed.

The August before I began my senior year in high school, my father died suddenly. He was very young, forty-six, and he had a cerebral aneurism. It was an awful time, and to get out of the house I started doing plays my last year of high school. Of course, I suddenly realized I was meant to be an actress.

I had already enrolled at Purdue University, where I thought I would go into landscape architecture since I couldn't think of anything else I wanted to do and my mother thought that would be a good idea. Then at the last minute I became a drama major and still went to Purdue. I just realized that I wasn't really going to be happy drawing trees against buildings my whole life. You know, I'm looking at the curriculum and I'm thinking, I've got to take agronomy? What the hell is agronomy? Anyway, I wasn't a prodigy but I was allowed to be in the graduate acting class as a freshman.

I wasn't bad. I was one of those people where they would say, "This girl is a mess," until I would actually act and they'd say, "Oh, okay." I ended up leaving after three and a half years, thinking, I don't want to do this, I clearly am not going to be an actress. I liked the actual moment I was acting, but I didn't like anything else. Everything preceding it and following it was just sheer hell for me.

I moved to Nashville thinking, I'll get some kind of a job until I figure out what I want to do and go back to school. I had family living there. I always thought it was a beautiful town and I loved the music. My sister and her family had moved to Lebanon, Tennessee, which is about thirty miles outside Nashville. Then my mother ended up moving there and so it became our second home in a way. My family is still there. I was working in a department store or something like that, but there was an Equity theater there and I went to audition because they put an ad in the paper for extras. I worked up a couple of monologues and the director said, "You should be doing this full time." And I thought well, I can see I'm destined, you know?

I came on board as the apprentice because they had already hired the company in New York. I think there were one or two native Nashvillians who were in the company, but it was mostly people from New York. I stayed until the theater closed due to lack of participation from the community. They didn't really care about seeing Arthur Miller plays. I think it was a year and a half before it closed. Then I just started working as a waitress again.

I was a very unfocused person. I mean, I was an extremely confused person. I still am, but at least I know what I want to do. But for years I didn't know what I wanted to do. And I kept thinking, I'm supposed to be doing something, and I didn't know what it was. Also I had a wild streak a mile wide and I was just hell-bent on having a good time. And that's what I did. I mean, I basically just waitressed and did that thing.

THE WEST COAST

I ended up moving out here in 1982 because I decided I did want to act. My whole life was constantly deciding that I did, and then that I didn't, and one of the times that I decided that I did, I decided to move out here. I knew it was either L.A. or New York, and I thought well, gosh, I hate cold weather, I don't want to have to pay for heat, I have a car I'm not going to get any money for, certainly not enough to pay for heating bills for one winter. Based on those kinds of decisions, I moved to Los Angeles.

So I did, and I attended the Strasburg Institute and waitressed. I didn't really try very hard at getting jobs, you know what I mean? Every time I would go see an agent they would say things to me like, "You don't really wear enough makeup," and things like that. Well, I thought of myself as a Debra Winger type, more of a character actress, and I really didn't think wearing a lot of makeup was going to help me. I finally came to the conclusion that I didn't want to do it because I really couldn't make myself do it. I had head shots done, but the thing of going out every day to meet these people and basically groveling on your hands and knees for some crummy acting job was just not in my nature. And I was a good actress. When I was in class, people would always tell me that I was great. I got plenty of positive reinforcement, not so much at Strasburg—at Strasburg they never tell you that you're any good. I could live with that, I felt that I had some kind of talent for it. But I wasn't as motivated as I probably should have been. And I'll tell you, it was an odd thing because I had a lot of feeling for it and I really felt that a lot of the people that were in the classes didn't take it seriously enough, that they didn't feel responsible enough about what they were doing.

It seemed as if there was this unspoken kind of game going on, where the whole objective of the other person was to try and get you to tell them that they were really great. You know what I mean? I didn't really care if they told me I was really great; I didn't want to tell them that they were really great unless they were really great, but it was just like everybody's ego was always in the way.

Anyway, the final straw came when I did this play with a friend of mine, aptly titled *The Funeral*. It was a little tiny theater which I later found out was a heavy kind of homosexual theater. I didn't realize it at the time, but the play was kind of a lesbian play and it was really bizarre. Actually, a friend of mine had been cast, and the girl who was going to do the play with her was all of a sudden not able to do it. They gave me one page of the script to come in and audition, and I got it. And then they gave me the rest of the script, and I thought, Oh, God . . . no!

I miserably lasted through this play, which I think was only six weeks. I think I probably would have killed myself had it gone on another day. And when I finished that, I just thought, that's it! I quit! And again, I just floundered for a while. I was so incredibly confused and troubled. I fought depression for years; I thought I had some kind of horrible problem. I thought maybe I had some sort of chemical imbalance. I really didn't know what was wrong with me, but it was just frustration that was absolutely devouring me. And part of it was my own fault. I was, again, not a very driven person in terms of making myself work. I worked hard when I was waitressing—I was capable of working hard at any given task— but there was always this thing in the back of my mind where I felt like I was supposed to be doing something and I just couldn't get my hands on what it was.

MOTIVATION

Well, my mother was coming out and I didn't have a job. I had been on unemployment. I'd been working with caterers and things like that, but basically just getting into trouble, being in bad relationships and doing all the stuff that everybody out here did in their twenties. It was such a typical experience that it's kind of embarrassing because you always think you're somehow exempt from what you see everyone else going through, but really you're right in the middle of it.

So my mother was coming out and I thought, holy shit, I've got to get a job. Of course, I'd been talking to her about all this, trying to figure out what was wrong with me. I thought maybe I hadn't dealt with my father's death. He was an extremely driven person, very self-disciplined, and I felt like I was none of those things. I think I had a serious inferiority complex, just all kinds of basic youth problems that seemed a lot more serious at the time. And I think, at the time, they were serious.

Other people would look at me and say, What is your problem, why aren't you doing something? And I would just say, I don't know, I don't know why I am so completely ineffectual. Anyway, I got a job working as a receptionist at a commercials production company so that I'd have a job when my mother arrived.

I hated answering the telephone, but I loved working at this place. I started working as a runner for the company. They had just opened a music video division, so I started being a production assistant on music videos and then a production coordinator. At that time I met the guy who is now my husband. And he helped me a lot; he taught me a lot about production. Before too long I was production managing and producing music videos. And I actually found that I had an affinity for that kind of work because it was so task-oriented. I'd never had that in my life, where you actually started out with nothing, a piece of paper that said these are the things that you were going to do, and you turned it into something. I really loved that part of it.

The fact that all you had at the end was a music video was troubling to me. Also, it was very, very difficult to justify morally the almost abusive objectification of women in that particular field, you know what I mean? Certainly, only short of pornography. I really had a problem with it, and yet I was earning a living for the first time in my life, certainly above what I could earn as a waitress.

And I enjoyed being in charge. I really liked being the one that people had to answer to. I was still faced with the dilemma of feeling like I was supposed to be doing something more creative, and not knowing exactly what that was going to be. I kind of ignored it half the time and was consumed by it the rest of the time.

Anyway, I had been going out with David for a couple of years through that period and we had a terrible, terrible relationship and ended by breaking up. Then one night I was out with a friend of ours and I was saying that it wasn't that I was unhappy in the relationship, I was unhappy with everything I was doing. I liked the work, but I felt I was supposed to be doing something more. And he said, "In your secret heart of hearts, if you had to fantasize about what you really want to do, what would that be?" And I said, I don't know why, but I have a sneaking suspicion that I could write.

I had always been an avid reader but I had such an appreciation for great writing that I always felt it was out of my grasp. I still don't think that screenwriting is great literary writing.

Anyway, our friend said, "Aw, you don't want to be a writer, God, that's a horrible job." But you know, somehow when I said that, I felt as if I had lifted a weight off me because I had actually said the word or something. I had dabbled with the idea of it, but I had never actually attempted anything. I mean, maybe once or twice I had tried to write a sitcom script or something like that, but again, the discipline thing was a problem. And then one night, I was coming home from a shoot, and I had just gotten off the Freeway and I pulled up in front of my house and parked the car. And I turned off the engine, and I thought, two women go on a crime spree. That was about December '87. And I just sat there in the car because of that phrase. I liken it to being hit in the head with a two-by-four. That's what it felt like.

That idea stayed lodged in my mind. So I just let it kind of rest there; it never left my thoughts again. I was very intrigued by the idea of women as criminals, but not in the typical way. I wanted to see two women in an act of total rebellion, but I didn't want to see two black-leather hateable people doing these things. It just slowly started to evolve. I would ask myself, what would make me commit a crime? What would have to happen?

I've always considered myself a feminist from the time I was in high school, certainly in the Seventies when the movement was really in full swing. I was so grateful to be living in that time when people were shining giant klieg lights on problems that had just been swept under the rug. I remember reading *The Women's Room* and *The Feminine Mystique,* so I'd always had kind of a burr under my saddle on that subject anyway. And waitressing—and in the theater department in college—I had always been faced with these things that I felt were obvious expressions of sexism of the worst kind.

I was also very resentful of the fact that because I was a woman, I was somehow in danger. I had been followed home from work sometimes; there were times that somebody would be standing out in front of my apartment building and I would be afraid to go in. I just felt very scared, and it really bothered me because I know that guys weren't feeling that. And I have friends that had been raped. It really made me angry. I knew that other women were feeling angry about it too.

So, anyway, I just let this idea fall into place. And I finally decided I was going to write a screenplay. I felt that through my production experience, even though it was all music video of the most nonnarrative kind, music video production is one of the most hands-on kinds of experiences that you can get—you get a real feeling for it. I started to really figure out how to tell a story in pictures. And I read the Truffaut and Hitchcock books and things like that and I picked up the Syd Field book and looked through it, and I thought, this is just way too structured, I could never write like that. I'm just going to tell this story. I know what makes a good movie. I know what I want to see.

I sat down and I started writing. Probably a total of four people knew that I was doing this and they were all sworn to secrecy. I didn't want to walk around telling people, "Yeah, I'm writing a screenplay," because I knew I would never finish it, I knew I would just get nothing but negative feedback. It seems people are always so willing to believe that you're going to fail. Especially with somebody who didn't go to film school, I was kind of there by luck. There were certainly people who would say, "Well, what the hell do you know about it? You didn't go to AFI."

I just decided not to open myself up for that. And the challenge to me was to finish the screenplay; that was all that I was trying for. I didn't think about selling it, I didn't think about anything. I did think, though, that if I finished it, I was going to attempt to direct it. Because with this idea came a release: I am not going to say no to myself anymore. I have said no to myself my whole life. I've always told myself I couldn't do this, I wasn't good enough. In terms of acting, I wasn't pretty enough. I wasn't disciplined enough, I wasn't ever enough. Well, I just decided I'm not going to say that anymore and I'm not going to tell myself that I can't direct this. I had to tell myself to fuck off, that part of me that was going to try and keep me down—I was going to fight it. I was going to actually accomplish something.

I wrote it out in longhand and I would go to the office at night when nobody was there and I would put it into the computer, which didn't even have a screenplay program in it, just typing it on a computer, and it was incredibly difficult and I hope to God I never have to go through that again. But then I would print it out and I would look at this stack of paper getting taller and taller and think, I'm getting there. And I finished it and I thought, goddamn, this is good. I thought it was so good. And part of why I thought it was so good was that it was finished, I mean, I had actually completed something, and it was maybe the first thing in my life that I had ever completed besides a music video or whatever. I was just so blown away that I had actually done that.

I gave the screenplay to a very, very good friend of mine. We were kind of a producing team and we developed an extremely close friendship. I told her that I was writing this thing, and I said, when I'm finished I want you to read it and if you like it, we could produce it, and I could direct it. She was in London at the time and I sent it over to her and she called me up and said, well, this is what you're meant to be doing.

I was doing a shoot at the time and I just started crying. I went up to the production office and closed all the doors and just cried for a really long time. I felt, thank God, after all this time, there it is. And I felt like it had been handed to me on a silver platter, even though I'd actually had to mine the silver and hammer the platter.

It had taken six months, about a third of the time that the second one is taking me. We did start shopping the script a little bit and immediately it started to get very positive feedback. Finally it went to Ridley Scott. At first I was nervous about that because I thought, oh, I don't know if I want somebody like Ridley Scott reading my script. I was very insecure still, even though I thought it was really good. I'd had one meeting already where somebody had said, you know, does she have to shoot the guy? You know that kind of thing. But I felt so strongly about it, I felt so much that the story was right exactly as it was, that it had to be told that way. And there was nothing to be gained by mincing anything. Yes, she had to kill the guy because it had to be a totally unjustifiable act in terms of logic. In terms of emotion it's completely justifiable, but in terms of logic, it is so much the wrong thing to do.

So I said, sure, give it to Ridley. Well, Ridley read it and said he might be very interested in producing this film. At that point I talked to a friend I'd wanted to produce it and she said, let him do it. She didn't say, well, we made this agreement or anything like that; she just immediately said, your film will get made. To this day, my fantasy is that one day she and I will do a film that she produces and I direct.

I met with Ridley and he said, I just want you to know that I understand that the ending can't be changed. So we decided that he was going to produce it. He was extremely supportive, extremely open to whatever I had to say. He would just sit there and I felt he was trying to get in every crevice of my brain to understand why I had made this decision, why I had made that decision.

It was a dream experience. Sometimes I would be driving home and I would feel this strange physical thing happening, almost as if I could feel my life changing. It was the weirdest thing. I was talking to my husband about it not long ago because I can't even describe it; it was some kind of strange metaphysical experience, with the emphasis on the physical because I felt like I was being pushed through a wall. I would practically get dizzy. And then Ridley finally decided that he wanted to direct the film.

I think he'd toyed with the idea before, but I think he also realized it was very different from anything he had attempted to do, that he was certainly going to meet some resistance on doing a piece that was so character-oriented and certainly not the slick visual that everybody expected from him. At the same time, that was the thing that attracted him to it. When he finally did decide to direct it I was a true believer.

THE REASON D'ETRE

I don't think of Thelma and Louise as feminists; they would never call themselves feminists. Their idea of feminism is something so horrible that neither one of them would ever be able to ever ascribe to that, because they have a negative view of it, the fictional, stereotypical character with combat boots, the angry, man-hating lesbian who believes that man should be wiped off the face of the earth. But one of the things that came out of this is the moment where Thelma says, Do you feel awake? I feel awake.

At that moment, Thelma cannot see around the next corner. Around the next corner could be the end of their lives, and whatever is behind them is so far from where they started out that there is nothing. It's being so purely in the moment, few people ever get to experience it. It doesn't have anything to do with feminism; it has to do with purity of self. I think that men's lives are just as narrowly defined and I feel just as strongly for the condition of men in the world, the way their identities are defined by what they do and the fact that they are basically denied the privilege of living an emotional life without being thought of as flakes or wimps. One of the things that's hurt me about the criticism about *Thelma & Louise* being man-bashing and all that kind of stuff is that I'm aware of how sexism hurts everyone.

I want to direct, but just my own writing, at least at this stage of the game. I mean, I don't think directing is such a wonderful job. I have a lot of respect for people who are willing to direct something that somebody else wrote, but I think the only reason to direct something is to tell the story the way you want it. If you want to tell somebody else's story as badly as you want to tell your own, then certainly it's worth doing. But I'd rather tell my own.

I'm not very good at other people's ideas, you know? I like to think of it myself or else I really don't quite get the full experience out of it. There are a couple of things I've seen that I wouldn't have minded doing as an adaptation, but I don't really think it's going to be my strong suit in the long run. Probably there are going to be one or two things I'll feel strongly enough about to invest them with the same sense of emotion that I feel about my own work, because they just move me enough to get completely into them. I mean, you have to wear the story like a skin, you really have to inhabit it to make it anything. I'm not on the outside looking in, I have to kind of *be* it.

I know how hard directing is, you have the input of so many people, it's not like little pieces you can just move around a board. In an ideal world you would be able to imagine in your mind and project onto a screen, and that's not ever gonna happen. There are so many variables between the idea and how it actually makes it to the screen. There are so many things that can go wrong. God knows, nobody knows better than I do, that if one Production Assistant doesn't show up at this van at this time, you can lose four hours.

James Brooks is my idol. His way with dialogue was always astonishing to me. When I was writing *Thelma & Louise,* I would rent *Broadcast News* or *Terms of Endearment* and listen to the way the people spoke to each other. The first time I saw *Terms of Endearment,* I walked out of there and thought, what is the big stink about this, this was totally manipulative. I didn't get it. When I went back, I felt like I had been hit in the head. I couldn't believe I missed it the first time. I don't know what was wrong with me.

There were things in that script, like when Debra Winger confronts the girl that her husband is having an affair with, and says, "Well, if you see Flap, you just tell him that his wife and his baby have gone to get their flu shots." It was so brilliant. She never has the right word at her fingertips. She'll think of a million things later, but right now all she can think of is "tell him they've gone to get their flu shots." There were so many moments in that movie. But just the way people talk is so fucking wonderful. It's so fascinating to me, God, it's so beautiful.

I can only describe my working habits as totally spasmodic. I haven't yet found a way to get up every day and go sit in my office for three hours. In fact I'm having a big problem right now. Ordinarily I have to have a spark of something, a feeling of, oh my God, I've got to write this! Well, I'm finding that I can't really wait for that anymore.

I get ideas anywhere. But I can't just sit down and write anywhere. I need a feeling of isolation. Even in my own office, which I thought looked like a great working environment because I was in my own house, I still feel I really need to be where there are no people and there's simply nothing else to do but write.

I can think of fifty ways to rearrange the top of my desk before

I can write. My husband, on the other hand, is one of those guys who gets up, goes for a five-mile hike, closes the door to his office, and will work for hours at a time. He is so focused and so concentrated, and I always think, well, his work is really going to suffer. But it doesn't, it's good. I'm sure in some strange way he must be validated by seeing that I practically have to tie myself to a chair to write. And it was different when I was writing *Thelma & Louise* too, because I was trying to pull myself out of a pit and every time the pencil touched the page I was one step higher.

I still write longhand first, and then I rewrite when I put it into the computer. I just find that it's a more organic experience to write with a pen. I think I get the seed of the scene that way, but I'm really doing the hard part when I put it into the computer, and I enjoy that too. But for some reason, I feel more emotion when I'm writing it by hand; it's just the way the words look.

After *Thelma & Louise,* I have to work harder to keep the writing pure. It's not that I don't feel as strongly about it; I think I second-guess myself more. It's harder to get myself into the moment than it was with *Thelma & Louise.* First of all, when I was writing *Thelma & Louise* I felt that I was writing a story that hadn't yet been told; I really felt like I was doing something new. I don't know if writers ever have the luxury of having that experience twice.

WORKING ON THE PRESENT

So I feel I'm in a period of development as a writer. That first one was my gift, and from everything on it's just going to be really, really hard work. And I'm going to have to find the ways to do that. I certainly can tell a story with as much emotion—and I'm looking for that story which hasn't been told—but everyone who tells stories will tell you how hard that is to find. In many ways, *Thelma & Louise* was divine inspiration. Because it was such a cornerstone in my life, it was the foundation on which the rest of my life was going to be built. And so there was an intensity to it that I may never experience again. But that is what I now aspire to.

I can't talk over my stories with studio people. I've done it once or twice, but the thing is, if I have something I want to write, I'm going to write it, I'm just going to write the thing. I think many times when you tell something, it dissipates it or it somehow takes away that need to have to tell it.

Sometimes I pitch things to my friends. But I don't want to have to try to convince somebody who's sitting behind a desk or whatever, no matter how much they might want to hear it. Coming from an acting background, I don't have any problem throwing myself into it. I just hope that things never come to that point where I find myself sitting in an office, trying to persuade somebody to let me write this story. Because then you're in the same situation as being an actor.

I would love to be able to write comedy. I really don't know if I would ever be able to write *pure* comedy, where everything is just funny. I think that is a fantastic gift. And I don't know if it's mine. I hope that everything that I do will have a comedic overtone to it, but I like things to be a little more true to life in that they're horribly sad and extremely funny at the same time.

I did a lot of technical research for *Thelma & Louise.* I talked to the FBI a lot. I really enjoy researching. You always find things that you didn't expect. A lot of questions that you thought were going to be problems are answered. A lot of that stuff is missing from the movie too. But I did enjoy it, and certainly, even though it's not in the film, it made it possible for me; they weren't blank spaces in my mind.

WORKING ON THE FUTURE

I'm working on a Southern family saga now. Present day. A story about two sisters who come from a very traditional family. One of the sisters is married and a Junior League type and has always been the dutiful, good daughter. The other daughter works for the father; she's very, very business-oriented. She doesn't feel a lot of love in her life, because she's trying to prove herself and she's trying not to be vulnerable. To her, love is the way in which people ultimately show what fools they are.

The married sister finds that her husband has been cheating on her, and she has never planned on anything but being a wife and a mother. Her world is completely undone because she has given up all expectations outside her home. And she leaves her husband and comes to stay with her sister, who lives in a house right behind her parents' house. She has to deal with the pressure of her family saying, he's not leaving you, you have a responsibility to your family, you've made no provision for anything in life besides that, we're not taking care of you. And she's just saying, all I have to give up to make that situation work is my self-respect.

She finds out this is a game in which she cannot win. And her father is the most adamant about her sticking to her role. And we come to find out that the father has always behaved in exactly the same way as her husband; it's not something that you're supposed to take personally.

And the wife is angry with her mother, who has always pretended to be oblivious to it because she's never wanted to jeopardize her position. She's always loved her husband, she's always just figured it was her cross to quietly bear.

And the wife says to the mother, "Look, maybe you don't care if he fucks your friends, okay, but I'm not like that." And the mother says, "What do you mean, my friends?" All of a sudden it goes from being an abstract thing to the idea that she has been made a fool of her whole life. She'd never thought about it in terms of her friends. All of a sudden, all the years of humiliation come crashing down on her and she kicks him out.

The father is an incredible egomaniac and has bought an extremely expensive Tennessee walking horse and is going to take it to a contest they have every year in Tennessee where they choose the World Grand Champion. And along with the horse comes this trainer. And the married daughter ends up involved with him, because he's the only person who will say, you're not nuts. His wife was a nurse and left him for a doctor because he was never going to achieve the social position she thought was her natural place in life, and he understands what it means for someone to leave you or be unfaithful to you. They don't end up together in the end. But he does say to her, you have to make your life work for yourself. That's what he's learning; he's in exactly the same stage, he's just a little bit beyond her; he has accepted being alone and has accepted that he will find love again.

But he also says, if you have it in you to try to make your marriage work and that's what you want, you should do that, because now you have to discover whether or not you really love your husband. And that's where the movie ends basically, with him leaving and her kind of turning to face her husband to see. But it won't be on the same terms that it was before.

The other sister, who is so involved in the family business, is beating her head against the wall because the father wants to leave the business to the brother and the husband; that's just the way he thinks about it. It doesn't matter that she's running it. And she hasn't allowed love in her life; people think of her as an aberration because she wants to be a businessperson. And there's a guy who has loved her since high school and she's never given him the time of day. But her sister, the married one, tells him how to get around her defenses and it works. She opens herself up for the first time to the fact that she does need to be loved. She realizes she's in the same kind of stranglehold as her sister.

And the father has to finally realize that what he's doing has an effect on people, that you can't just live your life and expect everybody to take it. After being kicked out by his wife, he realizes that she was just as much a part of what they have as he was. There's a doctor in the town that she used to date before she married, and he always had a thing for her. He's widowed now, and she tells the father, I never did anything about it because I always had too much respect for our relationship. And now, I wish I had. And to hear his wife say this just galls the hell out of him. Because men can be unfaithful all day long, but they really hate it when it happens to them.

The mother ends up letting the father come back, because one of the things that the movie is about is forgiveness. It's a movie about fidelity, respect, love, and forgiveness. So that's what I'm working on now.

CRITICS

Well I've got tell you, I just think critics are doing what they've got to do. *Thelma & Louise* has gotten some incredible reviews, and in fact, a lot of the negative criticism that this movie has gotten hasn't come from film critics, it's come from gossip columnists, social commentators that are always looking for some grist for the mill.

For the most part, the film critics that I really respect have loved it and I've been very gratified by that. You can't please everybody, it certainly didn't come as any shock to me that every person who saw this movie didn't love it. I certainly would never expect there'd be anything in the world that everybody liked. I mean, there are people out there who would look at a movie like *It's a Wonderful Life* and go, oh what a piece of shit. To me, that is one of the most brilliant screenplays, or movies, the screenplay is so perfect, and yet you'll find people who think it's just a sticky, sentimental, boring story.

So I don't really think about critics. I have read one or two things. They did a thing in the *L.A. Times* that just foamed at the mouth for three pages. And I thought, you just so totally missed the point, and it's upset you enough to write three pages about it. It's a shame that you didn't understand it.

But I live in this house, I have my husband and my dog, and a very small group of friends. I'm not a big Hollywood type, I don't have a lot of friends who are big stars, and I don't hang around with a bunch of other screenwriters, and I didn't go to film school. My life is not remarkably different from before I wrote this screenplay. I can live with people not liking it.

Five years from now I want to have directed a movie that I wrote. I really don't know if I'll be writing the same kind of movies. I hope in a way that I am. I hope I'm writing things that are validating to people in a way that *Thelma & Louise* has been for a lot of people. I don't know, time will tell. I'll tell you on the one hand, though, I do shy away from things that have already been told. If I tell a detective story, I hope that I'd be able to tell it in a way that would make it a completely new story, and that the only thing making it a genre is that it was a detective story; everything else about it would be different. That is what I would like to do.

My father burdened me very early in life with the idea that if you're going to do something, it should be original, otherwise you're kind of just making noise. I think that's one of the things that kept me from doing anything for so many years; I just feared that it wasn't going to be original. And it is a huge burden, believe me, because it permeated my consciousness so completely. But it's like finally, after all those years, I can say, well there. There you go, Dad, now what do you think?

My mother is thrilled beyond all description, and, of course, she always thought it was just a matter of time. She has always been my biggest fan, so she's happy because she thinks, see, I was right, I always knew you were great.

But through this period, I have just wished that my father could have been around for it, that he could see all this happening. God bless him for saying that to me, because as difficult as it was for so many years, it finally was the best thing he could have said. He basically created the standard by which I will judge my work.

JUDITH RASCOE

J udith Rascoe quietly and unassumingly writes films of surprising diversity. From the adaptation of Who'll Stop the Rain, *with its tough, bloody mood, to* Eat a Cup of Tea, *with its eminently Chinese sensibilities, to the garish streets of pre-Castro Havana, and the complex emotions of* The Ruth Etting Story, *she manages to get inside characters who couldn't be more different from the woman herself.*

Almost uniquely in this industry and in this profession, Rascoe appears to lack the fierce drive and insecurity of so many screenwriters. She has proven herself enough to have a sense of her own worth and is self-confident enough to turn down a writing job if she doesn't find it interesting. Obviously, she does well in her profession, but money is not the issue. Her most obvious trait is an enjoyment of life, and her laugh is infectious.

She emphasizes that she's had good luck in her career and tells the story of her life as if writing screenplays had occurred through a series of coincidences, but her work indicates a solid professionalism that could only be achieved by discipline and understanding.

Perhaps Rascoe's grounding in literature accounts for her di-

versity. Or perhaps it's the vast number of subjects that excite her enthusiasm; she seems curious about everything under the sun. In any case, she achieves depth by having that quality herself, and her films bear witness to a formidable intelligence, unencumbered by pettiness.

I knew early on I was going to be either an artist or a writer. When I was in high school, I was very interested in playwriting. It was a kind of wacky thing to be interested in if you lived in Boise, Idaho. We had a little theater company and I worked in that, but it was the kind of theater company that did *High Tor* every year. And I read all sorts of books on playwriting, but the theater was an unimaginable distance away. I was interested in television because my Uncle Burton had become a television critic. We had a correspondence when I was in my teens. He even sent me some sample television scripts.

But it's puzzled me how I was sure so early. Even other people in high school thought of me as a writer. Probably because I had two uncles who were writers. So writing might have seemed a little more normal in my family than in some.

Then I went to Stanford, and they had a wonderful creative writing program; it was a very nourishing time for writers and I got a lot of encouragement. But after college I went to England for two years and I stopped writing.

I liked to travel. So I spent a year as a Fulbright Scholar at the University of Bristol and another year teaching school, and probably came as close to a nervous breakdown as I've ever been in my life. Fascinating, but it was a very isolating experience. As I look back, that's one of those things you can only do when you're twenty-two years old and you don't know any better.

I was pretty discouraged with everything at the end of that second year and I didn't know what to do, and I *had* been admitted to Harvard graduate school. So I came back and spent four years there. And then the prospect of writing the dissertation came up. Also, at the time I was getting less and less enchanted with English studies.

I'll say for the record that for anyone who has been around an English department for four years, Hollywood holds no terrors in terms of really mean-spirited, backbiting, vicious politics. At least in Hollywood it's *over* something, there's something at stake—and also, in my experience, people don't hold grudges in the same way. In the English department, holding a helluva grudge for thirty years is nothing.

At that point two things happened that were funny. One was I decided to write my dissertation on the Hollywood novel, about which I knew zip, but it seemed like an interesting subject. And so I came out here one summer and went to UCLA, where there was the only existing dissertation on the Hollywood novel.

I was still trying to think of how I could get another spin on this topic. At the same time, I became disenchanted with the employment situation for women in the academic world. This was just before everything changed, and I remember asking someone at UCLA, "What would be my chances of getting a job here?" and they said, "Well, not very good because we already have three women on the faculty."

At that point I decided I would apply for a Stegner scholarship; a friend of mine had gotten one the year before. I applied and got it. And so I left Harvard. You know, when you're writing your dissertation and you've finished all your courses, they don't care where you go. I spent a couple of years in Palo Alto and then really started writing with some application.

This is making it sound much more linear than it was. For instance, when I was a student at Harvard, I had been a reader for the *Atlantic Monthly*.

But I wrote some short stories and they were published, and I was doing some pieces for *McCalls*. Then I got a call one day— now, you have to realize I'm living in a shack, a day laborer's cottage in the hills of Redwood City, California—and the switchboard operator at the *Atlantic Monthly* phoned. She said, "Judith, we've had a call from a fellow who calls himself a motion-picture producer. He wants to get in touch with you, but naturally we wouldn't give him your number. We'll give you his number if you want to call him."

And I thought, now I have to pay for the damn toll call because they're so fastidious. But I made the call, and it was Joseph Strick, who wanted to meet me. I was going to the East Coast anyway to see some friends, and I met him in New York, and he told me he wanted a screenplay. He had stolen the plot from the *Epic of Gilgamesh,* but it was to be a movie about truck drivers. Because you know, his family had been in the trucking business.

I sent him half a written screenplay and he said, "I think that's pretty good, and I'll give you a couple of screenplays so you can see the form. And just write and I'll read it and I'll tell you what you can't put in a movie."

I was just keen as anything, and I went out, and for a while there I knew a lot about independent trucking. I just had a whale of a time.

A GIFT FOR DIAL

What was quite interesting was that two other people got in touch with me on the basis of the same short story that attracted Joe, a little story called "A Lot of Cowboys," published in the *Atlantic Monthly*. It was just about a bunch of cowboys holed up in a motel in Montana during a snowstorm. I guess they sort of liked the dialogue in that, I don't know, because nobody was ever very serious about making that story into a movie, but three people liked it. But I knew Joe was the real thing. It was just instinct.

He gave me a little contract. I'll probably always remember that as one of the most lighthearted days of my life. I'll never forget walking out of that building; it was a sort of overcast day, but I'd finally got to Broadway. I was finally in show business. And I hadn't even realized I wanted to be there so much until I was there!

The astonishing thing is that Joe actually made the movie, for a budget of about fifteen cents. No one ever saw it; it's one of those things that appear in very esoteric film guides. It was instantly dated because it was completed about seventy-two hours before CB radios came in and changed the face of everything. But the miracle was that I was a screenwriter.

Now, what I knew about screenwriting you could put in a teaspoon, but Joe is just a remarkable man. An editor working for him on another project took me aside and said, "You know you're really being spoiled, because you're being introduced to this business by one of the most deeply honest, deeply serious, generous, good people. You're not getting the whole picture here."

Of course, I wasn't really in the movie business. He made that movie, and I bought a car.

Joe brought me to London that summer because I was supposed to write a treatment and possibly a screenplay for him. I had a lot of fun writing the treatment. While I was in London, I met a guy who'd worked with Ray Stark in Hollywood and was now an executive of United Artists. He was actually like the captain of a beached ship, because the whole American movie business was pulling out of London. So he was in a ghostly office, doing nothing but planning his escape from the ship.

He had an idea for a screenplay and wanted to collaborate. Being a sucker for foreign travel, I wanted to stay on in London. So we cut a deal, that I would stay there and he would provide me room and board and bowls of rice, and we'd collaborate on this screenplay.

But sometimes his old boss, Ray Stark, would come and knock on the door. Ray would always bring a bottle of the best wine you've ever had in your life, and they would sit around and have fairly hilarious conversations about this and that. Ray got to know me as a collaborator.

I'd forgotten the winters in London. By the end of the project, when spring came, I was really ready to go. I came back to New York, and I was on Fifty-seventh Street one hot day when I was approached by a small sturdy figure who said, "Hi, honey, hello!" and I said, "Mr. Stark, how are you?"

He asked me what I was doing and what I was going to do. I had gotten a contract to put together a collection of short stories and I said I was planning to do that. I might as well have said I was going to do chalk throwing. He patted my shoulder and said, "Honey, we'll find something for you to do."

I was staying with some friends in Brooklyn; at the time it was the sort of place where the cab drivers said, "Are you sure this is where you want to go?" We were all sitting in the kitchen, and someone said, "My God, what's that?" and outside the door was a limo. The driver had a pile of scripts and a copy of a book called, *The Way We Were,* with a note saying I was to read everything, then call Ray and tell him what I thought.

I read the material and wrote all sorts of opinions with the arrogance of youth. Then the limo appeared again and I was taken to Ray Stark's apartment on Fifth-seventh Street. There was Ray Stark and some other people, and I was invited to express my opinion on the latest script, which of course I did. I had no idea if they would listen to me. We were all taken out to a wonderful lunch. I was thanked for my help and told to give him a call if I ever got to California.

HOLLYWOOD

Some months later, I did go to Los Angeles because in those days, as we all know, Los Angeles was cheap and warm, a better place to starve than New York by a long shot, and more interesting than San Francisco. After I got an apartment, I called, and immediately I had a job; I was a reader. That was pretty astonishing; it was like being a fly in a corner in the midst of making *The Way We Were.*

People have often said, "Didn't you work on *The Way We Were?*" It's absolutely not true. I just had a cardboard box with all the drafts of the script. At script conferences, when someone asked, "Wasn't there a version where Bob walked outside the car?" I would say, "Yes, on the July 12 version there was that scene." That was my entire function. By that point, just by propinquity, I was sort of in the movie business.

I was around for the making of the film. That was fascinating. But then my agent got me a job with William Castle, and I quit. I'd probably only been there six months, but it seemed like a lifetime.

My script for Bill Castle never got made, but again, I learned something. Who's to know when you are irrevocably committed to a path of action—but somewhere around then I realized I wasn't going to go back and write that dissertation. Probably, somewhere before the making of *Who'll Stop the Rain,* I decided I could make a living at this.

I loved *Who'll Stop the Rain,* and it had such a disastrous reception. I was furious. It had been such a labor of love, and so well done; it was such a strong movie. I must say, thank God for videotape, because it has enjoyed a kind of life after death. I really thought everybody involved in that production was really splendid.

The next spring, I worked on one project, one of those things where you work on it for six months and they keep changing the occupation of the main character, always a dangerous sign.

I've never worked on spec. It's been a very bizarre career in that sense. But I'm terrible at pitching, just terrible. It's not my gift. There are some people who are very gifted at that. I think, of people I know, Paul Schrader is the best. I've heard him pitch things over dinner, and he has such a gift at telling you just enough to whet your appetite, but not telling you too much; he would have been great in the advertising business.

Probably my academic background didn't help. I get a little bit analytical, I start adding footnotes, it's terrible.

I've always thought people shouldn't adapt their own work. Any story can be retold and become another story. I think the thing I'm working on now is a case in point. Martin Bregman came to

me and asked if I knew the story of Ruth Etting and Mo Schneider. And I said, "Yes, I do." I'd seen *Love Me or Leave Me* many
years before. And he said, "You know it's based on a true story.
How would you like to retell the story as a possible vehicle for Al
Pacino?"

At first I balked, it just shows that sometimes you back into
things you enjoy most. I hadn't seen Pacino in a while. I kept
thinking, oh, he's too beautiful, he's too sexy for the role. Also
the last thing I'd seen of that type was *Star 80.* For a long time I
thought, can I tell this story, and not wind up telling *Star 80* again?
It was a fascinating movie, but not one I want to write.

But two things happened. First, I saw Pacino in *Sea of Love* and
I thought, he's not a pretty boy anymore, and also he's such a
wonderful actor.

And then I started doing research on the real story; there was
actually quite a bit of material. There'd never been a book written,
but because of the trial of Mo the Gimp for attempted murder,
there were enormous newspaper clippings, and so I read everything; I love projects where I have to do research.

By the time I'd done that, I was a million miles from *Star 80.* I
was also quite far away from *Love Me or Leave Me,* although I
thought I'd better watch that movie very carefully and not make
any unconscious dippings into its pocket. It was good writing, and
they came up with some very elegant solutions to the marital problems in that story. And I thought, drat, I can't use them.

You know, there are still a few people around who knew Ruth
Etting and Mo the Gimp, one of them a very famous man but I
guess I won't say the name. He had known them in Chicago, back
at the beginning, day one, and Bregman knew him and arranged
an appointment.

He'd been in Chicago in the twenties, when they were first starting out. And he said yes, he'd been fascinated by them. In fact,
he had tried to write something about them himself, he thought
it was such a strange relationship. The way he depicted it was
different from the way I saw it, more like the *Hunchback of Notre
Dame.* In fact, at the end of our conversation I said to him, "You
know, you never said it directly but you didn't like her, did you?"
and he said, "No, I didn't like her. I thought she was using him."

At that time, when I talked to him, I was in possession of most
of the facts, and at some point he started telling me about the
relationship. I don't know if you know the story. Mo Schneider
was a Chicago gangster who met, fell in love with, and became
obsessed with the young singer named Ruth Etting, the girl from

Nebraska. He built her into a big star, into a superstar.

But when they got to Broadway, Mo didn't get more refined. Eventually he became more persistent, then more brutal. She asked for a divorce and he let her have it, never believing that she would survive on her own. But a year later she turned up with a guy who had been in her company. When Mo found out about that, he followed him out to California and shot the guy, almost killed him.

Anyway, this man who'd known them in Chicago was telling me the story—and at a certain point I realized that he wasn't remembering the facts anymore, he was remembering the plot of *Love Me or Leave Me.* And I didn't have the heart—I was just not in the position—to say, sir, it wasn't that way.

The dramatic solution that *Love Me or Leave Me* came up with, simple but natural, was to have the piano player there from the beginning. You know, have a nice little love triangle where she chooses between the piano player and Mo and then gets reunited with the piano player. Terrific. However that's not how it was.

Bregman at one point said, "You know, why don't you have her meet the piano player in Chicago?" and I said, "Sure, if you're prepared to buy the rights to the book. I'll be happy to do that, but it's not true."

But I was fascinated with this man who knew them and had, over the years, substituted the plot of the movie for real life.

It's very seldom a novel actually yields a good adaptation, the better the novel the less likely, unless you're really lucky. If you happen to get one of those novels, it's swell. But so often a novel is working on several time levels at once. If I had my druthers, what I'd rather do is work on something like *Havana* or *Mo and Ruth*, where I'm working with a real place or a historical moment.

THE WRITING PROCESS

I'm not the best structure person in the world, it's not very natural to me. I tend to write by doing a lot of thinking about the characters. I get these characters in mind, and I think about what can happen when you put these people together. *Mo and Ruth* is partly trying to figure out who these two people have really been. What happened was that after doing a lot of research on Mo Schneider and Ruth Etting, I felt I understood them—but they're not the people I wrote the movie about.

* * *

I finally structure very carefully, but it's the end of the process. It's very hard for me to do an outline. I often write enormously detailed treatments that no one will ever see. They have a little dialogue, they have biographical history, they have scenes I know will never be released. I'm sort of improvising with the characters. I write pages and pages. And then, with tweezers, I can lift one little thing out of it.

I'm enormously admiring of people who can write very casual dialogue and moments. I guess I'm too understated; my natural tendency is toward enormous understatement. But I love writing stuff where nothing *apparently* happens. Trouble is, so often, nothing happens.

I have thought about directing. I was in the AFI directing program for a while, and I was so wrong about my choice of material, the casting, my aims. I really didn't know what I was doing, but it was a wonderful experience; I had a great time.

But part of the fun for me in writing screenplays is that I direct them in my head. I tell you, I know what the wallpaper is like and what the camera angle is, shot by shot. But then, if somebody goes out and directs it and does a good job, it's all brand-new.

Also, I see my director friends go into clinical depression at the first assembly. They have to deal with the fact that all those pictures in their heads, their intentions, aren't there. Then they've got to take that raw material and turn it into what is theirs. I think it's fascinating, but I don't know—I'm very ambivalent about it.

However, the writer doesn't win, generally, in fighting for things, unless you're in an extraordinary relationship. If you're in that good a relationship, and you have a fight, and you win when you're right. You can explain your reasons, if you're a lot righter than the other person, you're going to win because you make them see reason. But actually I'm a collaborator.

One of the reasons why I was particularly interested in screenwriting was that I'd written quite a few short stories, probably two or three dozen, and I felt like a sprinter who wanted to be a miler. I was thinking in short-story terms. I remember I sent one story off to some publication, and they sent it back and said, we'd be interested if this were longer, and I thought, well, I don't want to know more about this.

But I did want to write in a longer form. And now I think it would be quite hard for me to go back and get compression. I think short-story writing is like lyric poetry, something that people do more naturally when they're young.

As for a novel, I've never written one. I'd like to try it sometime just to see what it was like. The weird damn thing about the movie business, one of the seductive things, is that compared to writing novels it's very social. I very much admire my novel-writing friends who sit there day after day, going in there with that thing and never taking a meeting. I'm sure there are other people who'd say that's a small price to pay. And writing is a lonely profession, but still . . .

I've done my attempts at comedy. I occasionally write funny dialogue, but it's a very special gift. I tend to think of really good comedy as the highest form, and often underestimated because it's so skillful. The fact is, if you have a terrific performance and very emotionally moving moments in drama, timing is not all. But in comedy, it's all. The timing has to be perfect, the delivery has to be perfect; really high-class comedy is a miracle. And often people who write it are so businesslike about it.

I met Lowell Ganz one time and I liked him so much. And there's a very serious guy. He and Babaloo Mandel work nine to five, so carefully and methodically.

I've turned down innumerable projects for every reason in the world, often because I'm simply not interested. One of the luxuries I have, being single and keeping my nut low, is to have the luxury of not working on anything I don't want to work on. I've never worked on a project where I thought, I'm going into this because I need the dough. And I tell you, it makes your life much simpler. You may not end up with a huge share of the world's goods, but I don't seem to be very avid for the world's goods anyway. I mean, I like them as well as anybody, don't get me wrong, but it has been a great luxury to do only the things I've wanted to do.

I don't think I've turned things down because I felt they were unworthy, it's just that there are things I'm not interested in. For instance, I don't get anything to do with the ballet or dancing. It's an art but it's a mystery, a blank to me. I would rather be mugged than asked to write about a ballet.

I tend to think I need a quiet environment in which to write, a perfectly quiet study with beautiful light and a smoothly running word processor. I spend hours at stationery stores, making sure I have all that stuff. But some of my happiest hours have been spent writing on prop typewriters at the craft-services table between takes.

I used to worry about my work habits. At the beginning of a project, I wouldn't even like the producers to know how little time I'd work, a couple of hours a day. But something accelerates as it gets closer to completion, the hours get longer and longer. Usually when I'm in the last stages, I'm working eighteen hours a day. But I can't set myself a certain number of pages, I'm very undisciplined in that. And I do try to keep to the old Hemingway thing of not writing everything—leave a little bit unwritten.

Once, in New York, I sat in on an acting class for three months and it was a marvelous experience. Particularly for somebody with no theater background, no sense of how to talk to actors. Their approach and my approach was so enormously different. Only later did I think of things in common. And I remember the teacher saying to them, You don't just base a performance on a performance. And I thought, all I know of actors are their performances; I don't know them as people, I've never known one as a personal friend. So what I've tried very hard to do is create the characters as I would in fiction, which is some combination of invention and modeling on other people.

I try as far as possible to think about people I've known, for instance intelligent people I've known who are, because of circumstances, completely uneducated. Or intelligent people who, because of circumstances, have been disabled in some way so that the world to them is a completely hostile environment—which it's not to you or me or most people. We all know people like that.

A screenwriter reveals him- or herself to a lesser extent than a novelist. I think with the exception of some people like Truffaut, it's one of the least self-revealing media. Let's put it this way, the revelation is very oblique. Although in an interesting way, it may in fact be more revealing than the work of novelists, who can create a persona.

For instance, John Milius has created a persona, you know, the man's persona as expressed in his screenplays, but what I don't know about John Milius is everything. I make deductions from his work about him, but I don't know. And I'm sure people who have seen things of mine make deductions about me.

THE MECHANISMS BEHIND THE ART

I write too much dialogue. Every time I see an assembly, I'm completely catatonic. My first impulse is to say, get rid of the dialogue. I'm the first one in the room saying, you don't need that line.

What you've got on the page is description and dialogue. But if you get wonderful actors and they're really cooking, the dialogue is like sprinkles on your sundae, and very often the lines themselves are the least interesting part of what's happening. I tend to be one who goes in there and says, you don't need that line, do it on the look.

And sometimes the actors, those little devils, can't say it right. So that's another reason to drop it, when they don't understand it. I used to be of the Harold Pinter school of screenwriting, where you're very distanced, you never put any parentheticals in, you just describe it and let the imagination of the reader flow into the page.

But I've been browbeaten into putting in violence and description. I'm always being told more, more. Is this being said with a smile? Does he stare at her when he says this? I'm actually encouraged to write the performance. I'd think it would make the director and the actor crazy, but I know what's happening is that, first of all, there are a lot of studio executives. They need storyboards. They sure need parentheticals.

And I've seen in rehearsals that lots of actors are not going to bear down on the right words in that sentence unless it's underlined. And if they misread it, the line won't make sense; you'll have one of those senseless conversations. An actor's first job is to find out where that line is coming from. Sometimes, even with very solid actors, there are misreadings. It's like stepping off with the left foot when they should be stepping off with the right foot.

But sometimes writing is like that also. Sometimes it's like tears and death and I can't solve it. I've done it wrong. Probably there isn't a screenplay—I wouldn't feel like I'd really done my job if there weren't a screenplay—that hadn't caused me to literally cry. This is hopeless, I've killed myself, burn the manuscript, I'll never work in this town again, etc. It's funny, the other day a writer friend and I were talking about screenwriting and he said, "You know they teach you all this stuff in these courses. They never tell you that the first thing you do is put your arm on the table, take out a knife, and cut a vein."

I think there's something to that. It would be nice to think it were otherwise, but if it weren't a struggle it wouldn't be worth doing.

* * *

I think the way to make a statement in a film is to ask a question. I'm not much given to making statements because I'm not that sure about so many things. But I have a lot of questions, and the project had better say to me, boy those are interesting questions. Not to harp on ballet, but I don't have big questions about ballet. *Havana*, on the other hand, generated big questions—and not just questions about American relationships with Cuba. As my friends would tell you, I'm one of the most profoundly apolitical people they know. But I thought the questions that are posed by the Cuban revolution, then and now, are terribly interesting.

So sometimes there are questions of that magnitude, sometimes there are questions as in "Mo the Gimp." While I was trying to decide about whether I'd do that project, Martin Bregman started just telling me about personal managers he had known, or his own relationships with actors, what had happened when relationships break off, what happened when the one-on-one personal manager got too close, and I thought these questions were absolutely fascinating. I realized that relationship is so extraordinary, that identifying with somebody else, to the point where they're mouthing the words to the client's songs, they *are* that person.

I couldn't possibly imagine being in that relationship, but it's the story of Mo and Ruth. There is a pathology. I'm not writing a story about a psychopath, it's love, but it's something that also can be more sinister than that. Like that person is no longer himself, that person is you.

About the danger of identifying. A man I was very much in love with had been a magazine editor and a newspaper reporter and he worked full time at *Life* and so forth, and was a little bit more sagacious than many people in that field. He was talking about working in Washington, and he said the most dangerous thing is not realizing that what people respect is the *New York Times* or *Life* magazine, not you personally. The great trap for reporters is to believe that they're personally being taken seriously when in fact it's the institution they represent.

I can't see that I'm interested in following a pattern. I have a weakness for period stuff, which is a terrible liability. In a time when it's really stupid to be so, I'm very interested in American history. A lot that I liked about doing *Eat a Bowl of Tea* was exploring that period in American life through a particular group of people. I like that; I like thinking about what we used to think we were, how things were different. It's like time travel.

One of the things I enjoyed in my research about *Havana* was reading contemporary newspapers about these people, trying not to benefit from second-guessing. I like that sort of stuff. And also I said to myself, I've been writing so many characters who are kind of "deez and doze" sort of people, I'm a little tired of that at the moment. I enjoy it and it's fun, but I want to try people who talk some other way.

I love language, I love the different ways people talk. Often the most really eloquent people aren't particularly well educated. Their phrasing, their choice of words, is not dictated by reading books but by finding some word or phrase that is expressive for them. Once I was in a shop in New York buying stationery and somebody asked the clerk, who was from the South, how he was, and he said, "I've had better days and grumbled." I mean, it's so beautiful.

. . . WHERE THE WIND BLOWS

I don't know about the future. I'll probably discern it at the end of the trail, I just don't know. I feel in that sense that I'll go where the wind blows. I hope I'll be surprised somehow. That's just a matter of my nature, I like being surprised. One of the reasons I so enjoyed doing *Eat a Bowl of Tea* was I was grumbling to a friend about people sending me what I considered really dopey projects. He knew that Wayne Wang was looking for a screenwriter with more experience than he'd worked with before, and I was so delighted. This was a world I'd always been fascinated by, and again I had a zillion questions.

Some friends and I are always trying to come up with some supercolossal blockbuster. We all sit around and dreamily think about how we're going to write *Terminator*, but we can't do it. We don't think that way; we don't have blockbuster psychology.

But sometimes you just see small stories that are fascinating. Once I was working on a suspense film and they sent me off at midnight to see *Halloween*, the first one, and I thought, gosh that's an interesting piece of filmmaking, great throwaway dialogue. Often when people do one thriller and get noticed, that first cheap thriller is swell. And I'm sure it's partly because nobody's paying much attention. People get to go out there and make the movie. They don't have people coming in and saying the hero should be sensitive.

Whenever you read accounts of Hollywood—the most vicious, remorseful, scornful account of the movie business by movie people—when they actually get to the process of making movies, you can just see the Christmas tree going up. It's like once you get there and there's a camera, everything changes.

I've been very lucky in working with people who've let me be there through the making of the film, so I felt part of the team. I think I've been very fortunate in that way. I believe very strongly that I'm a member of the director's crew, I am not the coauthor of the film.

I love talking to actors, and, of course, who doesn't love the moment of being able to take the director aside and say, "Pssst, what if you did this?" I would never, ever presume on my own to address any member of that team independently. But it's very extraordinary to create a world using an existing location, sustaining it in our imaginations—a whole world of characters and different places—and making it as real to ourselves as possible.

I remember sitting there on the set of *Havana,* which had to be the biggest set I'll probably ever see. It was sort of a montage of the main streets of Havana, and I was being an extra. I was talking to another extra, who was Cuban. Now, he was a guy in his twenties who had recently gotten out of Cuba and was in Santo Domingo hoping he could get to the United States; he thought if he worked on this movie it would help. He had never seen the Havana in this film because he was too young. He had never seen Havana with the ads and the full store windows and things like that. And yet he was dressed up and playing somebody in this Havana he had never known. The ironies are so heavy, they exhaust you after a while.

THE CIRCUS

I get a little gloomy sometimes, as I think a lot of people are these days, at the feature film business. There are some things happening that I don't understand. I mean, on one hand we're really spending a helluva lot of money on what might seem to the casual observer to be pretty dumb projects. And you look at some of the successful films and wonder where the maturity has gone. And along with that is the thing of movies being thrown into theaters for two weeks; if they don't work, they're yanked out. You don't know what to make of it.

And yet I think there is a running-away-with-the-circus quality in people who make movies. And I think it's quite interesting that compensation or not, some people make a zillion dollars and some people make very little, or you can make anything in between. The real compensation is being part of that circus.

LOWELL GANZ
AND
BABALOO MANDEL

Lowell Ganz and Babaloo Mandel are not just comedy writers; they're a comedy team. While Ganz is more outgoing
and Mandel more shy and introverted, their mutual dialogue has the laidback feeling of an act they've done together in
many different venues. They feed each other lines with the ease of
old performers, although they're relatively young. The closest one
can come to their style is by summoning up Woody Allen's Broadway Danny Rose, in which the New York performers play off
each other like jugglers.

The philosophy of Ganz and Mandel is that anything important
can be said more effectively with humor, and this is apparent in
all their work. Everything they've written, from Night Shift to
Splash to City Slickers, from Mr. Saturday Night to A League

of Their Own, *has a bit of an edge. Their gift is that they can make you see the truth about life and still laugh at it.*

They're not just wise guys; they're wise, although both would scoff at the suggestion.

Above all, they genuinely love comedy, can't see the world in any other way, and treat it as a serious calling of which they are custodians. They've earned success through long, hard years of live TV, sitcoms, writing whether or not they felt like it—producing the words whether they wanted to or not.

They're likable guys, but cautious, veterans in a business where burnout can come early. They laugh easily, however, even at the hard times that brought them to such a well-deserved success. Probably they've taken a page from their own book—everything is easier if you can see the funny side of it.

GANZ: I didn't start out to be a screenwriter, I thought I'd just write jokes for comics or sketches for TV variety shows; when I was in college, there were still TV variety shows. Instead, I got into sitcom writing, not because I knew it was a better field but because I just happened to fall into it. That was great because situation comedies were a healthy industry in the seventies, while variety and sketch writing were not.

But after I wrote situation comedies for about six or seven years, I started to get interested in trying something a little more demanding—and that's how I flew the Atlantic.

MANDEL: I was a funny kid. In 1960, I was in Monticello, in the Catskills, and it was movie night and they were showing *Some Like It Hot.* I sat there for two hours and that was what changed my life. I sat with an audience, I laughed, they laughed, and I knew what I wanted to do.

But I always wrote jokes, and when I lived in New York, the first thing I'd read in the paper was Earl Wilson. They used to have jokes and I would say, "I can do better than that."

GANZ: I used to read Earl Wilson also. "Today's best laugh?"

MANDEL: "Today's best laugh."

GANZ: They'd have "Today's best laugh" and you'd think, that can't be today's *best* laugh. Maybe it's number eleven or something.

MANDEL: What was in it, that belly dancer?

GANZ: Always had a picture of a girl in a bikini in the column also; it was another reason to like that.

MANDEL: And I never looked at that, I went right to the jokes. I knew there was something.

GANZ: We found out later that we used to spend our summers a hundred and fifty yards from each other. He grew up in the Bronx, I grew up in Queens. But both of our families used to go up to Monticello every summer. We stayed at places that were on the same block.

MANDEL: In the Catskills. We would walk every day, I might've seen him.

GANZ: But we met out here. I came out in April of '72.

MANDEL: And I came out July like second. I graduated college, threw everything in the car and just came. It was like lemmings. Now, I'm talking about a guy who never left his house. I'm very shy. But something drew me, there was a hand, a force, something at work.

GANZ: I actually came west because somebody offered me a job, I came with employment—which only lasted a few weeks. But I was pretty practically motivated. Somebody actually hired me if I'd come out here, and I did.

We met pretty soon after we got here. I was living up on Sunset Boulevard. I think they had probably just opened the Comedy Store across the street, a place for stand-ups, and a lot of young comics and young comedy writers used to hang around there. Even if they didn't stand inside, they'd stand around in the street, watching the guy help people park out front. I used to bump into a lot of people, meet a lot of people there, and Babaloo was one of them.

MANDEL: And I lived not far down the street on La Cienega. A place across the street from Fat Burger where I paid eighty-nine dollars a month. I found if you stayed in the house at night, you'd end up joining the guy next to you who was beating his wife, so I decided to get out. And I found this place called the Comedy Store, and if you went around the back, they didn't charge you.

GANZ: I had a job for a while writing. I was assistant story editor on a TV show. I was in and out of work for a while until I finally hooked on with a show permanently. But you'd meet people who were in work, out of work, between work, used to work, who'll never work . . .

MANDEL: My days were like this. I'd get up in the morning. I'd pour some milk into a large box of Raisin Bran and I'd write until lunch. I'd go to the box, have lunch, and continue writing until dinner. Then I'd go across the street to Fat Burger. Then evening would come, and then pretty much I'd go to the Comedy Store. But I wrote all day.

GANZ: It was a rich, full life.

MANDEL: Yeah, it was great. My dad came. I don't know why, but he was carrying something. He made my mom wait downstairs and he came up and saw this place I was living in; it was smaller than this office and the only reason I took the place was 'cause it had a color TV.

When he left the room, he was white and my mother thought he was having a heart attack. He wouldn't let her upstairs. And to this day, she still tries to get him to describe what that place was like.

GANZ: At that time I had a partner I had met in New York, a guy I went to college with. We were working in TV together from '72 to '79.

MANDEL: I had no partner. I had a legal pad. I wrote jokes. That's how I got by. Six dollars a joke. You've got to sell a lot of those.

GANZ: My ex-partner and I started to do well in television. We became TV producers and we started to have some good luck, and we knew Babaloo and we badly wanted him to write for us.

We wanted him to come on staff and work for us, and he just didn't want to.

MANDEL: I wanted to go directly to movies. I was an idiot, I wanted to bypass the training.

GANZ: He just wanted to write. He had his yellow legal pads and he was writing.

MANDEL: And then my wife said after we got married, "You're gonna work in TV." And I said, "All right."

GANZ: When he got married, we knew we had him. So we used to hire him all the time. Whenever we had a show he would be the first guy we would want to write. And then my partner and I broke up right around the same time that I was thinking that I didn't want to work in TV much longer. And by this time, Babaloo and I knew each other real well. I mean, we'd worked on the same shows for several years. And he was always writing movies— nobody was reading them but he was writing them.

MANDEL: What was wrong with my imaginary friends? They were great!

GANZ: And I was kind of daunted by the prospect of writing something that lasted more than twenty-three and a half minutes, so we started to write them together. That worked out okay. By this time we had written quite a few TV pilots together.

The opportunity for a feature was brought to me by Ron Howard and Brian Grazer. They had a concept for a movie and they were willing to give us a chance even though we were *only* TV writers. This was about ten years ago. In the years following that, a *huge* number of people made the transition from TV to features, especially directors, very successfully. But in 1980 it was still a little more segregated.

I think Ron and Brian couldn't afford a real movie writer at the time. But it was Alan Ladd Jr.'s company that made *Night Shift*. At this time I'd had a lot of success at television. I was pretty well known in that business, but he had never heard of me.

MANDEL: But he was as nice as if we were William Goldman.

GANZ: He treated us as nicely as if we were important. He was a very nice man.

That picture was *Night Shift,* and it did okay. You know, it wasn't as big a financial success as everybody hoped because the previews were so successful and the scores on the preview cards were very high. But the studio had a little trouble opening it. It didn't have movie stars.

But still, we bump into people who can recite the entire movie, line for line. People who had rented it or bought it and have seen it twenty-four times and can actually just burn through the entire movie. "Give me a line, I'll give you the next line." So we're pretty proud of that.

MANDEL: These are people who will be later described as disgruntled employees with a gun.

WRITERS WHO WANT TO BE WRITERS

GANZ: I teach sometimes at USC and I used to lecture at UCLA, and one of the first things I always say is, "I'm a screenwriter and I actually consider that a profession. I don't consider it a stepping-stone. I don't consider it something I'm doing until my break comes along, or the dues I have to pay in order to become a director. This is actually a profession and a career for a grown-up human being."

People say to us, so you *just* want to write. The word "just" is put in front of it. "Merely" want to write. We've had all the opportunities to have development deals at studios. No. We don't want to option material. We don't want to have more things in development. We don't want to hire other writers that we would oversee. We like to write. Even when we don't take the title or the credit or the money, we do take on certain producing responsibilities, sometimes, when a picture of ours is being made, but that just generates out of the enthusiasm and interest and excitement of the project. We go into an editing room and we help cut, and we help cast sometimes, but it's always just that . . . we're associated on a picture with people we know and they know us and they trust us and they bring us in on other areas of the production and we're happy to participate. But we don't want to formalize that into a different kind of work.

MANDEL: We've been away three days to go on location for this movie we're doing and I missed my family and they missed me. Unfortunately we're not the Ron Howards. They're terrific, they're great, they go and they all have a great time. It's hard to do with a big family.

GANZ: We are never around socially. We periodically meet somebody who's famous. We met Norman Lear last year; we were with somebody and they said, "Oh, this is Babaloo Mandel and Lowell Ganz," and we shook hands and he said, "Oh, so you guys really do exist."

MANDEL: Once a year, if we're invited to Penny Marshall's party, because my wife tells me to come, then we stand in the corner looking for Barbra Streisand. This is it.

GANZ: Penny Marshall's birthday party. Once a year. That's it. That's our only Hollywood thing the whole year. We live in the valley and we don't hobnob.

MANDEL: We don't tennis, we don't beach in Malibu.

GANZ: We don't brunch anywhere and we don't Chasens. We're no place. We work and go home.

Sometimes people, producers or directors or actors, say, "Gee, how come there aren't more guys like you, who just keep turning out reliable material that's interesting." Because, well, ninety-five percent who are capable of doing it get out of the writing business just at the point that they're getting good at it.

You can't hire them if they are still getting better at it, because they're writing for themselves. We're unique in that we've had a certain level of success and you can still walk in and hire us. We are still available to be hired to write for you.

AGENTS

MANDEL: Let me tell you about agents. I wrote a spec "M*A*S*H." script in about '74. I submitted it to a guy at William Morris. The guy suggested basically that I go home and find a career.

GANZ: Same thing happened to me in New York. It's not even really their fault, you know?

MANDEL: So I get an assignment off the script. The same agent calls me after he heard and says, "I've been thinking about it. I've been thinking about it and you know, maybe I was wrong."

GANZ: I came out with a job, so an agent found me immediately. An agent actually called to inform me I had the job. That's how quick they are when they hear something. You got the job and I got you this much money.

MANDEL: I had that agent for about six months.

GANZ: I had submitted material to guys in New York who had told me I was just going to break my heart and I should figure out something else to do.

MANDEL: And I didn't get an agent until I was an apprentice on his show.

GANZ: Right now we have no agent. Our agent quit the agency last week. But CAA is taking care of us.

MANDEL: Making sure that nobody from any other agency comes up here.

GANZ: But we have different ways to protect ourselves. They're not foolproof, but neither is producing and directing your own material. Careers have arcs, they have up and downs. Right now, things are going quite nicely and we pick and choose.

We're very careful about the people with whom we work. Any project we do has somebody attached to it, either a star or a director or a producer—or more than one of those elements—who we either worked with before or know very well and have great faith in, not just as talent but as human beings. Have great confidence in their loyalty to us, in their integrity.

We do a lot of pictures with Ron Howard and Brian Grazer. We're on our second picture with Billy Crystal. We're doing a picture now with Penny Marshall, whom I've known for fifteen years. On our first picture together, I had faith that Penny would treat us and the script with professional respect and grace and friendship, and she has. We weren't buying a pig in a poke. We're very cautious. There's virtually always somebody attached to the project who we feel is a friendly advocate for us and the script, and who is more powerful than we are.

And for the most part over the years, our experiences in the movie business and with feature executives have been pretty good. We've been treated with good grace most of the time and the majority of what we hear, even if it's not what we agree with, is generally thought out.

MANDEL: Most of the men and women we meet in this business are pretty intelligent people.

GANZ: We don't get a lot of what we would consider "absurd" notes. Besides, I spent eight years in television.

MANDEL: Nightmare stories.

GANZ: To me, you can't believe the difference. The executive participation on a script by script, scene by scene, page by page, word by word basis in television is so vastly more pervasive than it is in features.

When you're doing a pilot, especially—"Does he have to enter the room with his left foot first; can't he enter the room with his right first?" I mean, I'm exaggerating, but only for effect. I was shocked.

We talked about Alan Ladd Jr. before, but the name comes up again. Because when we turned in a first draft of *Night Shift*, it was our first screenplay and we felt there were some holes in it. But Ron and Brian felt it was time to turn in a draft, and God knows, we agreed. Okay, so we're going in to meet Alan Ladd for his first draft notes.

Now, based on my experience in television, where you turned in a forty-seven-page pilot and stayed in the office for six hours taking notes, I told my wife, "I don't know when you'll ever see me again." 'Cause this is 122 pages or something. I assumed we'd be there until the crack of doom. And he came in and he had two key questions. He said, "Do you feel this character is doing what you wanted?" and "Are you completely satisfied that this ending is in the same tone as the rest of the picture?"

They were both pointed, intelligent questions. One of which we disagreed with, one of which we agreed with; one we didn't do what he suggested and one we did. It was completely different.

Our second picture was *Splash*. When that was in turnaround, I *will* say that we took some meetings with people who were considering picking up the project, and they gave us detailed notes about what would make it better, what would make it funnier, what line shouldn't be in, what line should be in.

We didn't like the ideas, although our reputation is for being very open. But we were open. We just didn't like the ideas.

MANDEL: What was that suggestion that they made about the grocery store?

GANZ: The mermaid is already on land and he bumps into her in the supermarket.

MANDEL: We're pishers, we're nobodies, but we're sitting there . . .

GANZ: At this point, we've had one semisuccessful movie to our credit . . .

MANDEL: This was the president of films at this particular place . . .

GANZ: So we're not arrogant; we do listen, we do think, "How do we know we're right?" But you just gotta dig in at some point—even if we're right or not—and say, "I just can't accommodate that idea, so it doesn't matter who's right, I just can't do it." We can't do it that way.

And then *Splash* made a whole bunch of money, and it's amazing how much smarter you are after you've made somebody a hundred million dollars.

But it goes back to that other thing we were talking about, when we have Billy Crystal or Penny Marshall or Ron Howard, we're kind of protected.

Then we've been involved with rewrite projects where we were given a script to take home—we don't do many rewrites.

MANDEL: A few.

GANZ: We'll do one or two things a year. The money's great. I mean the money's better than doing real writing. But we've gotten a couple of rewrite assignments where they said, "This is all in place, the sets are being built, it's cast already."

We figured we could go home and come back for the meeting and describe what we were going to do with it—and you realize that they've gone the other way. Rather than taking their shoes off and stepping all over it, they're barely familiar with the latest draft.

We'll say something like: "Are you married to the idea of the guy having the cabin . . . is that something that you all really love?" And they say, "Oh, is he in the woods now?" And they're going to start *shooting* in six weeks.

We've had people privately say, "His script is unreadable, none of us can get to the end of it, it's like we all have to put it down before we finish it."

Then how did it get a green light?! Well, the reason is, it's got a director and two stars attached to it. So you get it both ways. You get it where they've hammered a script to death and the other where they haven't really even read it.

COMEDY POV

GANZ: We've done pictures that easily could've been dramas. *A League of Their Own* could just as easily have been done as a drama or a romantic drama.

MANDEL: At least for me, it's hard not to see humor within drama. Look, I'm sitting in Evansville, I'm on the set with the producer, and he says, "I've been eating food on the set for three months now. Let's go. There's a little mom-and-pop restaurant." This is in Kentucky. So he drags me into the car. And there's this little, "How y'all doin'?" café, real sweet.

I'm sitting there and in walk these two couples, probably in their seventies. One of the women looks frail. I mean, if she makes it through the meal, I'm amazed. They sit her down—they're all three holding her—they get her into a seat, and I'm saying, Oh geez, there's drama. Look at this woman, I'm telling myself, seventy years, they been married forty. She's sitting down, the husband takes out the cigarette for her, the other friend lights it for her, they practically inhale it for her—and then I just turned away, the moment was over. But this is drama infused with comedy.

GANZ: *Parenthood* has several scenes that have no comedy in them, none whatsoever, and several other scenes that could just as easily stand up as valid structural scenes with no comedy in them. You know, if you're talking to us about our families or the ecology— we do a little work for the ecology people—we'll talk seriously. But comedy is very much part of life. Whether you like the style or not, it's very honest. It's how we approach things in our real life. I once had a surgery, years ago, so for years I had surgery anecdotes.

MANDEL: We were always taught to bend. To bend whatever you write toward comedy. They get the same message, just with a laugh, and then it sweeps over them.

GANZ: It's always been our goal creatively that no matter what the subject matter is, without forcing it, our laughs can be just as big, just as successful as the laughs in a balls-out comedy, a romp. We don't have to get smaller laughs than those pictures just because we have drama within the picture or because we're dealing with a real subject or a serious subject. When the audience laughs, they can laugh just as big.

That's a point of pride with us, that's a source of significant pride to us, that we don't have to be something *instead* of funny.

PUTTING IT TOGETHER

GANZ: We usually think of the situation first. But then, in the development process before we actually sit down to write, we want to know what the structure is, we want to have a basic sense of the beginning, middle, and the end. But in developing it, almost all of the conversation will be about the characters and our attempt to hear them, hear their voices, to be able to recognize their sound when they start talking. So yeah, we want to know the story, we want to crack the story but we won't take on an assignment because it sounds like a really winning kind of premise. Billy Crystal called us and said, "Three yuppies go on a fantasy cattle drive." Clearly that's a really good, commercial comic idea, there's no question about it. We knew it would be successful for somebody, whether we wrote it or not. We knew he was on to something, and we were on to something by being invited to do it.

But when we went home, the two of us, it wasn't to plot out the cattle drive, it was about, "Who are these three guys, who's the one guy particularly, what's going on with him, what's his attitude about the cattle drive, what does he sound like?" And then when we went back, we said, "We see you as this, and you would kind of be this way, can you accommodate that?" And he said, "Yeah, absolutely." And I said, "Well then, in that case, we can write it."

When we're in the office, we come in around ten. If we're in the middle of a script, which is usually, we read yesterday's pages.

We read what we wrote yesterday. We're either satisfied and we move on or we're practically satisfied and we just change a few words, or we stop and get depressed because it wasn't good.

But then we move on; we write. Our *best* time is right after lunch until we go home. Like one to four-thirty. We've read yesterday's pages, we've penciled them up and changed whatever needed to be changed, and then we can really write furiously for a few hours. Then we just dump the pages off on the secretary's desk. Very often we won't even reread them before we go home. Just get to the end of a scene, throw the pages on the desk, and read them the next day to see what they read like after a night's sleep.

I usually write. I find it very stream of consciousness to have a pen, to actually have ink come down through my arm, through my fingers, through the point of the pen. It feels very natural.

MANDEL: Longhand, yellow pads.

GANZ: We will not stop. We would rather write something that's bad and has to be thrown out than just sit there and spend the whole day not writing. If it's getting toward midafternoon and we haven't put pen to paper yet, we'll just start slogging through it. And if we come in the next day and it isn't good, we'll throw it out. If that goes on for a couple of days, we'll start to rethink the movie.

MANDEL: We've taken the wrong fork in the road.

GANZ: That's right. We have to retrace our steps and see where we got lost. We're clearly never going to find gas, food, and lodging in this direction. We took the wrong turn.

MANDEL: Usually if it's not comedy rich, we're looking at the wrong map; that's basically it.

GANZ: If we keep writing . . .

MANDEL: If something is not coming . . .

GANZ: If two days in a row, we're not happy with what we've written in the same spot in the same scene, then we'll start to retrace our steps. Why have we come to such a barren area? Why are we finding nothing interesting or amusing or emotional that we can write in this spot? It's been set up wrong. The structure's wrong.

Maybe it's ego—no, it's not ego, it's experience—that if it's a scene that should be in the movie, then we should find a way to write it so it pleases us. And if we can't, then there's something not valid about what we're trying to write.

We don't count pages particularly. Sometimes we'll leave if we finish a scene, look at the clock, and it's about four and the next one is a good-sized scene.

We'll talk out the next scene and we'll jot down some jokes. We write aloud a lot and sometimes we say something funny, and we'll jot down some points we think will be hit in the next scene and some jokes that have come up naturally in speaking the characters' dialogue. That's great when you actually come in the next day and we've got a few sketched-out thoughts on the next scene. But we don't always do that either.

We've always admired good dialogue.

MANDEL: Absolutely.

GANZ: I think always, even before we were professional writers, we romanticized the music of joke writing, the rhythms. Neil Simon, for instance, there's just something about the way the jokes are written, just the sound of them. The meter, the rhythm of it, the ability to repeat a good joke that we've seen in somebody else's movie and get it *exactly* right, not paraphrase the joke, but get it just right.

There's something very pleasing about the way a joke with just the right amount of words in it, all the words in the right places, hits our ears. A baseball player talks about when you really hit the ball solid—rather than all that extra noise, the rattling of the bat, you get that *click*. The right jokes just click instead of making all that rattling, and I think that's always been something that we have great affection for.

I did so much staff writing in TV where everybody's talking all the time. Where sometimes there aren't just two guys in a room but eleven, and almost all the writing you do is with your mouth. I think we're just very verbal. It gets very sound-oriented. When we can hear the character's sound, that's when we can really start to write.

But we come to the office because it's important for us to have a place where we write. I don't think it matters what that place is, but I think it's important that it's different from the place where we sit around and take care of our kids and watch television. I just like the idea of *going* to work. I like the idea of leaving where I live to go to where I work.

MANDEL: You have to strap on the guns. You can't do that at home because someone gets shot. So you get in the car, you strap on your guns, you come to work, you have your little shootout, you go home.

GANZ: Yeah, you put on your suit of lights and come to work. But you know, I've written in hotel rooms. I've written in a car. We wrote a couple of scenes in *Parenthood* in the van going out in the morning for rehearsal. The Teamsters pick you up, and you drive out—and sometimes if it's Ron's movie, we ride out together just for that purpose. "You know that thing we're going to rehearse today, I was wondering if maybe there should be a different element in it," or "That scene we rehearsed yesterday, that was pretty good, I was pretty happy with that, but then last night I was thinking, was this something we'd want in it?"

And by the time we got to the location we had a first draft, we had something roughed out, and then we'd talk about it again over lunch, and then we'd give it to somebody to type, and the next day they were rehearsing the new pages. And several times it got in the movie; once or twice it was stuff that we were really proud of afterward, because it was right.

When I was in TV, my first job was on the "Odd Couple" and sometimes we'd write the tag during the show. It was a live audience show and they'd say during the dress rehearsal, "I really hate that tag." And by the time the episode was over, by the time they had finished the body of the show and they had a one-to-two minute scene to do at the end, we had another choice of tags.

They were great studies, Tony and Jack, and they'd look at it for a minute and they'd say like, "Yeah, we'll try this." They'd go up and talk to the director and block it simply, "I'll be here, I'll be here, you'll be there, two singles and a master," and they'd play it and shoot it and it'd be in the show.

MANDEL: In movies, you have to do a rewrite for the star, a rewrite for the director . . .

GANZ: Still, better than TV. On TV you're tailoring every episode; it's their show. By the time you've been on for two weeks, it's the star's show. And I don't mean that as a big negative thing. But even if they're lovely, generous, gracious people who are very kind to your writing, by the time the show's been on twice, it's their show.

MANDEL: I think we've been fortunate, though. We've worked on a movie where Penny Marshall stood sentry over the script. We worked on it together, and there was someone else—another person who was going to be in the movie—who said, "The writers aren't adjusting to what I do," and it would've broken the spine. And Penny said, "Well, we'll have to recast." She protected the material.

GANZ: One or two didn't turn out so well but . . . no matter how gracious and enthusiastic about the writing an actor is, once you've hired an actor, you've hired a writing partner. Even if they don't change a word, even if they love every word. It becomes different because of their instrument. If you don't want that, then write a book. Then there is nothing, except for your editor, between you and the reader's eye. There's no interpretive artist between it.

If you're going to write movies, to me it's pathetic to whine and cry about how it has to go through the instruments of the director and the actor. That's part of it. Because you're not turning down those wonderful things they get you. You don't walk around and say, "Oh that's not my laugh, I only got that laugh because Steve Martin or Tom Hanks or Michael Keaton or Billy Crystal is so funny." You're taking credit for those laughs too.

They're taking a nothing joke and making it a medium. They're taking a medium joke and turning it into a touchdown. All you can ask is that they treat you with respect.

We're not very pushy. But that's one of the reasons we're not producers. We're not good at knocking on doors; we don't sell. We really don't. If you don't want to do our script, we'll write a different script. You read these stories about guys who have scripts that they got turned down in six places and they never let it die, and they carried it around for eight years, and they made it and made it and made it and the picture finally got made.

That's to me just totally beyond my comprehension. I can't imagine doing that.

We haven't even pitched much in the last couple of years, and we've pitched many, many movies. I had an enormous amount of practice doing it in television, a *huge* amount of practice. Once at Paramount TV, they asked me what I would charge to pitch somebody else's pilot at a network while I was there.

I don't miss it. We once pitched two movies in one day, both of which got written—two different stories, had a meeting in the morning, had a meeting in the afternoon. In the evening I was literally light-headed, I actually felt faint at the end of the day. And I was much younger then. It's a little intense.

THE JOB OF A CRITIC

GANZ: I'm holding them up to a standard that they have no intention of meeting, but I don't find them very illuminating. Basically, ninety-five percent of them are not essayists. I mean, essays are one thing. But the ninety-five percent of the reviewers who are not essayists are basically saying, "I liked it, I didn't like it," and then attempting to justify their opinion with objective truths. Saying, "It failed because of . . ."

Well, it didn't fail because of that; it failed for you because you didn't like it—which is certainly all right, God knows. But all that's happened here is that someone's made a picture you didn't like. "This picture succeeds because of blah, blah, blah."

Well, it succeeds because it found you somewhere. There was a nice mating here of a movie and an audience, and now you're going to explain how it happened, when sitting two rows away from you was somebody who thought it was a piece of crap! So what about all those wonderful things they did to make it work, how come it didn't?

It all boils down to that. I always feel like reviewers should be forced to say, "I saw this picture, I didn't like it, but you know, I saw the last three pictures this guy made and this is how I reviewed those," or "This particular actor I liked in this, this, and this, but not in this," or "This is how I reviewed movies on this subject in the past." So you can find where the inclinations are, where the prejudice is, and that sort of thing. Because I don't know what I'm reading or hearing when the guy comes on TV and says, "I saw this and it's a rip-rollicking-roaring hoop-de-do," or "It's a piece of worthless garbage." I have no context.

I mean, they matter, I do believe there is some impact on the general perception that America has about a movie when it's opening; they can affect that general perception. Not even whether they think it's good or not, but whether they seem to be implying that it's important, that it makes a space for itself in the marketplace. I think they contribute to that perception. I try not to read them.

MANDEL: I think they should all write a screenplay. I think they should be forced to, and let them criticize each other and then maybe they'll have a little more compassion.

CODA

GANZ: In the future, I hope I'm not writing the same movies, but I hope I'm doing the same work.

MANDEL: Yeah.

GANZ: Right now we've got a bunch of one-sheets up on the wall of which we're proud, to one extent or another. In a few years, I'd like to have several more up there that we're proud of, to one extent or another. I'd like to have a body of work, if that doesn't sound pretentious.

MANDEL: I'd like this room to look like Boston Garden with these one-sheets.

GANZ: But I worry about why this is going so good. What's the punch line? What's the trick ending? Where's the surprise? This isn't drama; it keeps being nice. Where does the sandbag fall? It makes me sound very healthy because in five years I just want to be doing what I'm doing, but the unhealthy part is that deep down in my heart I assume I won't be. That between now and then something is going to go drastically and terribly wrong.

But we're not trying to attain something we haven't had. We're just trying to protect the castle.

PHIL ALDEN ROBINSON

Phil Alden Robinson, a slender man with a thin face, a neatly trimmed beard, and an open expression, chooses his words very carefully so that there's no misinterpreting his meaning. In his late thirties, Robinson has paid his dues. There have been times when screenwriting was a very painful profession for him, but he is virtually a paradigm of the Hollywood axiom that tenacity is the prime necessity for survival. Out of his endurance came that very successful film with all the odds against it, Field of Dreams.

However, it's interesting to note that the same man who wrote the uplifting Field of Dreams also wrote the wildly funny All of Me. The variety of his work reflects the odd assortment of jobs he held, all of them in one or another field of communication, before the magic moment every screenwriter looks forward to—although, in his own words, the process of getting a screenplay bought is so slow and indecisive that there's never a moment of *heady success; by the time the deal comes through, you don't feel like celebrating.*

In common with our other writers, he obviously feels the pain is worth it. However, he feels writing is too painful to endure unless he feels totally committed to the story. He lives for the story, but he says, "You've always got to run through the pain, as the marathoners will say."

Perhaps as much as any of the writers here, Robinson illustrates that success in film writing may involve the ability to survive for weeks, months, and years on the belief in oneself. Sneakers, which he also directed, reflects years of work and innumerable disappointments before it finally came to the screen.

Robinson's experiences have left him cautious but enthusiastic, the perfect combination for a screenwriter who is in "the business" for the long haul and in the marathon to stay.

I started as a journalist. As a kid I was always writing something, but I never thought of becoming a writer. Then when I was in college, I started playing around with the college radio station. I was a disc jockey and I did commercials, news, and I was really enjoying it. So a couple of friends of mine and I decided, "Let's do something with news." And in the spring of '68 we went to Indiana to cover the Democratic presidential primary. We had called small radio stations all over the Northeast and said, "We're going, and for a nominal fee we'll send reports to you with your call letters at the end of them." Custom, on-the-scene coverage. That financed the trip.

We had a great time. And that summer one of the guys and I went to the Chicago Democratic convention and did the same thing. Then I went to work at a local radio/TV station in Schenectady, New York, where I was going to college. And I thought, "Well, this is what I'll do, I'll be a broadcast journalist." I was nineteen years old and I was on the air.

I got from that, really, into documentaries. I found that the day-to-day covering of news was fun, but I wanted to have something meatier to work with. And documentaries led to educational TV and corporate films and training films and educational films.

And I was writing and directing and producing and doing whatever had to be done.

I was in Los Angeles by then, freelancing in industrials and
educationals. And I literally woke up one night and said, "Oh, I
guess I'm a filmmaker." I really hadn't set out to become one,
but I realized, This is what I'm doing. Then, at the TV station
where I worked, I talked them into letting me do a documentary.
It's a shame you can't make a living at documentaries, not just
for those of us who would like to do it. It's a shame for the audience, which is not seeing good documentaries.

I had already gotten an agent, but I was still doing educationals
and industrials. Then a year or two went by and I was still doing
the same thing and I couldn't take it anymore. And I said to him,
"Get me into television, I don't care." I felt like I was in the minor
leagues, like I was stuck in the minors. And I was working all the
time and I was making a living and it was very gratifying, but I
really found that I wasn't satisfied; my instincts were more toward
entertainment, and the people I was working with didn't want
that. Some did, most didn't. I actually had a producer say to me
once, "The trouble with this script is you're trying to make it too
interesting."

That's when I saw the handwriting on the wall. If I hadn't seen
it till then, that was the clincher. "The audiences who will see this
film *have* to see it. You don't have to make it interesting to them,
to attract them. They're being told to sit and watch this film, so
just do the minimum legal requirement." So my agent said to me,
"We'll find a TV show that's been on the air for a while and that
has a big order so they'll take a chance on a new writer." We
settled on "Trapper John, M.D.," and I watched a few episodes
with a partner and we came up with six story ideas. My agent got
us a meeting through great persistence, and we showed up at the
meeting and the producer was very nice and said, "Tell me again
what you've done," and we said, "Actually, nothing," and he said,
"How did you get this meeting?" and I said, "My agent is very
persistent," and he said, "He must be. Well, okay, tell us your
stories."

We had written these stories out very well. We told him all six.
There was a problem with each one. They already had a story like
this one, the network said you can't do that—but he said, "We
like you, you've come up with good ideas, so come back with more
ideas and pitch them to us." We were heartened by that and came
back with six more ideas, worked out in great detail. One of them

they loved, they went crazy for it, they thought it was one of the best things they'd ever heard.

We went out and had a bottle of wine for lunch. Then I called my agent. He closed his office, took me to a bar, and we had a couple of beers. That night a whole bunch of us went to a sushi bar and drank sake all night long. That weekend was like a lost weekend. Monday morning the producer called and said, "The network hates the story, and we can't use it." I felt I had lost weeks, maybe months of my life, from having celebrated this great achievement. But the producer was great; he said, "Look, we're going to get you an assignment. Come back with one-line ideas. You don't have to work them out, we'll help you. We'll help you get an assignment."

We came up with twenty-two one-line ideas. They picked one from column A and a subplot from column B and that was that. We were very enthused; we wrote the script and they said, "This is the best outside script we've ever gotten. Do you want to write another one for us?" We said, "Yes," and they said, "Oops, SAG just went on strike." This was in '80. So it was back to industrials for six months. In January of '81, Trapper John called and they said, "Look, there's a pending Writers Guild strike in March, so the network is letting us order a few episodes early. Come write another script for us." We said, "Great."

At the same time, Avco Embassy had hired me to write a screenplay for them. This was in January and both of these had to be turned in before the March 1 strike deadline. So in two months I wrote a feature script and a TV script. Then the guild went on strike, so it was back to industrials and educationals and I really felt God was saying, "Are you sure you want to be a writer? Don't you really like industrials and educationals? Just give it one more chance."

Those were trying times. Not the most trying times I've had, because I thought that I was on the scent, I felt that I was . . . there was this elusive goal, but I was getting closer to it. But I did feel like that frog in the mathematical problem who could only jump half the distance to the goal line and never quite gets there.

Finally the Writers Guild strike was settled and I went back to the next Trapper John script. I got to do another feature script for Embassy, which was *Rhinestone,* and from that point on things took off. The career has been sort of self-generating, in the sense that I haven't had to stop and ask where my next job is coming from.

CREDITS AND REWRITES

I think the Writers Guild is a great organization that is flawed. I think that given how powerless we are even with a guild, I'd be terrified to be a screenwriter in this town without a guild. I'm in a position where I can negotiate a much better deal than the guild can negotiate for me. Still, we are protected in certain areas—not enough, but in certain areas—from what this industry has historically done to writers. The Writers Guild has protections based not on their fantasies of what would happen to us but based on forty years of history of what producers did to writers before there was a guild to protect them.

I have real problems with the credit arbitration process. It's very important that the guild be the arbiter of credits—and not the producers and the studios. I think that's good, but there is a built-in bias in the arbitration process for the first writer, which has helped me in some cases and hurt me in other cases. I've done a couple of rewrites, projects in which the studio wasn't going to make the movie because the script wasn't right. They hired me to change it and I changed it, and improved it enough so they said, okay, we're going to spend fifteen million dollars to make the movie now. I changed a significant amount of material and did not get the credit.

They say a full third has to be changed in order to get a credit. In that particular case, I thought I did change a third. I had a deeper problem than that which was, what's so magical about a third? The effect of the arbitration process is that screen credits are not true. One of the movies I did said, "Screenplay by . . ." and it mentions the writer. He's a very good writer and a wonderful guy, but the truth is the screenplay was by him and me and one other writer and the star.

So the credits don't reflect the truth, and I think that's unfair. One, I think truth is good, we should tell the truth. Two, when I get sole credit on a screenplay, I don't want people saying, yeah, but who really worked on it? I would like sole credit to mean what it's supposed to mean.

It's unfortunate, but that's my main complaint with the guild. Their process is secretive. Each writer submits a statement that no other writer can see, so I don't know in these arbitrations if these other writers lied in their statements. I'm not accusing them of lying, but I have no idea which one of them has the whole picture. The arbitration panel gets all the statements from these writers, but if somebody says something in one statement that is not rebutted in another statement—and how could you tell, if you don't know that they're saying?—then that remains the truth to the arbitration committee.

But it's probably better that we work it out ourselves than to fight the studio or the producer.

A rule of the guild is that you cannot question an arbitration decision except on grounds of procedure. It's binding and you agree not to criticize it in print. I'm not going to criticize specific decisions because that's the rule, but in fact I think it's a dishonest process. Not because the guild is trying to be dishonest; I think that they are so sensitive to the fact that traditionally the first writers get screwed that they're leaning way over backward, and now the second writer gets screwed. Who's to say one is more valuable than the other. In fact, you could make a very good case for saying it's the guy who got the movie made who has created a contribution that should be acknowledged somehow.

A friend of mine just went through this rewriting business, on a script that she and her partner had written on spec. They got a deal at a studio and they did another draft, and the studio said, we want to go in a different direction, and they brought someone else on. It's very painful.

This, to me, is something that the Writers Guild knows it wants to address but doesn't know how to address it, the fact that playwrights and novelists and poets and songwriters and any other kind of writers own their work, and you can't change that work without their participation. A screenwriter is not the owner of his work. In fact, when you sign a contract to write a screenplay, it says, "For purposes of copyright law the studio will be deemed the author of the screenplay." So the studio writes the screenplay, as far as the law is concerned.

On the other hand, one gets paid well for rewriting.

THE UPS, THE DOWNS . . .

This business is so slow, and so often scattered and indecisive, that you never get that one moment of Eureka, I've discovered the cure for a disease. What you get is, one day someone says, the studio wants to do it, and two weeks later you hear, okay, we're going to start negotiating, and a month later, something else . . . By the time you finish negotiating, you're so pissed off at them that you don't celebrate when the deal comes through. It's a very long process.

I've had a lot of wonderful moments. The opening nights of

All of Me and *In the Mood* were just thrilling. The great moments
to me are when you show a film to an audience that doesn't know
anything about the picture and you get this completely virgin response, and it's wonderful, it's really great, they haven't been
hyped yet, they haven't been told what's wrong with the film or
what's right about it, they haven't been told any of the jokes,
they're like a blank page, and it's really thrilling.

The really hard times, the times when I've had the most doubts,
were not in the hungry days, trying to get where I wanted to go,
but during the time when I had spent a year writing *Rhinestone*
and the studio loved it—and then let Stallone rewrite every word
of it. The day I heard he was going to be in the film was a low
day because I knew he was going to rewrite it. And the studio said,
don't worry, we'll try real hard to let you rewrite it. The day I
heard he rewrote it was a bad day, but I thought maybe it will be
okay because what he said was, I'm just going to change a few
lines of my own character's dialogue. And I thought, oh okay.

Two months later he turned in this ghastly script that was a
completely new thing. And the studio hired me to rewrite him
and what they said was, you can't change any of the dialogue he
wrote for his own character but you can change anything else—
and that felt real bad. But I said to myself, if this movie goes down
the sewer, I don't want it to be because I gave up on it. So I'm
going to try and be professional, I'm going to try to swallow my
pride and work on this.

It was very hard working with the material he had written because it was so bad and unfunny and unsympathetic, and it was
so over the top and obvious and on the nose, and full of all those
expressions that I had worked so hard to avoid in mine. And then
I turned that in and they said, we love this, we're going to fight
him to the death and if he wants to change one word, he's out.
He came back and put it all back.

I didn't really care about that until I saw the film. The night I
saw the film at a press screening was, I think, the worst night of
my life. Now may it always be the worst night of my life. I have
my health. People didn't lose their homes over this. It is, in the
great scheme of things, not a tragedy. But personally it was real
hard because I had spent a year on that script and I was so proud
of it; I really felt it was as good as I could write it. And when I
saw the movie that resulted from his script, I was so depressed. I
was rude to people that night. I was sullen. I was inconsolable. It
was to a certain extent an existential crisis.

But that's when I thought, this is a preposterous way to make a living. The lack of safeguards for your work—the amount of time and care and attention that it takes to turn out the work, compared to the lack of safeguards that work is given, is terrifying.

I realized I was at a decision point. Here it is the beginning of my career, I have just been shat upon by a studio and a star for all the world to see, and I have to decide how I'm going to handle this because to a certain extent, my behavior now will send a message to the industry: you can or cannot treat me like this. And it wasn't even a decision. I wrote letters and I gave interviews and I did a lot of press.

Looking back on it now, I don't feel that I had a choice. I couldn't do nothing. I mean, I was *doing* nothing and I couldn't keep doing that. There was too much pressure. And I thought, I'm going to take a lot of heat for this but it's worth it. I would rather take the heat for saying what I believe and for telling the truth than to just let the industry know you can do this to me. And so I did a lot of press and got no heat. Stallone called my agent and was furious but that was it.

People at studios, even at Fox, called to say we're glad you did that and it's about time somebody said these things. Writers, of course, were thrilled. I actually got calls from people who worked on the movie, and who were allied with Stallone, saying, we're glad you did that, we can't say this to Sly, but you're right. And I didn't do it for that, but that made me feel like I wasn't completely alone out there. But it was my little way of saying, look I know I don't have the power to fight you guys nose to nose or to arm wrestle with you, but it is a free country and I can say what I want. I can disavow it and just tell the truth about what happened. And if someone gets the message out there, if someone says, ooh, don't hire Robinson because he'll criticize us when we fuck up the script, I'd just as soon they got that message.

I don't want to work for someone who's going to mess up my material. I'm very collaborative, I have no problem with changing things, I have no problem with working with people, but I really don't want to be that powerless again and I'd just as soon people knew going in that I believe in the material I work on and I want them to believe in it too.

INFLUENCES

Robert Benchley influenced me more than anyone, I suppose. I think if there's a reason I'm a writer, it's because of Robert Benchley. When I was twelve, an aunt gave me a book as a birthday present, which I still have, a very dog-eared copy of the *Benchley Roundup,* which was a collection of his essays in the twenties and thirties. Brilliantly funny. Inventive and whimsical and he made me laugh by means of his language, his invention, everything but jokes. And it really excited me to the possibility of how a writer can create humor.

I remember in English class we had to write a series of essays on short topics, and I wrote them all in my ersatz Benchley style, which I'm sure would humiliate me if I saw it today. But they were the hit of junior high school. They were passed around like dirty magazines; everyone wanted to see these things. And I think it was the first time I felt like I could find my own voice this way. In fact I was finding his voice, but it was a way of finding mine.

I've seen some reviews lately that compare me with Woody Allen, and I have to chuckle because he was influenced by Benchley a lot. He's an original and fabulous talent, but there's a lot of Robert Benchley in Woody Allen. Particularly in his essays, if you read his comic essays, which are brilliant, very much like Benchley. And that's not to criticize him at all, but there's a thread that goes back to Benchley and Perelman, and I love that stuff.

COMEDY

I think that a good comedy is every bit as important as a good drama. Scientists know that when you laugh, somewhere in your system you secrete something that's good for you. Norman Cousins cured himself of cancer by watching Marx Brothers movies. To reduce it to its extreme, laughter is great to take people's minds off their troubles. If a movie does nothing more than entertain and amuse for an hour and a half, God bless it. There's enough misery out there, we don't need to add to it. Which is not to say that we shouldn't make films that are depressing also; there are some great depressing films. But it's too easy to slough off comedy as being not important and I think it's vitally important.

But everybody has a different idea of comedy. I've always been a fan of Steve Martin. Working on *All of Me* was the first time I met him, and there was a key moment in our relationship. There was a line in the script I thought was really funny; I've long since forgotten what it was. He said, "Let's take that out, it's not funny," and I said, "Gee, I kind of think it's funny," and I wasn't being argumentative, and he said, "No, it's not funny. It won't get a laugh." I said, "Really? I really think it will get a laugh." It was the only time he got impatient with me, and he snapped. He said, "I've been in front of live audiences," and I put on this mock bravado and I said, "Oh yeah, well I've been in live audiences." And I felt for a second, I've gone too far, and he laughed and he said, "All right, leave it in."

I've forgotten what the line was, but when the movie opened, he said to me, "You know what? That line gets roars." It just goes to show that nobody knows anything about comedy.

PROCESS

I don't think I can talk as well as I can write. I think I'm a pretty good storyteller, but I never really know what it is they want to hear. The truth is, until I've written a screenplay, I don't really know what it is I want to say. I may have an idea about the shape of it, or moments that I'm looking for, or the progression of things, but I don't really get who the characters are or where the comedy is or where the truth is until I've actually had to sit down and work the material.

And it's hard to sit down because I don't know what I'm going to do when I sit down, I don't know exactly what I'm going to write, and the hardest thing about writing is thinking. Once I know I'm going to write, I'll sit down and write and you can't dynamite me out of a chair. If I develop the symptoms of what other people call writer's block, it's not because I'm blocked, I just don't have any good ideas, I don't know what to write, and I found that there's a very simple cure for it which is, think of something. Pick one and write it, you can always change it.

The flaw in my process is that I'm much too plot-oriented. And after I work out this intricate plot, I always have to go back and say, now who is this guy, and why would he do that? And then I'm locked into a Chinese puzzle. I would love someday to sit down and say, I'm going to think of a character. Let me flesh this guy out and then come up with a story for him.

But let me expand on one thing about how you pick something and write it, the process. I have a rule never to show anything to anybody until it's damned ready to be shown. And that's not because of ego; it's because without that rule, I cannot write a word. The first four, ten, twenty drafts will be awful. That's part of the process. When a sculptor has a big piece of stone, it doesn't look good until he's whittled away all the stone he doesn't want, and the same is true of writing; you can't get it good the first time.

I'm sure that Shakespeare's first drafts were awful.

And when I get stuck sometimes on the first draft, it's because I'm too self-conscious, imagining what someone will think when they read this page, and I have to remind myself that no one is going to read this page. I won't let my dog see this page. Once I know in my heart that no one's going to see this, I can be very free to write badly and to experiment with the material, to find what works. You have to try stuff. You have to know that your mate is not going to see this. If you have friends who come over, you've gotta know that they will not look at that, because if they even see the page . . .

And you want to show things, but you can't do it; I can't do it. And you whittle away and you change it and you throw something out, you put something back, and pretty soon it starts getting good. And the only way I can do it is if I know no one's going to see it. It's the fear of writing something bad.

It kept me from smoking cigarettes. When I was a kid, I knew the first time you smoke a cigarette you hold it wrong and you cough and you look stupid, and I never wanted to look stupid. That's a good result of a bad quality—but it also kept me from skiing.

I do a lot of research. First, because it's a great procrastination. And it's a crutch that I'm comfortable with, having started as a journalist and having always been good at school, I'm comfortable having a firm base of facts beneath me. In the case of *In the Mood*, I spent well over a month in the library, going through every day's edition of three L.A. newspapers for the two-year period that the story covered. It was really fun. I learned more about the story than the main character, Sonny Wisecarver, knew about it.

Also, it's a wonderful way to steep yourself in another era, to really learn what was going on in the forties, what people were talking about. I'm sort of a student of the forties, I thought I knew the forties. But every day in the *L.A. Times* on page two, there was a long, long list of Southern California casualties. Every day. And when you're going through these newspapers day after day and you see this, you start to get a feeling of what "world war" means. It was really sort of staggering.

And even the conservative *L.A. Times* was very tabloidlike in its coverage—always a juicy sex scandal, an unsolved murder, or a story like Sonny Wisecarver's in the news. Much more so than today.

So I'm a big fan of research.

I need order around me. If the desk is messy it's a distraction.

Part of that is it's a good procrastination to clean up the desk. This house is very neat. You can tell a writer lives here who hasn't been writing lately. There's a great quote from Flaubert, I think, he says, "Be regular and ordinary in your life so that you may be violent and original in your work." I'm not violent in my work, but I sure understand what he's talking about. It gives me the freedom to cut loose if things around me are in order.

I also need a big block of time. If I know that I have an hour, I usually won't sit down and write. I just find that it takes a certain amount of time once you've sat down to get this train up to speed, and I hate putting on the brakes. You don't say, I did that many pages this day; you don't judge. I don't have a set schedule. There are times when I get up in the morning and go right to work; there are other times when I won't write for two days.

I was jokingly telling this to somebody and then realized it's not a joke. They asked, "What's your schedule?" and I said, I get up in the morning and I exercise and I read the papers and I play with the dog. And take a shower and eat breakfast and make the phone calls, write a couple of letters and it's time for lunch. You have lunch, on the way home there's an art gallery or a store you can stop in, you come home, there's the mail, you have to answer letters, there are more phone calls, you return the phone calls, it's time for dinner. You go out to dinner, and after dinner, you say, Gee it's eight-thirty or nine o'clock, I could write but I'll be fresher in the morning. So you go to sleep early, you wake up and the same thing happens the next day.

It's very easy to not write; not writing is very simple. Not writing is a full-time job.

It's funny, I had lunch with a guy a month ago. I told him, I'm stuck on this script I'm writing, it got so bad that the place is perfectly neat. I rearranged all the books in my den. And he said, "Yeah, sometimes what I'll do is I'll re-pot the plants," and I said, "Re-pot the plants! Thank you!"

I think I always imagine myself in the roles when I'm writing. I've never acted, but I think I have what most people have, an idealized view of how wonderful it would be to get up and emote and have people cry, and I think that I'll only achieve that in my dreams. I hesitate to say I think it would be fun to do it, because I have too many friends who are actors, and who have very hard lives. It takes a lot of skill and dedication and it's not the sort of thing that you can just waltz through.

Once the star is on the film, I will do another draft to tailor things for them, and that's really fun because it's for stars. In *All of Me,* one of my favorite lines in the script came out of just that. It's late in the film and Lily [Tomlin] is still in Steve [Martin's] body and Steve wants to go to bed with the stableman's daughter and Lily won't have anything to do with it, and this is the second time she's ruined one of these things, and in the original draft she just says no. And Lily said to me, "You know, I don't want this character to be such a prude through the whole movie. Why can't she say, ooh, let's try it?"

And I said, "Gee, it's such a big leap for her to all of a sudden be an adventurer." And she said, "What if she disagrees at first and gets talked into it?" And I said, "That's a good idea, let me take a stab at that." The first half of the scene was easy because that's when she says no, and I was used to writing that, and then Steve goes into the bathroom where there's a mirror and says, "Come on, let's do this." And she says, "What's so good about sex," and he says, "It's like laughing or the World Series or like Duke Ellington, it's one of those things that make you glad you're alive." And I thought, okay, now what is there about Lily that I can use in this scene, and I knew that Lily is enamored of the glamour of old Hollywood, she loves that stuff, and I thought this is good, she'll fantasize about Clark Gable, he's perfect. So she says, "I'll fantasize about somebody," and they go back in the bedroom and she's now fantasizing about Clark Gable and he says, "Wait a second, my head is filled with pictures of Clark Gable taking his shirt off." She says, "Isn't it great?" He says, "Throw in a couple of women on top of him and we're in business here," and he gets back in bed with the stableman's daughter and he says now, "I've got the whole cast of *Gone With the Wind* humping in my head."

Usually that gets one of the biggest laughs in the movie, strictly from trying to tailor something for Lily, knowing who she is and what she's interested in.

I was really very proud of that because I felt that I got something right, for the situation, for the actor.

CRITICS

I believe you can't take that stuff personally and I don't. I would rather get a good review than a bad review, I've had more good reviews than bad reviews. When I see a bad review, it doesn't depress me, I think, okay, that's his opinion. There are great movies that I don't like, and that's my opinion. There's one great filmmaker, and I've never liked one of his films: Ingmar Bergman.

I understand he's brilliant, I know he's great, one of the masters of the medium. His films don't speak to me. I won't say that they're boring, but I will say I am always bored in his films.

I recognize that it's probably my lack. I just think that what he doesn't speak to me says volumes. He is dealing with issues in a certain way that don't touch me.

Also, I'm so verbal that I'm very conscious of the fact that I'm not getting any of the nuances of language. I don't know if a character has just used a colloquialism, I don't know if he has said it with an ironic twist in his voice. I don't know, if he emphasizes a word in a certain way, if he means something different than he did in the last scene.

There are Swedish films I've loved, so it's not just the language, but that's part of it. So I figure if I give myself permission to not like Bergman films, I certainly have to give people permission not to like mine.

I just think reviews are people's opinions, they're entitled to their opinions, I would fight to the death to defend their right to express their opinions. I got a terrible review in *Premiere* magazine and I didn't cancel my subscription. I still love the magazine. It's just someone's opinion. I also take the attitude that the good reviews are right and the bad reviews are wrong. Although the truth is, there are points in some bad reviews that I've agreed with, where I thought, yeah, he's right, I didn't get that part right.

One other factor is that the first movie that came out with my name on it was *Rhinestone* and as I said, I didn't feel personally affronted with all those reviews because I agreed with them, it was a disgracefully bad movie and it wasn't my work they were reviewing; it just happened to have my name on it.

Now if I get a bad review, I think, my name was in the *Rhinestone* reviews, these guys can't hurt me. I've been vaccinated. There's nothing these people can say about me tougher than I've already seen. I have also seen wonderful reviews of my work that I didn't agree with, where I felt that they completely missed the point. I don't think my work is perfect; I think it's flawed, and there are things I don't like about movies that I've done, and some of the reviews point that out and I agree.

I do think I draw the line at statements of "fact" that are not true. I've seen this in some reviews. One review of *All of Me*—it was Rex Reed—described the plot in very crazy terms and then said, "Don't tell me they're not putting anything up their noses in Hollywood other than nasal spray." Now, I think that's a despicable thing to say. This was a drug-free movie. Who's he accusing of taking drugs, Carl Reiner? Get out of here! There were no drugs on this movie. Believe me, I would have seen them.

If he had said, this is the stupidest plot or the worst movie I've ever seen, I would have said, okay, that's his opinion. But to imply that this plot is the result of drug use, I think that's almost actionable, I think it doesn't have a place in serious criticism. That's the sort of thing I draw the line at, a personal attack that is unfounded. You know, if somebody wants to say that Phil Robinson has no talent, they can say that. But for them to say the plot is the result of drug use is really bad. And unfortunately you do see that in reviews.

I get a kick out of how some reviewers will misquote things, they'll put them in the wrong characters' mouths. And there's a sloppiness in some reviewers that wouldn't be acceptable in the movie. But they don't hold themselves to the same standards. They'll credit the editor with something the cameraman did. I've seen a lot of reviews where the actors are credited with the lines of dialogue. It's extraordinary to me that a writer—and a reviewer is a writer—doesn't understand what a screenwriter does.

STUDIOS, CARE AND FEEDING

Everyone has opinions about things. The big lesson I learned from *Rhinestone* is that you must pick and choose, to whatever extent you can, where you're going to work and for whom. Because the battle is won or lost there. If you're with people who understand what you're trying to do and believe in and will stand up for it, you have a fighting chance of getting what you want on the screen. If they don't feel strongly about what you feel strongly about, you'll never get it.

My cinematographer on *Field of Dreams* used to say, "We are surrounded by assassins and saboteurs." It's not always intentional, but there are always forces out there that will change the shape of something, and you have to have people around who will agree with you.

I've been fortunate in the last few movies because I was in a position, to a certain extent, to pick and choose who I was working for. So I didn't have the clashes. There are always disagreements, and you work them out. *Rhinestone* was a case of people saying, "We love this material," and then not standing up for it.

But I think one of the things I have going for me is that I'm sane and I'm perceived as being reasonable. So when I do have a disagreement with the studio, they generally take it not as a matter of power but as a legitimate disagreement. In fact, on *Field of Dreams* one of the executives at the studio really wanted the main character to have a teenaged son; he felt this would help bring out some of the issues in the script better. And I'd tried that about a year and a half before and it didn't work and I gave it up.

But he brought it up again; he said, "You really must do this," so I spent about two months trying to get this fourteen-year-old bastard into the script, and I just couldn't go it. And I spent a lot more time on it than I would have given *my* idea because I wanted him to know I was trying. Then I went back to him and said, "I've been working my ass off on this; I can't get it. I think it's wrong; here are the reasons I think it's wrong. But the big reason is, I just feel it's wrong," and I showed him the pages. And he said, "Okay, if you feel strongly about it, then drop it."

I'm sure if I'd said to him at first, "No, absolutely not, I won't write this," it would have been bad.

You win some, you lose some, it's the process. You have to let them know you're not fighting to protect your ego, you're fighting to do what's right for the script.

One thing I learned in *All of Me,* when I sat down at a table with these people who helped define American comedy, they're going to want me to make changes. I feel like any writer does, I feel that my ego is wrapped up in my work. I would love to hear them say, it's perfect, don't change a comma. That never happens; they're going to want changes, and there are some changes I'm not going to agree with. But my job is not to say no; my job is to figure out how to say yes. In other words, if someone says, you can't use that line, instead of saying I love that line, I would say, all right, tell me what your objection is and let me come up with something else that we both like.

I think that's one of the reasons they accepted me. I wasn't sitting there saying, who are you to say my line is no good?

WRITER AS DIRECTOR: FIELD OF DREAMS

I came out of a discipline in documentaries and educational films where I was both writing and directing, they were part of the same process. It took a couple of years of screenwriting before I could get to direct a movie, during which time I never thought of myself as someone who would never do it, I always felt that I would get the chance someday and I would just have to go on writing screenplays until someone said, okay, he's valuable enough to us that we will take this chance. So I guess I've always thought of myself as a writer/director.

When I'm writing, I say to myself, "This is so hard, I'm not good at this; I should be just directing and stop writing." When I'm directing, I think, "God, just get me off the set and let me write something." Writing and directing are equally important in the filmmaking process.

I think that Shoeless Joe [*Field of Dreams*] changed some people, how they look at the world, how they feel about themselves and their families. It's an adaptation of a brilliant novel by W. P. Kinsella, a great Canadian writer. It's a contemporary story about a man on a corn farm in Iowa, a small farm, with his wife and his daughter. He's the most normal man in the world; he's never done a single crazy thing in his life. And one day out in the fields, he hears a voice. And the voice says, "If you build it, he will come." And he interprets that to mean, if you plow under the corn from which you are barely able to support your family and build a baseball diamond out of the cornfield, that Shoeless Joe Jackson, who's been dead for thirty years and who was banned for life from playing baseball after the Black Sox scandal, will get to come back and play ball again. And he goes to his wife and says, honey, uh, I heard a voice and this is what it said and this is what I think it means and I'm supposed to do it. And she says, well, if you think that you have to, then do it. And he does, and with great love and dedication he builds a perfect baseball diamond. The grass is perfect, there's no pebbles in the dirt to make the ball bounce, he builds bleachers, he builds lights, and he waits and nothing happens. And it's autumn, there's leaves on the ground, nothing. There's snow on the ground, it's winter, nothing. Springtime, little robin is pulling a worm out of the ground, nothing. People in town are calling him funny names and they're going under, they're losing money. And one night his daughter says, Daddy, there's a man out there on your lawn; and he looks, and there's Shoeless Joe Jackson. And that's just the first chapter of the book. And he hears another voice and it tells him to do something and he is led onto a journey in which it's all about making dreams come true.

And in the end, it all comes back, and you don't know quite how these things tie together and in the end it ties together and when I first read the book, I got chills thinking about it, in a way that was so emotionally powerful and satisfying that studio executives and agents cried; they wept when they read the script. It's funny. It's original, it's very, very deeply touching. The story is so out there, but what it's about is so deeply personal and real that it was just an extraordinary piece of material.

The book chose me to a certain extent. I read it years ago through a series of coincidences. People who don't like that kind of material read it and loved it and gave it to me. I tried to get it set up; I couldn't. Two producers optioned the book. They couldn't get it set up anywhere. It took years of pushing and finally Kevin Costner's commitment put it over the top at Universal.

THE FUTURE

I've had more good times than bad times and I expect to have more good times than bad times in the future, but the bad times are a part of the business. It's like ball players who will say an error is part of the game. I think that I've finally reached a plateau where from here on in it's not about a struggle to get a better position, it's about the struggle to accomplish what I've set out to accomplish on this level. I finally got to be a writer/director of feature films. Now I want to make the best movies I can make. It's no longer about, ooh, give me a chance to write a movie, give me a chance to direct a movie. It's now about, okay, let me really dig deep and see how much I can do with this opportunity.

In theory, it's limitless what you can do. I'm in a good place and I'm extremely lucky. I know that and I don't want to blow it. I really want to give back what I can. Unfortunately it takes so damn long to make a movie. If you're a writer/director it takes a couple of years. I envy the old guys from the golden age of Hollywood; they could make three movies a year. I'll be lucky if I make one every two or three years. How many movies do I have before I retire? Do I have ten movies, fifteen? I doubt twenty.

On balance, I'm doing great. I am very, very happy. I would like to do better. What I don't want to be doing in five years is jobs for the money. I don't want to be another body for hire. I don't think I could do things that didn't mean something to me—it's too hard. Writing and directing, separately much less together, are so hard. They require so much stamina and dedication that if you don't really believe in it, I don't know how to do it.

They take over every instant of your life and they test you, they take you past the limit where you think you can go in terms of your stamina and your courage and your convictions and your determination to not compromise. You gird yourself for a certain amount of struggle; you always have to struggle past that.

You've always got to run through the pain, as the marathoners will say.

You have to go past that point, and every part of the process takes longer than you think it's going to take and it's harder than you think it's going to be, and I don't know how hacks do it. I could no more go through this process with something that I didn't want to do than cut off a limb. It's too hard, too painful. It's not worth it. And if I didn't have a story I was dying to tell, I'd do something else.

JOHN SINGLETON

There has never been a more distinguished directorial debut than that of screenwriter John Singleton's Boyz N the Hood. At the age of twenty-four he became the youngest Academy Award nominee for best director—eclipsing the half-century reign of Orson Welles—and the only black director ever so honored. Singleton's searing personal vision is aptly reflected in his piercing gaze from behind wire-rimmed glasses—a thin, intense young man whose keen intelligence is informed by an uncompromising single-mindedness. He's the opposite of loquacious—the quintessential man of few words—and prefers to define himself almost entirely through his actions. There is about him a restless and wary energy that generates a momentum all its own. Having just completed a music video with Michael Jackson, Eddie Murphy, and Magic Johnson, Singleton is embarking upon his second feature, which he promises will be even more thematically and technically complex than his first. Once you have heard Singleton talk about what he does and how he does it, you cannot doubt that he will have a long and prolific career as a filmmaker.

I'm from South Central L.A. and I got into writing from my English classes. I had one English teacher that especially influenced me. I'd always liked to read, mostly little novels and comic books, and was always an avid film fanatic. When I decided to go to college and tried to figure out what I wanted to study, the only thing I could think about was film. There was nothing else that really interested me. I couldn't be a business student. I barely knew how to multiply, so I couldn't be an engineer—you had to know how to do math. All I knew how to do was tell a story, so that's what I decided to do.

I don't fall into that age-as-hype bullshit, that I'm so young to be doing what I'm doing. I just do what I have to do. Ultimately, it's all about making a good film and being a good filmmaker.

I had no all-encompassing mentor, but I've had several mentors on different levels, from different walks of life that have affected me. In terms of filmmaking influences, everyone from Spike Lee to Martin Scorsese. My favorite screenwriters are Bob Towne and Paul Schrader. They're both my heroes. Bob Towne, because he's done so much like *Chinatown* and there are some scenes he wrote in *The Godfather* that I really love. Paul Schrader, because he has that edge that I'd like to try to have in my work.

POETIC JUSTICE

Last night I finished the screenplay to what will be my second film—"Poetic Justice." I started it in February and I hadn't really had a chance to write a lot of it until the beginning of this summer. And in May I was on page 29. In the last two months, I've just ripped it up. Before that, I had all the publicity to do on *Boyz*—I had to edit the film and take it to Cannes and all that kind of shit. But now I've finished and it's really good.

When I write a screenplay, I start with the characters. I think there are only like seven stories that have been told in the history of man, but there are so many types of people in the world. So, if you concentrate on the people, than that's what makes your stuff unique. For example, *Boyz N the Hood* is a coming-of-consciousness story, a rite-of-passage film. And rite-of-passage films have been done all the way from *Rebel Without a Cause* to *American Graffiti* to *Risky Business* to *Boyz N the Hood.* "Poetic Justice" is kind of like a romantic tragedy, and romantic tragedies have been done from Shakespeare through *Love Story* all the way to the present day.

In "Poetic Justice," I've deconstructed the whole romance genre and done it as an actual war between men and women. I concentrated not on the uplifting cliché but instead on what it's really about. Emotions between a man and a woman are a very volatile situation. Passion has many different levels and sometimes passion is not just sex; passion is fighting too and I want to get into that. This film is like *Apocalypse Now* meets *Heart of Darkness* with real hearts. It's a road movie moving up the California coast from South Central L.A. to Oakland instead of moving up the river.

"Poetic Justice" is going to be miles ahead of *Boyz N the Hood.* Both technically and in thematic depth. Some of the same themes will continue from *Boyz,* like the family getting back together. The family unit will always, always be a recurring theme in my work.

I make tough street films for the whole family.

WRITING AND DIRECTING

In terms of filmmaking, writing is my first passion. I write and I direct to protect my vision because I can't get anybody to direct the kind of films I do. It's not just a matter of being black, it's a matter of being in the know. There are people working now who don't know where my generation is coming from. How can somebody like Alan Parker or Phil Joanou direct Ice Cube in a movie?

I look at the eighties as kind of a downtime for American film. We had a real fucked up government that told us, "Don't worry, be happy," and all the movies seem to reflect that too. Nobody was dealing with real life. Whereas in the late sixties and early seventies there was a renaissance of filmmaking led by Arthur Penn, Stanley Kubrick, Steven Spielberg, Martin Scorsese, Francis Coppola. And then what happened in '79 and in the eighties, everybody wanted to look away from reality, and I think society stopped questioning itself because of the government and because of the film business. And now we're going back to questioning ourselves because the government is not in tune with the people. The cinema and the other arts are going to start reflecting that.

FILM SCHOOL

I recommend film school to get the fundamentals. But I recommend life to learn how to make a good film. I think if you're not in the constant process of looking at life and observing and taking from it, being able to look at it with an objective, then you're going to have problems. You can't make anything original.

I would recommend the formal training of film school, but nobody can teach you how to write. You can teach yourself how to write by doing just that. I used to go to class and tell my teachers, "Don't fuck with me, I'll be back with a screenplay in two months, I'm not coming to class." They'd be like, "Damn, you know . . ." and I'd say, "Well, the deal is this—you have all these people who are in class who don't even know if they want to be writers in the first place, and they're procrastinating and the reason they come to class is to complain about the fact that they can't write, and then they want you to give them a good grade at the end of the semester. I'm not asking for that, I'm just asking you if I give you a screenplay, you give me an *A*."

PROCESS

I'm not one of those people who sit at the typewriter and just crank it out. I think if you do that you open up yourself for more rewriting, and I hate to rewrite. So, what I do is, I daydream and I come up with the beginning and I come up with the end and I have the characters. And everything else, getting from point A to point B comes from setting up the characters to combat each other. Creating static.

I really try to say things without saying things. I'm not partial to dialogue-heavy screenplays, I'm partial to saying something visually—like the recurring helicopter theme in *Boyz*. And I strive for simplicity and try to talk stuff in terms of the senses—smelling and hearing and seeing. I use a lot of "we see," "we hear," "we smell." I use a lot of metaphors—comparing things to certain things so automatically there's a process within a person's mind to link that to something else.

I think it was Jonathan Demme who told me—the power of directing lies in the subtext. You allow the audience to discover the film; you don't tell them, that's television. You allow them to discover the film, that way they are really, truly viewers. They're involved in the act—you allow them to create also. You do things offscreen—you work with their imagination.

I write like I talk. My screenplays sound like I talk. I use certain diction and slang in my screenplays that the ordinary reader won't understand. Executives don't want to fuck with that because they're like, well, we don't know what that means, but we'll just let him do it—it sounds authentic.

I write my screenplays on a computer. Some people write in a notebook and give it to somebody, but I write on a computer and format the thing myself. Everything. Even transitions. Beforehand, I know how I'm going to get out of a scene and into a scene on the first page. I don't work from an outline. I just find it right on the computer. The script I just finished last night could be shot now. The scenes are full, the rhythm, the pacing, the transitions are in place.

My first drafts are equivalent to some people's third or fourth draft after they've had somebody else go over it. I try to write so it's ready to shoot—a skill I tried to acquire in film school.

WORKING AT THE MAJOR STUDIOS

The studios can't really mess with my scripts because there's things in my films that they don't understand. So it's like, how can you mess with something that you really don't understand. They don't understand until they actually see it.

I originally wanted to be an independent filmmaker, but I had an opportunity where I had somebody telling me, I'll give you six million dollars to do your movie, what you gonna do? Especially when all the independent filmmakers are out of work and all the independent distributors are being squashed. So the only choice is to go with a major now. It's going to be very difficult for independent filmmakers in the future, because majors not only have all the financing but they own the exhibition process. How can you make a film if it's not really going to be shown anywhere?

VIOLENCE

New Jack City came out, and the media neglects to say this, but when *New Jack City* came out, earlier in that week, the L.A.P.D. lynched Rodney King in front of a million people on television. So automatically the kids in L.A. are going to have a mind-set, "fuck the police," you know? That's what they were saying and it's what they chanted when they broke into those stores in Westwood. They had their money taken away from them, $7.50, then the police shaking batons in their faces. And they were like, "We ain't standing for that . . . fuck that, this is war."

The Rodney King video had national ramifications. It's something that black people have always known about and it's something that I expressed in my film. It's funny, because the only scene that I had problems with the studio were the scenes with the cops. They said, "God, do you have to show the cops in that light?" I said, "This shit is real." And then after the hassle with Rodney King, they were like, well, we're glad you left that in.

A lot of people attributed the violence around *Boyz* to the gang thing, but *Boyz* wasn't a gang movie. When the movie opened, there were a lot of instances where there were fistfights in the vicinity of the theater, and there were reported to be violent incidents linked to the film. But *Terminator 2* and a lot of other movies opened where there have been fights around the corner from the theater and those are not reported. I think it's a subliminally racist kind of thing, well, maybe not even so subliminal. CNN gets on with their cute little map and tries to attack anybody that's saying something socially relevant now because there's too many people who aren't saying anything of social relevance.

SOCIAL RELEVANCE/ ENTERTAINMENT VALUE

I think that filmmakers have the same obligation that once fell upon novelists and journalists to say something relevant, because nobody reads anymore. More people go to movies than read. If I had come around thirty or forty years ago, maybe I would have been a novelist because I wouldn't have been able to make a film. But I've always had a strong visual orientation, and now everybody gets their information from visual means. We have to say—if we feed them bullshit, then the population thinks like bullshit. Tell them to think, then they think.

But if you're making films in America, your first obligation is to entertain and the second is to inform. I write movies that I will go see with my homies—something that's relevant to them.

In the past—and in other films—the inner-city experience has never been truly represented in its complexity. Hollywood has ignored or distorted the minority experience because they don't know about it, nor do they really, truly care.

BLACK FILMMAKERS' RENAISSANCE

The sudden surge in black-oriented films is first of all due to money. A couple of films came out that made a lot of money in the last couple of years, starting off with *She's Gotta Have It* to *Do the Right Thing,* and then *House Party* came out and busted out eighty-six million from a two-million-dollar budget. Those numbers talk. Initially that's what the hype was about, but now it's really about just making a good film. The recent renaissance of black filmmakers will last as long as they continue to make good films. When people start selling out and not making good films, then problems will arise. I think there are very few filmmakers, true filmmakers out here, and a lot of film "mockers."

Some people say what will really entrench this whole renaissance will be if a black filmmaker were to direct a movie that was a white-theme picture with mostly white characters set in a white environment. I disagree with that. I think what is more important is that appreciation is made for different types of aesthetics in film. It can only help American cinema as a whole.

If there are more black filmmakers, then hopefully there'll be more Mexican-American filmmakers, Asian-American filmmakers, some Native American filmmakers documenting what's going on with their culture. People say that this country is about multiplicity of culture, but that's one big lie if it's not reflected in the art. In the past history of film, there's only one type of art aesthetic that's pushed forward.

Any filmmaker can make a film about anything that he or she feels is important. I wouldn't do anybody any justice if I made a film about white folks, because that's been done thousands of times over again. But nobody has made *Boyz N the Hood.* So there's so much room to be gained on the front that I'm on, there's no need for me to go on another front.

PITCHING

When I pitch, I just give the general idea. If it was up to me, I would just write, I would just give somebody the screenplay and say, give me the money. Because after you pitch, then you have all these other opinions; some of them are good, but a lot of times people don't share your same vision, they won't know until they see the screenplay, or even until they see the film, what it's going to turn out to be. You can't pitch your way into being a screenwriter.

ADVICE

Learn how to write good screenplays. Don't concentrate on dialogue; concentrate on saying things visually. And if someone wants to write movies, you can't be concerned with looking for the kind of ideas the studios look for. You have to ask yourself, what kind of movies do I want to see? And if you don't have any contacts in the business, then you need to bring your ass out to L.A. and find some. You can't make movies if you want to be in Peoria, Illinois.

LESLIE DIXON

L eslie Dixon's San Francisco home, where she relaxes when
she can get away from Hollywood, is old-fashioned, multi-
storied, with many windows. Like most houses in that area,
the front door is at the top of a flight of stairs. The rooms are
generous and welcoming but somehow a little formal, like Dixon
herself.

She is slight, with a delicate face and dark blond hair. She is
clever, glib, straightforward, and funny, all at once. She speaks
fluently and quickly, which gives what she says a surface gloss even
if she's saying something meaningful, but she speaks meticulously.
As she says, "I've never had a problem shooting off my mouth."

Dixon is a capable, practical person who manages to write very
frothy material, the more outrageous the better—as is apparent in
Outrageous Fortune. But it's not surprising that she intends to
produce much more of her own material in the future.

Outrageous Fortune earned the highest first weekend gross
ever seen by Disney Studios at that time. Much of that was due
to the material given Bette Midler and Shelley Long, dialogue that

mirrors the sensibility of Dixon, a fastidious but somehow slightly wicked tone.

In spite of her irreverent attitude, one never doubts that Dixon will be a hell of a producer, which she wants, as well as a writer— or virtually anything else she attacks as single-mindedly as she attacked the profession of screenwriting. A motivated woman, she has the kind of tenacity it takes to succeed in Hollywood, and the impetus of a silky juggernaut.

Intelligence alone isn't enough. Sometimes talent alone isn't enough, and certainly determination won't make it happen if it's not backed by ability. But when you put them together and add a clearheaded view of the motion-picture business, continued success is certainly more likely. We expect that Leslie Dixon will be around for a long time to come.

I was raised by a movie freak. My mother was always dragging me off to revival-house double bills, as well as anything current, so I probably saw every movie in release with maybe the exception of Roger Corman's C-pictures. From the time I was very young, I was more interested in movies than anyone else I knew. And I definitely wanted to be some sort of a writer, so it seemed like a marriage of the best possible worlds to just try and combine the two.

Oh, I dicked around with journalism and free-lance articles, some of which were published, and wrote a play that a number of people liked. But the amount of money those things ultimately netted pushed me even more definitely into the direction of film, where it was possible to make a living as a writer.

My goal really was to pay my bills as a writer without having to have an outside shit job. That's what I wanted to be able to do, and it seemed like screenwriting was the obvious choice if that was my goal.

I didn't have a miserable childhood. I guess one of the reasons I don't feel particularly accomplished, and I haven't talked to people about this too much, is that my grandparents were quite famous artists. And they are the stars of my family, so anything that I might do, particularly in the realm of popular entertainment and not fine art, is not going to measure up to what my grandparents did.

This in no way intimidates me; it just keeps my perspective rational. I don't compete with them, but my grandmother was Dorothy Lang, the documentary photographer, and my grandfather was Maynard Dixon, the Southwestern painter, and they're both now renowned artists. And so every once in a while, when I'm feeling like hot shit, I just look up at the wall and there's my grandmother, and I say, "Hmmm . . . get over yourself!"

I was raised here in San Francisco and I visit whenever I can, and it is the height of bad taste to move to Southern California. No one gives you any encouragement or support, and can't possibly imagine why you want to leave all this clean air and great Chinese food and go "down there." And so I did not muster up really the bad taste to do it until I was twenty-five, and it took me a full year of saying good-bye to people and justifying why I was doing it.

But you have to go to Los Angeles. I think you *have* to. In the ten years I have been in Los Angeles, I know of one person who broke into television writing without living in L.A. first for a period of time.

Anyway, I did not hit the L.A. soil until I was twenty-six years old. I knew enough to know that one really cannot sell a script without being in Los Angeles first and getting a sense of the marketplace. I was very serious about selling. I was not out to expose my personal vision of life, death, and art; I just wanted to make a living.

So I moved there. I did not know anyone and I certainly didn't know anyone in the business. And I kicked around in fairly menial secretarial jobs, many of which were not in the entertainment industry, and wrote at night, because I did not have any financial support from anybody. I lived in Los Angeles for over a year before I even started trying to write a screenplay. I read a lot of scripts; I kind of wanted to learn what kind of movies were being bought and made and what weren't.

I was very encouraged right away because with some exceptions I didn't read a single good script the entire time I was there. It seemed like the average screenplays that were being submitted to producers were of such an encouragingly despicable quality that I was cheered up and felt I had a shot. I took a year, and when I finally came up with an idea for a script that I thought had a shot, I came at it from the point of view of an actor or actress who might want to play this part. Because it seemed to me that that helped to get pictures bought and made.

I came up with an idea for a script in which the hero would

get to play four different parts, because I thought maybe an actor's ego would not be able to resist that. And indeed, I managed to get an agent with the script, which I wrote with a partner. The agent managed to get two offers on it. So, although everyone told me I would have to write nine screenplays and maybe I would sell my tenth, I sold my first—but I think that is because I put a year of study into it before I even picked up a pen.

That script was called "AKA," and it's still in development at Paramount after various incarnations. Years ago, I threw up my hands and said, "Do whatever you want with it." At a certain point, your first screenplay is something that you don't want to work on forever and I think it has some basic story problems that no one, including me, has ever been able to solve.

I don't care if it ever gets made at this point. It's my first script and I have a lot of affection for some things about it, but I do not consider it to be my finest hour as a writer. I'm just wonderfully grateful it sold and started me off, but I think, at a certain point, it's wise not to go back. It's wise to go forward and I'm just letting them do what they want to it.

That was the only script I ever wrote with a partner. After that I went on by myself. My agent was able to get me another job doing a rewrite for Interscope. It was a very new company at that time and since then has had tremendous success with *Three Men and a Baby* and *Cocktail* and whatever.

When Robert Cort came in to run the company and read the rewrite I had done, he said, "Well, this is a pretty stupid idea for a movie, but whoever did this rewrite is a pretty good writer." So he came to me and said, "Why don't you write us a female buddy picture? We've had several crack teams of male writers come up with various ways to try this and they haven't done it, so why don't you try?" And I said, "Can I come up with a whole new story?" And he said yes, and we worked out the story together, and that became *Outrageous Fortune*.

That was the beginning of my career really, because I was a working writer, had become a working writer with an agent, and that changed everything for me.

I'm a big believer in a beginning writer starting with a small agent who will hustle for you, as opposed to an established and arrogant jerk-off who won't return your phone calls. My partner and I found a very small agent who probably had four clients and had been an agent for about a year, but we liked her. And she had such a voracious desire to get her hands on this piece of material that I really felt she would hustle for us, which she did.

I'm happy to say I'm still with her. She went up the ladder and I went up the ladder and we're still together.

I feel very fortunate that early on I met somebody that I can actually put that level of trust in and have it rewarded. I know most people bounce from agent to agent their entire careers, and often with good reason.

Interscope, which liked the property, had a first look deal with Disney, so they sent the script there and Disney did their usual, "Well, hmmmm, no. . . ." But Bette Midler decided to make it and then that pounding Disney machine went to work with pitbull tenacity and it got put together pretty quickly.

WRITING CREDITS AND VERACITY

I think I've worked on too many rewrites in my career, alone and as a writing team with my husband. We discovered late into our marriage that we could write together without marital explosion. So, singly and collectively, we have done a lot of rewrites.

But about a year ago, I realized I was getting other writers' movies made for them. Because of the way that the Writers Guild works, you can write every line of a screenplay and maybe even make huge, significant changes in the story and still never get any credit. And although the sums of money for rewriting are attractive, ultimately your career can erode when there is a dearth of produced credits. I realized I had to write one, or possible two originals a year, if I wanted to stay in the game as a heavyweight.

I'm glad that I came to that realization before any damage was really done. If I continued to take this rewrite money for another couple of years, I think I would have started to slide to the B list. Maybe I will do one a year still. It's always easier to see what's wrong with someone else's script. But I just decided at a certain point that I did have stories of my own I wanted to tell and I've started turning down rewrites.

It's just that when a year and a half goes by and you haven't written an original, it becomes problematic.

But I wish that writing credits were more accurate. I understand and empathize with the guild's desire to protect the original writer at all costs. If someone invents a piece of material and that picture gets made into a movie, that person should be entitled to a very large percentage of the money and the residuals attendant to a produced credit. But I think the guild is very fast and loose with the words "written by."

The way the guild works is that the word "story" really means premise. And "written by" really means story. And dialogue gets no credit at all. That's how it really works. Now if "story" really meant story and the bulk of the residuals and money were attached to that, the "written by" credit could be accurate.

There are such famous, famous cases like *Pretty Woman*, like *Fatal Attraction*, where pictures have gone on to do a couple hundred million dollars in the marketplace and the original writer— who did not write a word of the final script—gets directing deals and half-million-dollar development deals based on something that they truly didn't write. I find that incorrect.

So I would like to see accuracy, even if money is not attendant. Maybe an additional "dialogue by" credit. I don't think that it will ever happen, because any union exists to protect the weakest of its members. And I'm certainly glad the Writers Guild exists, rather than not. I would not want these credits to be determined by studio executives, but at the same time I'm sorry that they're so inaccurate.

Audiences and critics across America, and even people in the entertainment business who ought to know better, really don't know who wrote what. They really don't. And it's a very depressing experience. I've had experiences where you wake up, you open the paper, and a critic is calling you a bad writer for something you hate and did not write in a picture which, for various financial reasons, you must leave your name on. Or I've opened the paper and the critics were praising someone else for scintillating, witty lines of dialogue that I know were written by me. Both of those really hurt.

So I do wish the guild could find a way to compensate the original writer while still being accurate. That would be nice. And if there are eleven writers on a picture, let them all get their names on there; maybe that will discourage studio executives from putting eleven writers on a picture, if the embarrassment of having to list them is commented upon by every critic.

These are small problems, granted, compared to the ability to get together rent and food in a given month, and I am not one of those writers who feel their lives are terrible. I remember when I first moved to Los Angeles and I was living on fourteen hundred dollars a month and driving around without auto insurance because that was just not a financial possibility. I would go into meetings with development executives. And you sit down, and you do the five minutes of schmoozing and say how are you, how are you; I was just basically trying to get my first or second deal. And they say, "Oh, I'm just going through hell with these workmen. I mean, I'm having this house in Bel Air remodeled and the sixth and seventh bedrooms are thoroughly torn up, the bathrooms are flooded, I mean, these workmen, I just can't . . ." And I would just sit there staring at them and thinking, I hope I never get that far gone, that I've so terribly lost touch with what normal people go through.

THE LUXURY OF CHOOSING

Just as the bottom has completely dropped out of the spec script market, my interest is at its highest. I've had the luck to work with executives who have given me a fair amount of creative freedom and support, so I haven't had a problem writing on assignment. But writing a screenplay is never easy, it requires the mental concentration of a chess game. And the more screenplays that you write, the more the attraction increases of not having to tell anyone what you're doing, or why.

So I have been writing on spec for the last couple of years. And on an original script, my desire to set up a development deal is fairly low. Not to excite some frenzied bidding war or auction when the script goes out, just for the simplicity of not having to account to anyone for the choices that you make. At least for that first draft. At the end of that point, it's nice to have input.

I really, really like screenwriting. I like the brevity. I like the challenge of having to tell an entire story in 110 pages with very limited description. I am a person who functions best within limits. If you say, "You may not have more than one hundred thousand dollars to shoot this sequence," I'll come alive trying to figure out some clever way to work within those limits. If you tell me that this character can't leave this room for a half hour of screen time, I will enjoy finding a way to make that interesting to an audience. But if you say, "You may have any sum of money and you may do anything you like; you are completely in control and can describe anything," I become paralyzed with indecision. Screenplays are about very finite limitations.

GETTING AHEAD

Everybody asks me if I want to direct. I think it's because I have a bossy, authoritative personality. No, I've never wanted to direct for one minute, ever. Part of that is because I truly know what directing entails. I've been on a lot of sets and I've seen experienced people hovering on the brink of physical and emotional collapse from the pressure.

So it's never been a big goal of mine, but I'm being pushed in that direction for a lot of reasons, the largest of which is the serious dearth of comedy directors in Hollywood, since what I write is comedy; just putting together a comedy director's list is intensely depressing, as we all know.

And for various reasons, you're not going to get the first eleven choices on the list, and then you hear from the director's agent that he wants to do a drama next, because comedy is the bastard stepchild. Even though it is a bread-and-butter staple of this industry, it is still considered by both actors and directors to be inferior even to a thriller, and certainly to a drama. And you will almost never win the Academy Award for a comedy. Once in a blue moon, it is sort of a necessary evil.

But rather than directing, I have been producing. I actually produced a low-budget film for Orion called *Madhouse,* which my husband, Tom Ropelewski, directed. It was fun. I was good at it. I am now the producer of all my original scripts.

It's not as tough as directing, it really isn't. There are very few producers I really respect, who bring something to the party. It just makes more sense for me to do it myself where I am in my career right now. It also helps keep you from getting replaced by other writers.

I can't see any enticing reason to hand over the control of something I have invented on spec to another person. Ultimately when a picture gets produced or made, one must hand over that control to the director, or you aren't being realistic. And there are many things that can happen on the set spontaneously that an experienced writer would be stupid not to take advantage of and applaud and work with. But before it gets to that point, why give it away?

But basically my identity is tied up in writing. I would say my writing career is so far ahead of my producing career that, among other things, it would be financially idiotic for me to stop writing. But the bigger issue is that I still really enjoy it and I don't feel that I've even begun to hit my stride with it creatively. You can't write enough scripts to ever learn everything there is about how to do this well.

And yet, writers who I really admire are drama writers, because they do something that I don't understand. I don't understand how to sustain an audience's attention without a few jokes. I mean, I suppose it's the story or the performance or whatever, but the writers I really admire, somebody like Richard Price, who I just think is a terrific screenwriter, or Nick Kazan—I don't know how to do that. Robert Towne is a friend of mine. I look at what he does, and he looks at what I do, and we don't understand how we do those things. I think you admire what you can't do yourself.

Also, I'm constantly disappointed when I see on film what I've written. For instance, *Outrageous Fortune* is certainly the best picture I've worked on; part of that has to do with the fact that it was so correctly cast. But I have ambitions to make much better movies than any of the things I've been associated with. It's a relative disappointment compared to word processing for a living; I never lose sight of that. I have a number of things in the pipeline right now I'm really excited about. I hope they will surpass, at least creatively, anything else I've worked on.

DEALING WITH IT

Overboard was a writing assignment. I have gotten stuck working on pictures with the worst premises, going back to the dawn of my career where I was lucky to have a job and somebody said, "We'll pay you to do this." That's how I ended up writing a picture with amnesia as the central plot device.

For me to complain about how *Overboard* turned out is a little silly, because how good can any movie with amnesia as a central plot device ever be? I mean, let's get real here. It's silly. And also because I contractually had to work on *Big Business*—identical twins switched at birth? I am the queen of dopey premises that get handed to me. A studio head once told me, "Stop breathing life into corpses."

Anyway, given the premise I was stuck with, I tried to make the most amusing script that I could. Any writer will tell you, "My vision is better than what they ultimately made," so take that with a grain of salt if you will. But then these real heavyweights got involved, Goldie Hawn and Kurt Russell and Garry Marshall—and I was very tired and burned out because I had just come off *Outrageous Fortune*. I staggered back from that set and had to start another one.

I don't believe I'm the first person to have this problem and I don't believe I'll be the last. Garry was a sweetheart and I always liked him, and Goldie and I never had too much interaction except that she was very, very nice to me the couple of times that I met her. I think one of the problems with that movie was that you had dueling producers. Garry had his own producer whom he brought, and Goldie had her own producer that they brought, and there was going to be a power struggle before a frame of film was shot.

Garry works in a very improvisational, freewheeling style, with writers coming and going, and they were backed up against a release date. I think the result was fairly predictable.

There are things in that movie that make me cringe in embarrassment, that I never would have written in a million years, particularly in the last fifteen minutes of the movie. As a result, since then I've asked for an unlimited right to a pseudonym in everything subsequent my agent has ever negotiated for me. The emotional investment in a premise like amnesia is just simply not what it might have been. If that had happened to *Outrageous Fortune* I would have been much more distraught. That was a truer reflection of my spirit. There are people that love *Overboard*. They come up to me and say it's their favorite movie—it was a huge hit on video. But my own personal taste is more edge and less sentiment. I'd rather be Billy Wilder than Frank Capra.

Because I basically started my career off with a big hit, I have usually been treated pretty nicely. Generally the horror stories that you hear have not really happened to me. I haven't been lied to, I haven't been double-dealt. Disney, for instance, is great in that they are actually fairly honest in their ruthlessness. That is just what they do. At least it's kind of aboveboard; they have their agenda and it's fairly predictable.

I haven't even had to pitch for a really long time. The first couple of times I did it, I remember thinking, "This is why I haven't done any acting since junior high school." I hated the idea of auditions, that gut-clenching terror, or going on the stage, which I did in junior high or high school. And there it is. That old feeling back, in spades, when you're about to walk into somebody's office and there are thousands of dollars and a possible movie on the line.

But I found that feeling only lasted for about ten seconds. I never had a problem shooting my mouth off. Talking is not scary. I think a very talented but shy writer is at a big disadvantage in this business. I tell a lot of people, "Your personality is a big asset, if you have one." I'm not shy.

So I just have not been abused—yet. But also I have to say, my agent and I plotted together very early to stop me from being abused. This is why I'm still with her, because she says, "Don't go work for *these* people, they're horrible assholes and they'll make your life miserable. Yes, it's a lot of money but you can make just as much or almost as much over here with *these* people, who are wonderful.'' And she's tried to steer me to humane studios and decent producers. There's always someone in every studio who's got a speck of humanity.

I think she realized that she and I were in it for the long haul and I wouldn't leave her in a year, so she's helped me try to plot for the long term, not just thinking, ''How much money can I make off this client this year and next year because of course the year after that they'll leave me.'' So I think I've been a little luckier than most. It *does* help to have an agent at a big agency if they're really working for you, because they're very connected on a pure, visceral, gossip level. There's that web to every studio and producer in town, and they get a sense very quickly about who is a jerk and who is dishonorable, who to protect their clients from.

AH, THE CRITICS . . .

I think the critics vary wildly depending on what their medium is and what city they're in. For example, I did not realize the entire time I was growing up that the San Francisco critics were out of step constantly with every single other major critic in America. Much more arty, much more pretentious, much less liable to enjoy a mainstream film that audiences love. I did not realize that every time I opened the paper, this would be a contradictory opinion to everyone else's in America. Now I get up here and I read the critics and I howl with laughter at how out of it they are.

I think if I were a Siskel or an Ebert, I would be really tired of movies. In print, one critic doesn't review everything, so most of them see two movies a month or even a week. But poor Siskel and Ebert have to see every piece of shit that's released. And if I had to see *Beverly Hills Cop 14* or *Ninja Turtles 16,* I think I would start to hate movies, which to me would be very depressing. Or I would stop enjoying mainstream films and only be attracted to pictures that were very weird and different because I would be so used to seeing conventionally plotted movies.

And I think that my judgment might begin, and I'm speaking for myself—I don't know what happens with those guys—I think I might begin to stop performing my function, which would be to tell normal people whether they would enjoy a movie or not. So I think that when a critic has to see every piece of shit that's released, there does tend to be a judgment problem.

Regular critics, I think, are usually very ignorant of the process by which movies are made, and occasionally they can be out to get somebody they don't like, a director or a filmmaker. But by and large they perform a function, and it's just part of the process that you may produce something that will have them all on your back. Only once in a blue moon does a movie come along that critics like, and I'm mystified by why they like it—or hate, and I'm mystified by why they hate it. Generally speaking there is a reasonable consensus. I also know a number of them are failed screenwriters and hate all of us with a great passion because they know we outearn them by twelve to one. All I can say to that is, "Ha-ha."

WRITING

Writing is never easy. But it helps a lot if you have a good story and there's actually something happening on a story level in the scene that you're writing. If two people are sitting on a couch yapping at each other about life, it's going to be a lot of harder to write than if one of them attempts to kill the other one. So I like a tight outline with some degree of plot. If anything, I might tend to err on the side of overplotting, just so there's something going on in scenes. I've read a lot of scripts where the premise isn't clear until page fifty-one, but I like the sort of French comedies that start on page one and fly off. So it is much easier to write when you have a tight plot.

I use a scene-to-scene outline in which I try very hard to have something on a plot level happening in every single scene. Sometimes that is just not possible and you have to do some connective tissue, but I'm a big believer in plot.

I do think preparation is very helpful, but again you also have to allow yourself not to be boxed in. My husband and I just wrote a spec script that we finished a few days ago and we were typing along and we found a character from Act I popping back up in Act III because we sort of missed him and wanted him to come back, and that wasn't at all part of our outline. But we tried to have the elasticity to allow that to happen, partly because it was a dull scene and he livened things up. Generally speaking, I find that the more prep work I do, the easier the actual writing process is, and I've gotten a lot faster over the last four years. I haven't had that long a career.

I never do research. I fake everything. I fake absolutely everything. Once in a blue moon, if I can just do it by calling somebody on the phone, I will. For comedy you don't really have to. Well, actually, if I really thought the material was going to suffer from my not doing research, I would, or I would pay someone to do it. But so far the genres I've written in have been things either with which I'm fairly familiar or that are so farcical that faking it is fine.

Tom and I are about to take a writing job together, to do an adaptation of a French film, most of the protagonists of which are ten and eleven years old. And I think I'm going to have to hang around some eleven-year-old kids and talk to them a little bit about their attitudes toward some things in order to really write that script as it should be written. I think it would be irresponsible of me not to, because I don't have any children. I'm going to have to hang around my friends' kids and really suck up the vernacular. But that will be one of the first instances of my ever having done that.

A WRITER'S LIFE

I get up at eight-thirty or nine, have coffee, read the paper, take and make business calls, sit down at ten-thirty, write until one or one-thirty, take a lunch break, preferably not a business lunch, preferably in, not interrupting my concentration. I try not to take business lunches if I can possibly help it. Get back to the typewriter as quick as I can.

Work again from two to seven or seven-thirty, maybe a couple of more business calls and that's it. Tom, my husband, will not allow me to work at night, and it's really a shame because I'm much better at night. Usually that's the schedule five or six days a week unless I'm getting to the end, in which case I can go seven days for two weeks in a row and not really be too much interested in anything else. But evenings I try very hard to be social, and we go out a lot. I put a fair amount of energy into sustaining friendships.

I have real friends in L.A., but none of my friends up here are in the business and I do like that. But there are still a few trustworthy people in L.A., there are a few. I have friends in L.A. I did not make through business. But it is difficult to be real friends with a producer or a studio executive because there's always a mixed motive there, whether or not they're even conscious of it. It is achievable, but I'm much more suspicious than I used to be.

I'll tell you, I've really bent over backward to get a couple of talented friends jobs, and that really bit me on the ass; the people involved totally flaked out. As a result, I've been much less generous and much colder about helping people, which is really unfortunate because I was very generous-minded that way in the beginning. Now I'm at the point where if some friend of mine has written a script, I will not read it, because if I'm working on something similar they could sue me and I'm suspicious enough to believe that's within the realm of possibility, which I did not use to be. It's really sad.

I like to be by myself and have it quiet when I work. There's a reason I don't have children or pets. I can't have any kind of music because I'm sort of musically inclined, and I'll start listening to the bass line and separating that out from the tenor sax, and listening to the harmony—it's impossible.

I try to set a goal for myself every day. And I've slowly played tricks on myself by increasing the pages even if it's crap. I think the day is approaching where I can write a passable screenplay in two or three weeks. Right now it's longer, it's six. But I think I can do it without a loss of quality, just in terms of being a more experienced writer and being able to make better use of my brain and time.

It doesn't have to be a very good screenplay. Personally, I wouldn't let it leave the house until I'd revised it enough. For me, rewriting is the name of the game. Almost nothing turns out right the first time you do it. I rewrite and rewrite before anybody ever sees it. I have a project at Universal that I've done four drafts of since they said they wanted to make it—without being asked, simply because I wasn't satisfied.

I never think something is perfect, ready to shoot, verbatim. That's a ridiculous attitude because it negates the director's and the actors' contributions. Actually, *Outrageous Fortune* was shot pretty much verbatim, but if I were directing, I probably would shoot even less so. I found that when I was producing a film and my husband directing, we were freer about letting the actors contribute than any set we'd ever been on. Once we finally got the reins, we were allowing them a lot more. A talented actor is often a better writer than most writers.

I've been very impressed with things actors have done on the set. You work with them a little bit and you shape it. They often don't have a sense of shape, but sometimes they know the character better than the writer, and it's a resource, so why not use it?

I almost never write with stars in mind, although sometimes it is impossible not to think about Bette Midler when I am writing female characters. She is able to put across a kind of outrageousness, even a borderline vulgarity, without anyone ever being offended, and that's the edge of the envelope I like to push. I just think she is so multitalented in every possible way that she sneaks into my mind. She's the only one really.

There are never characters in my scripts that are based on real people I know. Never. Although there may be people who represent some side of my own nature, I'm writing in my own voice and I'm saying exactly what I would say if I were standing there. I draw on myself or on sides of myself but not on anybody I've known.

Certainly little nasty truths that bubble up out of an appropriate moment will creep into my work, where I can slide them into something I am working on. But the big criteria is: do I think it's funny? But people often say to me now if they make a joke, "Now don't put that in one of your scripts." And I think that's very funny, because it's like, "Oh, so you think you're interesting enough to be in one of my scripts. You think audiences would be riveted to the screen by you?" It's just such a funny thing to say, it's so unwittingly egocentric for people to think that they could possible sustain an audience's attention. You really have to do a big sleight of hand.

In the future I'd like to be producing my original scripts, just getting them made into films. I don't want to be doing anything different, really, from what I'm doing. If possible, I would like to not have to end up directing, I would prefer not to be producing other people's scripts, even if they're good friends. That is an option that has been available to me several times and I've just said no. I don't want to do it because then I'm eight months out of the writing marketplace, which I really enjoy. It's what I do.

I think there are a lot of people who can produce films and who really need the jobs, or are personally desperate for the jobs. So, no, I would like to be producing my original films, that's what I'd like to be doing.

And I don't want to start a company. I don't want development people working for me, I don't want a phone in my car, I don't want a suite of offices on a lot. I think all that distracts from just simply getting work done, and I'm very sensitive to work-avoidance mechanisms that writers use. Like the telephone, like musical instruments, like the psychiatrist. Like gardening. Becoming a cottage industry can also be work-avoidance in a way.

I would just simply like to get as large a number of films made as I can, with scripts that I write and care about and produce.

TOM RICKMAN

Tom Rickman's story is particularly American, and he himself reflects what we'd like to believe about opportunity in America. Brought up in a world much like that of Huck Finn or Tom Sawyer—and with about as much incentive to become a writer—he could have lived out his life in Kentucky, as his family had for two hundred years.

But he loved to write, though he hadn't planned to go to Hollywood but to New York, where he intended to be a playwright. Rickman got into movies by accident when a small film he made for fun at the University of Illinois found its way to the American Film Institute. He ended up on the West Coast, at the beginning of a career distinguished by his ability to summon up an America that many Americans haven't seen; his writing invariably strikes notes from the heartland.

This ability won him an Academy Award nomination for Coal Miner's Daughter. But before and after that screenplay, he has produced a body of work that places him in the tradition of Will Rogers and Mark Twain. Quietly and without fanfare, he contin-

ues to turn out writing that has earned him the honest admiration of his peers.

He is a dynamic, cheerful man with prematurely white hair, sardonic rather than cynical despite a career that has had the requisite disappointments. He writes, he teaches, and he seeks out new talent at the Sundance Institute. He takes the time to bring out the best in his students, which is rare in a working writer with a schedule of his own.

But Rickman himself is like the people he writes about; quite aside from his ability, he's a good person with an underlying toughness. He calls himself a "hardy perennial" and seems to have earned the title honestly.

My movie background was a little bit different in that I grew up out in the country. Although there were movie houses in Paduka, which was ten miles or so away, the family went to drive-in movies. There was a drive-in close by, the Kentucky Lake Drive-In, which usually showed movies that were anywhere from five to ten years old. For instance, in the early fifties I must have seen Randolph Scott in *Gung Ho!* from 1943 about ten times. They also showed a lot of old Republic westerns, and the kind of Technicolor westerns that used to have Ray Milland in them, or Rod Cameron and people like that. And they had religious movies like *The Robe* and *Dimitrius and the Gladiator,* those kinds of things.

I don't think I ever saw a classic movie until I was a teenager, or even later. Nor did we have a television set; there was no television channel in this part of the world at that time. So I can't say that I had much of a movie childhood at all. I had an interesting one, it was kind of like the late show with no television.

But in terms of entertainment, I was much more interested in two other things. One was radio. I loved listening to it and still do, dramatic shows, suspense and comedy shows, and so forth. And the other was comic books, DC comic books particularly, which were very visual and had to tell a story in eight pages. Generally they were very ironic and intelligent stories, war stories usually. The difference between their war stories and others was that we almost always lost.

I was interested in music too, jazz and bluegrass, really kind of eclectic stuff; and especially pre-Elvis rhythm and blues. There was a black station in Nashville that we used to listen to, Randy's Record Mart, which would play rhythm and blues twenty-four hours a day.

So that was what got me interested, I think, in storytelling and entertainment—much more than having any sort of real movie background. Because I was really ignorant, even when I started at AFI. I wasn't much past the point where I thought that the actors made up their lines and there wasn't such a thing as a director. At least I didn't know what he did.

My family had been living in the area since the seventeen hundreds. It was a real country-boy life where you went swimming naked in cattle ponds and roamed around in fields through kind of unsettled country. I'm grateful now that there was no television then. Later on, when television came in, it tended to take the kids out of the fields and put them in the living room.

I sometimes feel like I grew up in the nineteenth century, that I don't have much in common with the way people I meet now grew up. It may not be true; everybody's nostalgic about their childhood. But this really was kind of a media-free, turn-of-the-century childhood, I think.

My mother always liked to read, but I can't say exactly that we had an artistic household there. She was very interested in anything I would draw or write or say, and it's nice to have your mom encouraging you. I think the difference is that the career possibilities of life were not enormous there. Not that anybody was telling you that you had to do this or that; it just seemed to work out that way. Very few people got out of town or left home. Most people I grew up with are still there. And so, you know, you tended to dream a lot.

I think *Life* magazine was another thing that I used to pore over. Oddly enough, everything I was looking at was a good decade or fifteen years before my time. It was like the drive-in movies. The *Life* magazines I liked belonged to a neighbor, and they were all from World War II, so as far as I was concerned World War II was still going on in the fifties.

I always wanted to write, and I began with comic books. But as a teenager I got very literary. I wanted to be like James Agee or James Jones, because one of the things that fascinated me then was war—books like *From Here to Eternity,* and *The Big War* by Anton Meyer, and *Battle Cry.* These were the things that really got to me as great storytelling. But the kind of literary, Southern, poetic writing that James Agee represented, that was something, I thought, that was real writing: that's what I wanted to do. I really admired the James Agee who wrote the Knoxville, Tennessee, prelude to *A Death in the Family*, the very poetic section that starts that novel. He was already dead, unbeknownst to me, by the time I was interested in this, as were James Dean and others.

That was a true movie fixation I had—with James Dean. Whatever it was that was in James Dean went straight home to me and I would do anything to re-see his movies. I must have seen *Rebel Without a Cause* twenty times. I would hitchhike to wherever it was on and watch it, and I didn't know he'd been dead for some time.

I think I was headed for teaching. But when I got out of high school I worked in a shoe store for a while, then joined the Marines. I'd never had any intention of going to college, and it took going into the service to make me think that that might be a good thing to do.

Joining the Marines was a direct reflection of movies and books. I was absolutely fascinated by war, war as portrayed in World War II movies and novels and *Life* magazine. I thought of little else. I certainly never thought of what war actually was. I only thought that it looked exciting. And that also, if you went to war you could write a really good novel about it.

However, I wasn't in the war. I was out before Vietnam and didn't have a war. And as far as being any use to me as literary material, it wasn't. The only thing I liked was that feeling, especially in the Marines, that you've come through something. That camaraderie and sort of self-destructive pose has been kind of an interesting thing to know about.

In college, I had a double major in English and history, and a minor in journalism. I worked on the college newspaper, and then I started my own. It was in the early sixties and we were already rebels, even in western Kentucky. I started an alternative newspaper, printed on a mimeograph machine, hand-distributed by my sister and me and a few other "communists"; that was a lot of fun. I drew a comic strip, I wrote editorials, she wrote columns. We had gotten my friend and roommate to run for student body president and he was the first independent ever to be elected, so we felt like we were Castro taking over the western Kentucky equivalent of Cuba. And there were attempts at doing literary magazines and that sort of thing.

Then I went to the University of Illinois for graduate work, which was also supposed to be in English, but by then I'd gotten really interested in theater. I'd always had a problem with being very shy, I couldn't talk in public or in class. As therapy I'd gone out for an Ionesco play, *The Lesson,* and gotten cast. Well, in that play the male character talks all the time. And after I'd done that I said, "I really like this."

So when I got to Illinois, even though I was there on a fellowship that was for English, I knew I didn't want to teach. I never did want to teach, I always wanted to be a writer. Now I thought I wanted to be an actor, so with some friends I rented an old central train station and converted it into a theater. And all the time I was there we did plays and concerts and so on, which is how I got in the movies.

This was in the sixties still, the late sixties where everything was going nuts. And there was that great feeling, whatever else you can say about the sixties, there was a terrific feeling that you could do anything. All you had to do was just do it. So I decided, I'm going to make a movie. I'd never done that, never been on a movie set, never written a movie script, certainly never directed a movie, never seen one directed.

But there was a big movie boom then, it was in the air. And so I adapted a story, a short story, and we rented some equipment and cast it locally and shot the film in 16 mm sound, black and white. The cameraman on that film mentioned the American Film Institute was starting a conservatory for advanced film studies in Beverly Hills and he said, "Why don't you send the film," so I did. To my surprise, because that was the only film experience I had, they asked me to come for an interview. And whatever I said in the interview was the right thing I guess, because I got in and it really, literally changed my life.

My plan had been to go to New York and be a playwright and an actor. So I'd already tried to get a place to stay and had a connection that I thought I could use. Suddenly this came up, and really without my ever even thinking much about it, here I was. Also, at that time you could do feature films at AFI. The original goal there was to do a feature film a year, and so we all started writing features. When I say all, there were Terry Malick and Paul Schrader and Jeremy Kagen. There were only, I think, fifteen of us, and some interesting talent there.

At AFI I wrote a feature script that got a very good reaction from the people there. It was called "Roots," and it was a very autobiographical thing about growing up in western Kentucky, kind of rough and interesting, I guess. It got me an agent, it got optioned by an actual real live producer, and I got a deal at Paramount. And for one reason or another it was not done. It was optioned a couple of times by David Susskind but it was never done.

But meanwhile, the script was circulated and soon I began to get offers to do things and rewrite scripts. And Jerry Freedman, a friend of mine, a director whom I'd never met, asked me about rewriting a movie that he was about to direct with Raquel Welch, called *Kansas City Bomber*. So I did that, and that was my first screen credit.

Things were happening kind of fast. I didn't have a period where I had time to worry about, "Is anybody going to hire me?" or "What am I doing here?" I was still thinking, "I'm not even sure I want to be here." I hadn't really committed to being in the movies yet, I don't think. And then I was given this opportunity. And really it had to be done from scratch, it was one of those projects that had been completely written out of existence. Since then I've seen many of those; at that time I didn't even know such a thing could happen, but there it was.

So I was really excited and turned on by it and wrote it really fast. I wrote a draft of a 110-page screenplay, starting from page one, in two days. Thrilled to pieces, I gave it to Jerry, who liked it a lot. And the producers seemed to like it, so I thought, "Boy, oh boy, is this great! I really have a knack for this."

Then, of course, pretty soon the studio came into it. It was the last days of the James Aubry regime at MGM, and Ms. Welch herself came into it, and then suddenly it wasn't so easy anymore. So I got a really classic introduction to what it's like to work professionally, from elation to utter depression, in a matter of seconds or so.

I was very industrious then; I wrote a lot. And everything I wrote was at least getting optioned somewhere. I think when people first begin here, they think something's going to happen to the movie if it's optioned; it's going to be made or something. And it almost never is. But at least I was working, working as a screenwriter when I never even planned to be one. And I should say that I had written and directed my AFI project, which was a slightly esoteric piece, again western Kentucky autobiographical, but eliptical and "poetic." But it won the National Student Association first prize in a film festival in Washington, D.C. I got a special prize from Jan Kadar, so that was great.

First prize was a light meter. I'm not a photographer, even with an Instamatic. Suddenly I had a terrific light meter but I didn't know how to use it and knew that I would never use it for anything.

Nobody gave me a break in the sense that I met somebody at a party or happened to be at the right place at the right time and all that. Nobody knew me. I never saw anybody, I didn't know anybody in the movie business very much. It always depended on somebody reading something I'd written and wanting me to do something. So that, I think, was what it was. I mean, I would have liked to have had a break.

But I was writing my own things which were, as I said, generally getting optioned someplace. Somebody, somewhere, always was wanting to do them; they always seemed to be on the verge of being done. But I was also getting jobs, and many of those things were Southern or very American anyway. For instance, the next picture I did, the next credit I had after *Kansas City Bomber,* was a picture called *Laughing Policeman,* which was done at Fox. A kind of very hard-edged detective movie with Walter Matthau, Bruce Dern, Lou Gossett, terrific cast. But that was one of those things that are rewritten later. I got sole credit on it but it was rewritten and I felt that very little of it belonged to me.

This was my odd introduction to Writers Guild credits. I had previously written every single word of a Hallmark Hall of Fame show which I thought was going to be my debut into screenwriting and about which everyone was very happy, only to find that I got no credit for that. Whereas with *Laughing Policeman,* I had written very little of it and got sole credit for it. So something was balancing out, in this little bizarre way.

I haven't been involved in a Writers Guild arbitration lately. I think there are probably very few writers who will defend the arbitration process, but nobody can quite figure out how to make it equitable. I thought then that it was very, very inept, and that there had to be a better way of apportioning true credit on a picture.

Usually the first guy who writes it is favored, which is fine if it's an original. But if it's an adaptation, that's nonsense. That means the first guy failed to adapt and the person who did adapt, the person who actually succeeded at it, suffers because he wasn't there first.

An original script is different. You have an original idea and create original characters; you should be credited for it even if it's rewritten down the line, because that's yours. Adaptations, to me, should have a different set of criteria.

* * *

But I've done some uncredited rewrites. In fact, I actually always liked doing these kind of hot-zone rewrites where it's less for the joy of writing and artistic satisfaction than it is for the circuslike atmosphere. The picture is in big trouble and somebody has to come down right now. And already there've been twenty writers and everybody's fighting and shooting each other. The movie is probably shut down and nobody's doing anything. And you come down and start typing and it starts happening again, it starts being shot again, and now everybody's more or less happy and things are going along.

So you did it and there's no credit involved, and there's not much satisfaction involved either. In a way, if it starts as a disaster it's probably going to stay one. I remember this old bluesman who was in *W.W. and the Dixie Dancekings,* this eighty-year-old delta bluesman who died shortly after that. I remember asking him how he was doing one day and he said, "I may get better, but I'll never get well." And I always thought that was the truth about these kind of rewrites.

I think romantic comedy, believe it or not, is my favorite genre. I find the pictures I like to watch over and over again are the Howard Hawks comedies or some early things like *Twentieth Century* and *Bringing Up Baby.*

And I like Capra, without the Capra-corn. Capra's never been as satisfying to me as some of the more cynical directors. Of course, George Stevens isn't cynical, but to me he did wonderful comedies back in the thirties. And I love Hawks. Preston Sturges, I would say, more than anyone else, shows the way to write a comedy. They're always funny, and funny in a very original way, and they always have a serious theme beneath them, greed or whatever. I would really like to write about things in the way he did.

GOOD TIMES AND BAD

Disappointment goes with it. It's very debilitating, disheartening, when you see what can happen to a script. I've been lucky in a way because it's happened to me less as I went along. And as usual, or as always, I think it depends on a relationship with the director, someone who's directing your material. If the director respects the material, then you can be satisfied.

Any screenwriter, any playwright, for that matter, knows that things are going to change in production. You want them to change for the right reasons—to accommodate a piece of casting or a location or something that just hasn't worked, rather than to please an ego or to be censored. Or, in this odd kind of world we operate in now, there's kind of a reverse censorship, which is to make it dirtier or make it more offensive.

Any rewrite that's done for some sort of business or ego reason is wrong. If it's done for the good of the project, any writer who's any good doesn't mind doing it, in my opinion.

I was taken off *Kansas City Bomber*. I was taken off *Laughing Policeman*. I was taken off *W.W. and the Dixie Dancekings*, for that matter, but then I came back on. But that was purely an original script, based around that drive-in I was talking about earlier. The inspiration for it was that very same drive-in theater. And when I was taken off, I thought, "Well listen, if it's this way all the time, then I don't want to do it."

I think that period was about the worst. I mean I know I felt the unhappiest about that time. A lot of it is subjective, in that I think John Avildsen did a good job, and Burt Reynolds, and there was interesting casting. I run into people every now and then who seem to like it. And with the passing of years it all gets softened.

In general I've always gotten along with directors. I've never had fights and betrayals with them, because we've worked together very well. I've never been satisfied with what came out, however, until *Coal Miner's Daughter*. Because I think I can truly say that the flaws in that picture are mine, are the script's flaws. It's a perverse kind of pride to take, but it's true, I think. What the actors did I thought was perfect, and what Mike Apted did was just right, and if the script had had a better third act, it would have been a much better picture. So, in a strange sort of way, you can take satisfaction in knowing that.

I guess I didn't feel successful until *Coal Miner's Daughter*, and by then I'd been doing it for eight years. *Kansas City Bomber* was in 1972; *Coal Miner's* was in 1980. Up until then, often I wouldn't even go see the movies. I didn't see *Laughing Policeman* for years. I'm not sure I've ever seen all of it. I didn't want to talk about it. If anybody would talk about it, I never liked giving my credit. I still don't like giving my credits in a sense. I'm proud of *Coal Miner's* and a couple more, but I don't like to talk about the others.

There was a picture I always was fond of, which was *Hooper*, a rewrite I was asked to do—another one of those things where you have to come in and really concoct something. But it had a feeling about it, and to me it was also about something. It was about directors endangering the lives of stuntmen for frivolous reasons. And I liked what Burt Reynolds did in that, and Robert Klein especially was very good.

Yeah, I liked that. Larry Gordon asked me to do it and I came down and met with Burt Reynolds and Hal Needham and we talked for a while. It was very fast. Went back and did it very quickly, came back, talked again, and I did it again very quickly. Next thing I knew it was in the theaters. And so I had very little to do with it once the script was in. But I was fond of it without it being something I wanted to go around telling everybody about.

Coal Miner's Daughter changed my life because there was an Academy Award nomination in it, which helped me get a directing shot. And it made me feel good. I felt good because it was a successful movie, both commercially and artistically. But I also felt good because—being from Kentucky, and traveling in the South quite a bit—the picture seemed to mean something to people that I'd meet. They genuinely were touched by it in some way, especially the early parts of it. I liked that a lot, that they could tell me scenes, they could quote lines back to me.

It's not a picture that gets mentioned very much, because it's outside a genre. Or there's a genre there that's never been a movie favorite, or a Hollywood favorite, which is the country, the movie with dust in it. But that's fine. It was taken to China—the AFI had a showing in China—and the Chinese seem to like it. I was happy about that, I felt proud of it.

WRITING

The writing isn't the hard part; the concentration is the hard part, and the focus. I never do outlines and I never do cards or any of that. I'm one of those kind of writers that improvises. I start the script always, "Fade in, first scene," so that scene follows scene. And characters come in that I hadn't anticipated would be in the picture, and you have to see if they really need to be there, if they have a function, if they're going to show up later. If they do it's terrific. If they surprise you, they'll surprise somebody else.

And if your concentration is right, then it can be easy in the sense that you like doing it and want to do it, want to get up in the morning and do it, want to get to the end of it. Because once you've gotten to the end of a draft, a rough draft, that's when the writing really starts and you can make right all the stuff that may be rough and unfocused, that you've gotten through just to get to the end; you want to go back now and hone it and really make a good piece of work. So it's not drudgery for me if it's working, or rather if my concentration is there.

Research is one of the pleasures of it. I especially like doing things based on real people or real incidents. You go and talk to them and, basically, act like a journalist for a while, up until you start doing the screenplay, at which point you have to begin to act like a dramatist. And that means that you can't do what a journalist does and be concerned with pinning down facts and so forth. You have to make composite characters. You have to—in that dialogue that was never spoken—try not to bend the truth, try to get the essence of whatever this experience is. But it has to be a piece of drama first before it can be anything else.

When you start something original, sometimes it's a milieu that's interesting, the Mississippi River for instance. Sometimes you don't know. *W.W. and the Dixie Dancekings* is far from a movie classic, but it was interesting, I think, the way it was written. I sat one day trying to think of something to write, and I thought of this drive-in theater I used to go to, and I thought that *The Robe* was playing on the screen, with Victor Mature. And then I thought, "Well it's the middle of the movie, and there's a car coming out, only it isn't going out of the exit, it's going out the entrance.

And there's this boy there, who's the ticket taker, and the car stops and there's a fast-talking, flashy guy in the car. And he robs the box office without threatening the boy. That is, he convinces the ticket taker that it's in his best interest to be robbed, in a populist kind of way, that he's being exploited by whom he works for. That is, the guy will take all the box office receipts and give the boy as much money as he makes in a week in return. All he asks is that when the boy describes the car and the robber, that he just not be truthful about that."

So that was purely an improv. And that led on to the next thing. And I thought, "Well, now what's he doing?" And pretty soon there was a story there. That was interesting. That character then took over, the character of the robber took over, a guy with some sort of native wit.

Whatever the original impetus for a story is, what always makes it work for me is the character's beginning to behave in an interesting way, that you do get interested in what he's going to do next. I get interested in exploring that until the end of the story. In other words, the character drives the piece.

I'm pretty methodical. I think if I'm ready to write, and have done the research and gotten myself to the stage where I can actually start doing it, I really like to hit every day, I mean seven days a week. I don't like having days off. There comes a day when you get burned-out and you can't get up and do it. And some days are one-hour days and some days are ten-hour days. But I like to do it every day if I'm doing it.

I also like binge writing, when you get down to the final deadline and you have to do marathons and stay up all night. Which is fine provided you've left yourself a period to cool off so you can read it in the cold light of a couple of days later, and then fix it again. I like rewriting. I like rewriting over and over again. It never gets finished, as far as I'm concerned, right into the editing stage.

But I'm not methodical in setting myself a schedule. I never like to think, "Everybody wants this by next Friday, that means I have to do twenty pages a day." I don't want to think about it. I just do what I can. And I think a lot of writers, including me, have a tendency to get hung up on one scene or one segment and spend three or four days on that, and then you might even throw it out. Whereas, entire acts could go by in a single day or two days and never be looked at again.

I try not to write with stars in mind unless there's an actor already tied in somehow. But then, I don't think actors like it if you are writing, say a Jack Nicholson character, so that your character talks like Jack Nicholson and walks like Jack Nicholson does. I don't think an actor likes that. I don't know about Jack Nicholson, but I think what an actor likes is finding some sort of psychological depth and some sort of interesting behavior that the actor can take and make his own. If it's tailored for the actor, they feel you're doing their job. You aren't supposed to do their job at all—although sometimes they want to do your job.

So I try not to do it in that way, especially if there's a real, living person involved. I think the thing to do is to get that real living person down on paper, because that's what the actor will want to do. The actor is going to want to spend time with that real, living person and find out what that person is like. So you should be doing the same thing.

Sometimes I have to rewrite for a star who has just been hired, but then I try not to write to tricks. If there are actors who have cute tricks or do a certain thing pretty well or something. I try not to do that. I try to get a sense of something that would be interesting for them to do, and concoct scenes around that.

As far as having a place to write, I can work anywhere pretty much. In fact I have kind of a prejudice against people who can only write in Kauai or Acapulco. I like to think I'm a great hotel writer. I like it, being on location or something and holed up in a hotel and looking at an awful rug and awful wallpaper and doing it.

I really try to write only things that I'm really interested in. But I think the truth is, if you have any sort of reputation here, you never really write on spec. If you have an idea that interests you, generally somebody will want to buy it.

One thing I don't like, which no writer likes, is to write things that aren't produced. It's too much trouble and there's nothing more worthless than an unproduced screenplay. Nothing can be done with it, it's wasted ideas and energy. You don't want to do that, so you try to always be writing under some auspices where the movie will actually be produced.

I think my favorite unproduced script is one of the early ones I wrote, which would have been in the early seventies, I guess. It was about a hobo and a criminal, and I won't go into the whole plot, but I always thought it was a pretty nice piece of imagination. One of those things, it was on the verge several times and was never done, and it never will be done probably; its time has probably passed.

I think it's a myth that if you grabbed everybody's unproduced screenplays, you could go out and do them now. Most screenplays, even if they're about another period or if there's something timeless about them, are pretty susceptible. There's a moment in which something can get done, and that passes pretty quickly. And it doesn't just apply to genre pictures, it applies to whatever happens to be in the air at the time.

It's not just to be paid, it's the fact that as you spend more time on this earth, you have less time left. You certainly have less time to waste doing things that will never be seen.

DEALINGS WITH THE STUDIO

I like pitching stories to studios. You get the idea after a while, how to get somebody interested in something. It obviously doesn't always work, and sometimes the worst pictures you make are the ones they buy, and some fairly good ones aren't bought at all. But I like going in and batting something around. I mean, I don't have any strategy for it, I just like to talk about stories anyway.

One of the things I like to do now, before I start writing a script, is talking with the producer or whoever's involved in it first, sitting there and making everyone feel that if they have an idea they should contribute it. Sort of open it up.

I also think it's a good thing in a pitching session, where basically you're talking to somebody who wants to buy it, or who you hope is going to buy it, to be honest about the part you haven't worked out yet, but to be concise and interesting about the part of it that you have—the part that might intrigue them as well as you. And you kind of leave it open for ideas, suggestions, and so forth, because you're the one that's going to have to do it. Chances are that in a pitching session, nobody else remembers anything except you. They won't see you again for months. By then, they may have the very vaguest memory of this whole incident.

I haven't been in an adversary position with a studio recently. When I started, yeah. Because they don't know you, you have no reputation, you're just a kid, they're not paying you anything. And if they don't pay you anything, that means automatically that you're supposed to be treated like shit, and you are.

But I haven't had that lately, I'm happy to say. In fact, I've noticed an interesting thing. I do a lot of teaching and seminars and so on, and I always find the assumption that all studio executives are morons or venal or, in some way, destructive in the filmmaking process. The truth is, some are and some aren't; some are very helpful.

When you can say that you work with a studio and the studio's interest is really in the picture, and they aren't ham-fisted about twisting it for perceived commercial reasons, people always seem to be surprised that such a thing can happen. But I think it does for the most part. All studios are different, but there are a lot of intelligent, interesting people working there, who aren't particularly filmmakers but whose job it is to cause films to be made, and if they have something good to say you should listen to them.

I suppose it's just being honest after a while. If somebody's telling you something that's utterly ridiculous, you have to find a way to say that it won't work and you can't do it. And chances are, at least in my experience, people tend to be fairly reasonable.

If you give them a good argument, they'll agree. There are maniacs that nobody can get through to. But I haven't worked for any maniacs lately. And I don't need to work for any maniacs.

I find there's another reason why studio executives spoil a project. It's that they don't like it, and didn't like it from the start. It's not that they like it and want to make it better. If that happens, then you have a basis for discussion and it can be a reasonable, fruitful experience. But if somebody just doesn't like your picture, then there's trouble because there's no basis for discussion. They may be saying they like it and they may be saying that everything will be all right. But what's happening really is a gutting process.

They don't like failure any more than anybody else, maybe less than anybody else. My reading has always been that somebody thinks, "We've made a mistake here, we're going to live with it."

Hope dies hard. I think even in the worst disasters, everybody, right up to the last moment, has some kind of hope that it really isn't going to be that way. But then it gets tough because now you're not talking about the film anymore, you're talking about something else.

COGITATIONS

When I was at AFI, a student was a director, of course. Then there was no separation. You were a filmmaker, a guy who wrote and directed. Now it's compartmentalized, I think. But then it was the AFI attitude.

However, I wasn't ready to direct. As I said earlier, I'd done a student film that won awards and so forth, which now I think was a way of getting a job. I wasn't ready to direct, that's the truth. I wasn't ready to do the donkeywork on a television series, or prepare myself properly for it. There was something that intimidated me about it, and I know I shied away from it. And then later I wanted to direct. Later I thought I knew a little more about it.

When I directed *River Rat*, I shot it in my hometown in Kentucky. I had set the story with specific places in mind, not thinking that the local hero part of it is more of a liability than it is an asset. But you have relatives coming out of the woodwork that you never knew you had.

Well, you know, they're very nice people back there, so I didn't have any problems about that. It didn't make the film more difficult, but I don't think it made it any easier either, from the production point of view.

I still like writing. And I like writing things that interest me period, without tying them into anything else. I wrote a play that was produced here in Pasadena and in San Francisco, and another play in San Francisco a few years ago. And, like everybody else, I'm working on a novel.

But I have trouble planning next weekend, so I never thought of what I might be doing in a few years. I think it's a personality flaw in me, in a way. At least I've been told it is. It might have something to do with my writing style, which is the improvisatory nature of things, without a master plan or without a goal to achieve, a five-year plan, or whatever it is that you want to be doing then. I think I would try to look around for things that are interesting and that I would like to do—and do them.

CAROLINE
THOMPSON

There are few screenwriters on the American scene with such a singularly original cinematic vision as Caroline Thompson. Her darkly humorous portrayals of the fringe dwellers of this world are clarion calls for acceptance of the qualities we most desire in ourselves even as we seek to extinguish them in others. As she herself says, her films are driven by character rather than plot, featuring aspects of human nature that always manifest in the unexpected.

She lives in a one-story hacienda-style Burbank house equipped with backyard stalls for her five horses and a converted stable in which she writes. Her spectacles and well-spoken demeanor suggest just a hint of her bookish background, but her irreverent humor and openness, her ready smile and sometimes girlish giddiness, betray a love for the innocence and the spontaneity of eternal youth. One can imagine that Caroline Thompson at eighty years old will not be so different from the Caroline who before her thirtieth birth-

day had already penned Edward Scissorhands *for director Tim Burton* (Batman, Pee Wee's Big Adventure) *and cowritten* The Addams Family, *which has to date grossed more than one hundred million dollars worldwide.*

I was born in 1956 and raised in Washington, D.C. I always wanted to be a writer and wrote my first short story in sixth grade. It was about a blind flower vendor and this gold pocket watch he had. I don't remember what happened except that he finally had a customer and ran across the street with some flowers and got hit by a car. The last image was of his watch in the gutter. It was supposed to be really sad. I've been rewriting that story ever since.

After going to Harvard for a year, I switched to Amherst College for the last three years, where I studied English and also ancient Greek. I learned a lot from studying the classics—like how to sit there for hours and hours and hours, stumped, staring at pages of gobbledygook, staring and staring and finally cracking it. There was also the joy of reading one book a year, spending a year reading *The Odyssey*, getting to read so closely.

After college, I lived in the Amherst area for a year. I wanted to be a writer but didn't know what, how, or when. I made the attic of my house into my office, and it looked like Emily Dickinson's room—it was so perfect. Little perfect desk, little window, little rug on the floor, little chair. But still I couldn't write a word—it was awful.

I managed to squeeze out three short stories. Each word was agony. I was lost and had no idea. Maybe the reason I had no idea was that as far as I was concerned nothing being written or published made me excited or angry enough to respond. I remember reading or being told that the reason Henry James wrote *Portrait of a Lady* was because he was so pissed off at Gustave Flaubert for writing *Madame Bovary*—that it was really unfair to women, really cruel treatment, and he was going to show him how to do it right. There was nobody who was really getting my goat, so the need wasn't there to show them how to do it right, whatever right was. I just wasn't engaged. I was writing in a void and had no idea what to do.

I had a map of the United States on my bedroom wall. I knew

I wanted to go somewhere—I didn't know where, but I was drawn to L.A. I had come to Los Angeles in 1964 with my parents and announced to them that that's where I'd be living when I grew up. I guess I meant it. So the next summer I got in my car and came out here. The movie business stuff was very incidental to being here. My memories of L.A. were the deco buildings and Disneyland and the strangeness of being at the top of Mulholland and seeing both valleys at the same time. I had been eight years old when I was here before and literally hadn't been here since, but felt at home the minute we arrived. It was a lot like the Washington I grew up in, which is to say it was long and low and flat with lots of driving and a one-industry town.

I felt immediately comfortable here and had the social life that I didn't have in college. I knew a bunch of people and had names of people to look up when I got here, and everybody was extraordinarily welcoming to me. I had people to dinner just about every night for two to three years. It was amazing. Never had a life like that before or since. I couldn't do it now and I don't know how I did it then. I guess I wasn't working very hard, but it was really fun, a great phase. And a lot of those people whose names I had were in the movie industry, and I became really fascinated by the business of it. The concept of "the deal" was really funny to me— how people could get all worked up over the abstractions and forget that a movie was a story that you saw on a screen. It cracked me up. I thought it was hilarious and fascinating. Now I don't think it's funny at all.

I had this great urge to write a book. That's what I'd always wanted to do from the very beginning, and that's what I did. I supported myself doing a little journalism here and there and also by doing book reviews. That was actually a great gig. To make a hundred dollars a week was a lot of money at that time, and I was fast and I enjoyed it.

So I wrote a novel. It took me about eighteen months to write the first draft, and when I finished it, I'll never forget, it was Valentine's Day. And I read it and thought, this is horrible, and I threw it out. I had no choice, it was just terrible. So I spent about a month dazed; I have no idea how that time passed. Then I wrote the next draft of the same story but from a very different perspective in about nine months and liked it. A friend of mine who was a lawyer at the time, Nan Blitman, volunteered to agent it for me, and she asked me where I wanted it sent. I had been a big fan of Stephen King's early stuff, and he'd written a lot about his editor, Bill Thompson, no relation to me, unfortunately. Stephen

King had written so glowingly about him, I thought, well, I'll send him the book. So Nan sent the book to him, and it must have been a slow day, because he read it and bought it the next day. What a dream that was.

The book, *First Born*, is about a very uncomfortable subject for people—the story of an abortion that comes back. I thought of it as a black comedy, but the politics of that subject matter were pretty dicey at that time. Actually they'd probably be scared of it now, too.

For me it was a metaphor—I grew up knowing that I'd been an accident and that if abortion had been legal in 1956, I might well have been one. My parents already had two kids and had no plans for a third. *First Born* was about the unwanted child who's like, "So what, here I am. . . . " To me, that's close to as strong a metaphor as you can get. But the book basically was buried and died and may well have died anyhow, but it was buried because of the subject matter, and Bill couldn't get the publisher, Putnam's, to treat it any other way.

But it was a great thing in the sense that it was what I'd always dreamed of and there it was. And on the other hand, it was so filled with the reality of the politics of that company, the politics of the book business, the politics of this country at large. It was so fraught with issues that I had never considered, and so much happened behind my back that in a way I turned straight to the movie business because at least they fuck you to your face. They don't pretend it's all a gentleman's agreement and that there's a lot of gentlemanly stuff going on. They just do it to you. And I can handle that.

I had hopes for the novel to be a movie and had three directors in mind. I wanted it to go to David Lynch because I loved *Eraserhead*, Brian De Palma because I loved *Carrie*, and Penelope Spheeris because I loved her documentary, The Decline of Western Civilization. A friend had introduced me to an agent that he knew at ICM and basically strong-armed him into representing me. When I said that I wanted it to go to those three people, fortunately, Penelope was also represented at ICM at the time, so that made it easy to get the book to her. So he got the book to her, and she loved it and immediately responded to it and wanted to make it into a movie. I agreed *if* I could cowrite the script with her so I could learn about screenwriting.

We spent a long time writing the script on spec. We actually got a deal at MGM for it, but that fell through the cracks when the administration there changed. Then Hemdale wanted to do it, but ultimately it never went anywhere. It did a lot for me, though, because it was a script that everybody said, "What the fuck is this . . . this is really weird . . . I've got to meet the person who thought of this. . . . " So I got to meet a lot of people, and they were always surprised because I look pretty innocent, and they were always amazed by what must be underneath that sweet, young façade. "Who is this girl who writes these dark, grisly things?"

Penelope's agent loved the script and asked if I'd come over to William Morris with him because my own agent basically didn't have any interest in helping me. So I was eager to make the change, and John Burnham's still my agent today.

EDWARD SCISSORHANDS

Tim Burton and I met after *First Born*. I had a spec script set up at Universal when Frank Price was the head, and it was a very confusing time. They basically wanted the script to be something else, and I tried to give them what they wanted. It was a typical first deal—I had an office on the lot, felt really important and completely miserable. It was a disaster.

John Burnham did not know what to do with me, and so he had this brainstorm of introducing me to this other William Morris client that they had no idea what to do with—Tim, who'd just done *Pee Wee's*. John sent him my book, and they sent me a copy of *Pee Wee's*. I hadn't seen it, and I loved it. I thought, this was the most stylish, silly, goofy, charming, witty . . . I just thought it was spectacular. Tim was very embarrassed by it, at that time anyhow—he was very shy then. He really liked *First Born*, and we really liked each other, so we decided to work together, and that's how *Edward* came about.

Scott Rudin, who was head of production at Fox at that time, recognized Tim's talents and basically would have made a deal for the phone book with him. And Tim wanted to keep as much creative control over this material as possible. So we made a deal with Fox—Tim told Scott the barest bones, basically the image; we never really pitched the story. We took very little money up front in exchange for creative control all the way down the line. It worked. It sustained itself through three administrations at Fox.

I wrote *Edward* really fast, the first draft in three weeks. Tim was in preproduction on *Beetlejuice*, and when he is working on something—he's a little better now—but when he is working on something, he cannot for the life of him think about anything else. So it was literally six months between the writing of the thing and his reading it. And Fox had a very short turnaround period, so when I turned in the script, which was actually more than a year after I wrote it, they had a month to say whether they'd green-light it or not. I never took a meeting at the studio. I never had studio notes. Nothing.

It probably wouldn't have stayed so unique-feeling if we hadn't set the deal up the way we did. The only time the studio ever came in with remarks was during the tests at the end, things like why don't we try to trim this, or let's move that around. And by that point, Tim felt close to and comfortable with Joe Roth, who was the head then. It was more like a friendship, trusting thing as opposed to the studio ordering what should be done. That's how it stayed as clean as it was and how it kept its purity—which is really unusual.

One funny thing is that I've gone from being called weird—that's how my work was described before *Edward Scissorhands*—to being called imaginative. It's the same material, but now it's no longer weird, it's imaginative.

Edward opened me up a lot in terms of the surrealism that interests me, and it was all in all a great experience. The best part was sitting in an audience, listening to the girls do these puppy responses, "Aawwwhhh." I loved listening to the laughing, and I loved it when I could hear the crying at the end; I just loved it. It still gives me goosebumps to think about it. It was a really great first experience.

THE ADDAMS FAMILY

While Tim was off doing *Batman*, I trusted him that *Edward* would happen, but I knew I had to do other things. I couldn't wait for the four years it took *Edward* to get made. Literally, it took four years from the time I wrote it, and not because it was in development hell, but just because Tim was involved elsewhere. I wrote a spec script during the strike called "The Geek." It's still alive over at Disney, but I don't know what'll happen. It's about a guy who thinks he's a chicken, and it's about people's efforts to rehabilitate him.

I was still working on that when Scott Rudin approached me about doing *The Addams Family*. And I said absolutely not, nothing could interest me less. First of all, it's derivative. Secondly, the TV show was exploitative of this wonderful, original material. The TV show has some cool things in it because it has such a tone of the time, but who wants to get on this yuppie resuscitation bandwagon? Plus it's a huge studio movie, which I was not interested in doing. I guess with somebody like Scott all you have to do is say no, and boy, he gets so overstimulated by trying to change your mind. I kept saying no, and my agent was saying, "You should do this, you're not really doing anything now, it would be good for you to do this." And I said no.

I don't know how it happened, but Larry Wilson really wanted the job, and Scott wasn't sure about giving it to him. And then Scott had a brainstorm about putting the two of us together. And I guess I wasn't having a very easy time working or something because I said, all right, I'll meet the guy. Also because I had said to Scott, "I don't know from big studio movies; I don't know how to do it." I think instead of saying, "I don't want to," I said, "I don't know how," in my usual pretend-I'm-modest way. So the thinking was here's a guy who could help me do big studio movies. So I met Larry and he's smart and he's sweet and we liked each other.

And he understood the studio process because he'd been an executive and he'd been a screenwriter. Within a couple of days we were laughing a lot. He's a really sweet guy. He's a very funny guy. So I said yes. We saw a couple of the old TV episodes, but mostly we worked from the Charles Addams drawings from *The New Yorker*, where he introduced the characters and developed them. I was a real stickler for including his captions in the dialogue wherever we could, and actually the tableaus in the thing are from his drawings. We spent the next year and a half writing ten drafts of the thing and getting progressively in hell. A lot of them were so-called producer's drafts, which is the new mystery where the producer says, "I don't like it; I'm not showing it to the studio yet, do it again." And you sputter, "But, but, but." You never get paid for it, and it's something I think is terrible. But the whole experience made me want to be a producer.

I'm proud of *The Addams Family*. I think we did a good job. Should I have done it? Probably not. Did I enjoy it? I enjoyed the social part of it because it was a good time for me to have a partner. Did I enjoy the writing of it? Not really. Did I think that it was the right material for me? Not really. Would I do it again? Who knows?

AGENTS

I've been really lucky with agents. Not the first agents; they couldn't have been less interested in helping me. John Burnham has been wonderful, though. First of all, he was completely charmed by this very bizarre script. The fact that it was weird was what was good about it for him. And he had a knack at that time for collecting the sort of outré, fringe people—he represented a lot of the "Saturday Night Live" writers as feature writers, and Penelope was a client of his. He kept me working. He introduced me to people, and therefore I got the work or he found me work, and I worked steadily even before *Edward Scissorhands* got made. Nobody was interested in me until then. I don't know anybody else whose agent kept them working so steadily. I'm a real exception. He just kept me working all the time.

Another reason I like having him as an agent is I don't know if he even reads my work. I don't think it's his job anyhow. There are enough critics out there. Besides, we get along and we laugh at the same jokes—we're *sympatico*. I used to bait him and ask if he liked the gas station scene and he'd say, "Oh, it was great," and of course, there never was a gas station scene—in any of the scripts. I'd get a big kick out of it.

But honestly I feel that if I'm writing a script for Lucy Fisher, for example, I want Lucy Fisher's response. I don't really care what other people's responses are at this point. I have a pretty strong voice inside that tells me if something's good or not, and my bullshit meter is really strong.

I don't remember what I write. I have writer friends who can quote pages of their work. I can't do that. If somebody says, "Well, in the third draft, I like the way that so and so is handled," I'll say, "How was it handled—I don't remember." I don't sit on what I've done very much.

ADAPTATIONS

About two summers ago, I took on tons of work that I'm still trying to get out of the way. I actually work about ten hours a day now. For a while I was working on two things, one in the afternoon and one in the evening, but now I'll work on one thing really intensely in three- to four-week chunks. These are not originals, generally speaking; these are adaptations, so that's a lot easier. I think those adaptation gigs are just the best because it's already like having a first draft in front of you—you have somebody to argue with. Again, it's that old "argue with" thing.

PROCESS

I've been writing really fast this year. I've been doing first drafts in three, four weeks.

Computers are great. I learned them quickly and could compose on them immediately. I never could compose on a typewriter, and I wrote my book longhand, but I could immediately compose on a computer. I can't really explain why except that it was very comforting having a blank page only once. When you write "Fade in"—that's the only time you face a blank screen; your material is always there. Whereas on a typewriter, every time you put a new white page in, it's a blank—it would just drive me insane. For some reason, on a legal pad, having all those sheets of paper, I could do it.

I doubt I'd ever be able to dictate to anyone. It comes out my hands; it doesn't come out my mouth. That's one thing that's really hard for me in pitch meetings or story meetings—if someone asks me what I'm going to do with a piece of material, I really can't tell them because it doesn't come out my mouth. Fortunately, now I'm in a position where I just say, "Look, trust me or don't trust me, hire me or don't hire me." I'm not going to tell you what I'll do because I can't. Obviously that doesn't work across the board, but generally, people seem to respect that—right now anyway. I figure it's not going to last forever, nothing does . . . .

THEMES

I never took a screenwriting course, and I never read any of those books. I find them very destructive. They're bullshit because they make you think there's an answer. And there isn't an answer. There's no set response to any problem. The story should solve it for you; you shouldn't solve it for the story.

And I've watched enough movies in my life that it is an intuitive rhythm. Writing a screenplay is like writing a poem in that it is a very specific structure. But for me, it's so deep in there that I don't even have to think about it. The rhythm is there; it fills itself in. In terms of "the antagonist in the third act should do blah-blah-blah" or whatever, I just don't believe in it. Because that way you start forcing the material.

Everything I do is character-driven. That's where Larry and I both conflicted and complemented each other. He's a very plot-driven writer, and I'm a completely character-driven writer. In fact, I don't really understand plot. To me, it's like, can the character do this? I can't make a character do something that he or she wouldn't do. Ideally, when I start out, I know the characters so well that I set them in a situation and they respond.

There are a couple of things I'm always interested in. I'm always interested in outsider/insider themes. *Edward* is a perfect example of an outsider who comes into a community, and they accept him because he's different and they're pleased as all get out that he's different because it relieves their boredom. But then fundamentally he's too different and so they reject him. *First Born* was the outsider who wants to be inside. It's always the outsider who wants to be inside. Either people fucking them over or them fucking themselves over. Usually a combination of both.

The other thing that interests me is metaphors. I loved *Edward Scissorhands* because having these scissors for hands is a perfect metaphor for not being able to have contact. It's an obvious one, but that's what makes it such a good one. And *First Born* again, there's the metaphor of abortion. It is what it is, but it's also the perfect metaphor for unwantedness. That interests me a lot, and those metaphors don't come often, but I love them anyhow. *Edward* is a perfect example of the metaphor telling me what the story should be. It was a story that I just ran after. It just told itself, and my favorite writing experiences are when the stories tell themselves. Whether or not they're the best scripts, I don't know.

I really enjoy writing dialogue—but what's weird when a movie gets made is that often the dialogue gets winged on the set, and it's really hard to watch. It's hard not to have any say. Tim respected me enough to let me alone during the writing process. He did not try to control me or ride me or tell me what the story should be or what I should do. And I figured, well, I owed him the same courtesy during the directing process, because I respect him completely. But it was very painful sometimes. An actor would sometimes do something little like recasting a line but other times basically rewrite a scene. I find it really hard because it throws the whole thing off kilter. Your job as the writer is the overview, and it's very frustrating when other people don't respect that. Then I went through a period when I was throwing away dialogue because I figured, who cares, nobody's going to pay any attention to it anyway. And then I came back to being careful with it.

I really enjoy scripts. I love the form. I really think of them as a literary form. I think of them as a reading experience, and I work hard to set a scene for somebody and set the atmosphere and get them to feel the feelings that the script intends them to feel.

Francis Coppola is the producer of *The Secret Garden*, and I had one really long, six-hour meeting with him. And he said, "Well, you don't put stage directions in here." And I said, "I don't do that on purpose because I think it's the director's job and I don't want to insult them." But if you'll notice, I sculpt the script so that you are focused on what I consider important, so that if I want the shot to move to a new character, I'll put that character's name in capital letters and set it off. And do the description as the next— And Francis said, "Ah, the geisha method. That chair is not as comfortable as this chair. Come sit over here in this chair." It's a very subtle way of attracting attention without making it look like a piece of techno-garbage. Instead of making it techno-jargon, which is what a lot of scripts read like to me, it's a seductive experience.

I use some adverbs. I try not to use participles; I try always to make the verb active—instead of "is running," I'll say "runs." I try very much to keep it alive. My first draft is never for a director; it's for a reader. It takes me many drafts to get to a draft for a director, but I think of them as two really distinct things. I'm not sure if the studio people realize the difference and realize what's being done to them by my scripts in a way. Maybe they do. I'm always told how well written they are. I don't know about the "well" part, but they're certainly written; they're not throwaways. It's never just get the scene down.

I think scripts can be a wonderful reading experience. I really enjoy reading scripts. It would be nice for them to be published as literature. I'd hate for it to come to "the director has done damage to the movie." But screenwriters work really hard at what we do, and it's a very distinct job. I did feel hurt by the pieces written about *Edward Scissorhands* when it was always Tim Burton's vision, or ninety percent of the time it was Tim Burton's vision. There was a lot of me in that movie, and anybody who knows me can see me in it. But to the public at large, it wasn't mine at all, it was Tim's completely.

DIRECTING

I'm scared to death of the prospect of directing and also exhilarated by it. I don't know if the instincts that I've depended on my whole life will remain intact. I write scripts by instinct, by what feels okay—this feels right here, this feels right here, this feels right here. Well, when I stand up there, am I going to know what feels right or not?

One of the most fun jobs I ever had in this business was years ago, every Friday, being the music coordinator on a soap opera. It was my neighbor's job, and he took a psychiatric leave every Friday, and so I filled in for him. It was really sweet of him to give me the job because I needed it terribly and it paid great, a hundred bucks a day. And I was really good at it considering I have very pathetic musical sense. I can't sing or anything, but I spent my teenage years watching soap operas and I had right-on-the-money instincts about what music went where and when it came in and when it went out. I had no reasons, it was all gut.

I keep thinking, well, I've watched a lot of movies; I hope my guts tell me what's right and what to do. I'm sure my first two weeks directing will be spooky. One reason I want to do a directing debut for a major studio is Larry Kasdan's theory—which is to say it might be the only chance I ever have, so I might as well put everything in that movie that I ever liked about movies. Which is a good theory. And secondly, do it at a major studio because then you can afford to buy the people who can hold you up where you're going to fall down, like a cinematographer who costs some money and an editor who costs some money. If you go low budget, you are bound to get people who are as inexperienced as you are, so you're all sort of flouncing, flumphing, and floundering together. And I don't know if it's the truth, but it's certainly what got in my thinking.

I've noticed in my life that people like doing things for me. They like to take care of me. They worry about me, so they step in to take care of me, and I think that's a really good trait for a director to have. I've noticed, like Tim, that's how he gets such good work out of people, because people are always worrying about him. And he's real good at certain aspects of the job that are up and above the fact that he's got a great eye. He's really good at blocking people out, keeping them from asking him a lot of questions that they shouldn't be asking. He's very good at isolating himself and keeping himself unapproachable. Which is a good thing.

The fact is, I'm not trying to trick anybody. If they want to give me an opportunity, I'd like that opportunity. I helped Tim with a documentary this summer about Vincent Price. It's still in very rough stages and Tim's theoretically the director, but I directed a few of the interviews that he couldn't do, and I really liked it. I came home, and I was just full of myself . . . . *Ay yi yi yi yi* . . .

Though I must say, I don't know how much I like the way a director is chained. I love my freedom—it's the same thing about not having kids. I love that I can go write when I'm writing. I'm about to go to Mexico on Saturday for ten days to write a script. I love that I can do that.

In *Edward* there was a long time between the writing of the script and the making of the movie, and the parts that I didn't like, I didn't take personally, particularly. But I took very private parts that I did like, and I just enjoyed that process so much. Where if I had directed it, it would have been a completely different experience because of the responsibilities. Whereas not being responsible ultimately but being connected to it in such an intrinsic way was such a joy. I brought my parents out for the premiere, and when that red carpet came out it was just great to show them—see? And that meant a lot to me, going to the premiere and having it filled with people.

I'm a shy person, and I don't really enjoy any of the little taste of celebrity that I've gotten; I don't enjoy it at all. Which surprises me—I actually thought I would enjoy it, but I don't. And I dress less well than I used to. The success that I've had has given me enormous confidence, but enormous confidence to be me instead of enormous confidence to become an image of myself. It gives me confidence to go back to the sort of slovenly, withdrawn, self-involved at its worst, horse-crazy kid. I guess that's maybe why I would never want to be an actress; I wouldn't want to go out and promote myself. It doesn't appeal to me. Which is interesting. I had thought that I would want to be photographed or whatever, all those things that I haven't wanted.

I don't know what I would do if I didn't have my horses. They mean childhood and they mean fun and they mean something to daydream about besides work, and they literally keep me alive. Last week I was in bed sick and I didn't ride for six days and I was so depressed.

When I was a little kid, horses meant a lot to me, and then it stopped. It was classic: horses to boys and back to horses. I've always been a real girl that way. And the thing about horseback riding is that it's not about what people think it's about. It's not about dominance or anything like that. It's about cooperation. I think that's why women like it so much, because it's not about bullying this fifteen-hundred pound creature into doing it; it's about finding your common ground with this beast. And it's not about taming the beast; it's about joining the beast, which is really a girl's thing. It's about equals. It's not about who's in charge here.

In contrast to this business, which is all about power and dominance. Growing up where I grew up and going to the colleges that I went to, everything was so competitive. And I was never good at competitive sports and wouldn't play them. I watched my mother screaming at my brother and sister on the swimming team to win, and it made me fold up inside. I've always been competitive with myself, but I couldn't play tennis as a kid because if the other person really wanted to win, I thought, well, let them, who needs it, who cares? If they want it that bad, they should get it. But then if people try to bully me . . . As a youngest kid, I learned real early how to get around that. You either give them a look or you just say no, and I can be very stubborn.

In meetings with executives, I'll say no if I think they're wrong. But I'm very accommodating if they have a good idea. I've always thought of meetings as if they were cocktail parties. I think of it as my party—I'm trying to make them comfortable even though it's their office. Otherwise I can't see where I fit. I can't see myself as their servant, which sometimes infuriates people.

More than one producer has told me that I don't behave like a writer. Well, I don't know how writers are supposed to behave.

NICHOLAS KAZAN

Nicholas Kazan by physical resemblance could be mistaken for the fifth lost Marx Brother—with his bushy mustache, retreating hairline, and surprising wit—but he would definitely be the black sheep of the family. His peculiar perspective of the American scene includes such dark nightmarish scenarios as At Close Range, Frances, and Reversal of Fortune—all of which deal with themes of betrayal, family warfare, and frustrated carnal desires. His early work as a playwright and his journalistic pieces for Newsweek and the San Francisco Examiner included such inclinations toward violating societal taboos. And while his reputation has always been as a writer of solid craft and risk-taking substance, he has, with an Academy Award nomination for Reversal of Fortune, emerged from the quiet obscurity of production company A lists to top-drawer prospect for rewriting big-budget studio blockbusters. On the cusp of a directing career, he will always remain a writer at heart, steadfastly maintaining his individuality and independence.

I never wrote fiction.

I began writing plays, because one day, during my senior year in college, I heard voices. Literally. One line of dialogue. And then another character answering. And the first character (whose name I didn't even know) responded. So I rushed to a typewriter and wrote those three lines down. And the characters continued to speak, and I continued to write down what they said. As if I was taking dictation. This went on for an hour and a half, and when I finished, I had written the first draft of a one-act play, a play which was professionally produced some years later.

Around the time the play was produced, I began writing screenplays. And in the same way that I "heard voices," I saw pictures. And the pictures seemed even more vivid than the voices.

I believe I have more of a gift for screenwriting than I have for playwriting, but I wish that wasn't so. Playwrights have far more control over their material, and if they are successful, because of that control, they seem to be a generally happier lot.

The first plays I wrote in college and after college were scary and funny. One-act plays mostly, but I did have a full-length play done in Berkeley in '71. After that, I worked with a bunch of friends, and I wrote mostly comedy. Some edgy comedy, some more benign, but always comedy. And then I read an article by Michael Goodwyn in the *Village Voice* about the *Texas Chainsaw Massacres*. I went to see the film after reading this piece, and I thought it was fabulous—very scary and very funny, a really macabre sense of humor. And that inspired me to write a horror script.

I wrote the script very quickly. I finished it, looked at it, was revolted by what I had written, and put it away. Took it out again nine months later and said, "Well, this is really pretty good." Worked on it, refined it, finished it, and sold it. Everyone felt that this script was substantially more accomplished and more interesting than the comedy stuff that I had been writing. It got made poorly. Destroyed. I took my name off it.

That led to my getting the job to rewrite *Frances*. Both of these scripts were written in an extremely visual style—primarily a sequence of images without a great amount of dialogue. It was the process of seeing those two films in my mind that made me feel I'd found my calling.

Based on *Frances*, I was hired to do *At Close Range*. Although for two years I got compliments on the script of *At Close Range*, it didn't lead to a great amount of work until the film was made. That was my break.

Before filming, there was a reading of the script *At Close Range* with all the actors. They laughed all the way through it. They said, "I can't believe this script. I didn't realize it was funny." But the director and the actor Sean Penn both felt they were making a tragedy and that there was no place for humor in tragedy. So they systematically took the humor out of the film as they made it.

I wrote *Patty Hearst* as a black comedy, and Paul Schrader, whose work I greatly admire and who made a very good film, was not interested in the humor in my script. I had wanted to write a play about Patty Hearst when she was still in captivity, and I very nearly got a commission to write it. It was going to be very, very wild. Essentially, there was going to be a series of scenes, each a fulfillment of various fantasies the public had about her—because every time you had a fantasy about Patty Hearst, it would turn out to come true. She joins the gang, robs a bank, sleeps with gang members. So I was thrilled when I was approached to write the screenplay many years later.

Afterward, I read that when Patty Hearst saw the film Schrader made, she was very relieved because she had been afraid that the film was going to be sex, drugs, and rock and roll. And I laughed because I thought that my original script *was* sex, drugs, and rock and roll. Paul wanted to make—and did make very well—an austere film that concentrated on the horrific aspects of her experience. A film about personality and how personalities change. I was shooting for something broader and more raucous, and I think she probably wouldn't have liked my film at all.

So it wasn't until *Reversal of Fortune* came out that I lost my reputation as a humorless writer. A reputation I found rather amusing because, prior to selling my first screenplay, I had supported myself, albeit not in high style, as a comedy writer.

REALITY-BASED MATERIAL

It appears from the outside that my interest or talent lies only in reality-based material—I hope that's not the case. A few months ago, I counted it up, and I've written fifteen scripts, of which six were based on real people and events. But it happens that almost all of those six have been made.

Even wild flights of imagination should feel true. And what often happens when I'm watching a Hollywood film is that I'm quite excited and engrossed, and then all of a sudden something happens that is fraudulent and I'm thrown out of the movie. It was good up to a certain juncture, but that's it, good-bye.

When you're writing something that is based on real material, you have landmarks. You know that you're going from this tree over to that rock. You can go anywhere in between, but those two landmarks are there and cannot be moved or changed. And then you try and find the true path between them. I've written other scripts that, while they may not be wild flights of imagination, I hope have the same ring of truth—the feeling that events follow a natural and inevitable order.

I wrote a script about the conquest of Mexico, about Cortés and Montezuma, and I did research for four and a half months before I wrote a word of text. Fortunately, that was during the writers' strike, so I had no distractions and I could afford to do research for four and a half months. Then I wrote the script in a month. Usually I write the script very quickly, but I write extensive notes first. I calculated that my notes on that film were three times as long as the script.

For *Reversal*, I did research for about three months. I write notes to myself about the characters, about the situation, about the story until I just can't do it anymore and I'm ready to explode—I've reached critical mass. Then I know I'm ready to write the script, and at that point I write a draft in ten days. I lay off for a couple of days, then rewrite it in ten days, lay off for a couple of days, rewrite it again in ten days, and at the end of that time, I have a draft. But my notes will contain whole scenes in rough forms, snatches of dialogue, many fragmentary or tentative outlines, and so forth.

After the thirty-four days are finished, I tinker with it and read it over until I can't stand it anymore. Usually I read it once a day, make a few changes, put them in my computer, print it out, and do the same thing the next day. Finally I start showing it to my friends and get their reactions and then make the changes based on what they say. When I've run out of friends, I turn it in.

The other script I wrote during the writers' strike, I didn't write any notes for whatsoever. I just sat down and wrote it. I don't know if it will ever get made—it's a very strange little film—but I wrote it the way I used to write plays: just by writing what came to me, letting the story guide me, rather than the other way around.

I write six, six and a half hours a day, sometimes a little more, but I find it very draining to write at that pace and concentrate. I start more or less first thing in the morning. Otherwise my attention is elsewhere, and when my attention is elsewhere it's hard to bring it back.

WORK ETHIC

If I take a job, I do whatever's required. A lot of writers are rip-off artists—if they can get a couple hundred thousand dollars, a half million dollars, to rewrite a script, they do it, and if people don't like it, the writers say, "Fine, I've got my money." Their reputation may suffer a little, but if their next script is good, it doesn't matter. But I believe that if you are contracted to build a house for a certain price, you should build a house for that price. If you're contracted to write a screenplay for a price, you should write a screenplay for that price.

I don't mean that I will do endless rewrites for free—usually what happens when people don't like your work is that they want you to rewrite it for free. And almost invariably that's a prelude to getting fired. When they say, "I want you to do this for free," what they really are saying is "We're going to give you a last chance to fix it, but we really don't think it's going to work, we don't want to pay you anymore, and when you finish doing this last thing for free, we're going to fire you. In fact we're already talking to other writers." That's usually what that means.

However, if you *suggest* doing the work, if you say, "Oh, I see, there's a problem, let me fix it"—that's another thing. I've been very involved in the last three films I've worked on—in the production on some of them and also in the editing room. I volunteered my time—I wanted to make the pictures better. And I believe I did.

STRUCTURE

I don't use any cards, I've never done that. I never think about a film's structure in terms of acts. To me, an act is for a playwright and a play because the audience *gets up* and leaves and goes to have something to drink and you've got to have something to bring them back. In a movie, there are different rules. The audience doesn't get up; you *don't want* them to get up for popcorn.

You have to keep them in their seats. So the rules are quite different, and I think this emphasis on acts is misleading.

You *do* have to have a novel premise, and it's helpful if the piece can shift one way and then turn another, and in the end you should have a resolution that feels like a natural fulfillment of everything that came before. That is true of every story. If I tell you a story about something that happened going to town today, that story will have a beginning, a middle, and an end. It better, or else you're going to say, why the hell did this guy tell me this boring story.

There are many movies now that start with a bang. Something happens, bingo, someone's kidnapped. You know what the thing is about. But you don't *have* to do that with film. You can start at a leisurely fashion with nothing seeming to happen, and as long as the audience is entertained they will stay there, provided that by twenty minutes into the film, you've given them an idea of what the movie's about. You can't do that on television. You have that leisurely twenty minutes and you cut to a commercial, they're gone. In a three-act play, you're going to have a break after about forty minutes. By that point, you want the piece to be sufficiently involving so that the audience is buzzing at intermission.

In essence, there are *no rules* with film. It's like a dream: it can take many different forms. The important thing is that what happens should be continually surprising and in retrospect seem inevitable. If you have that it doesn't matter what your structure is.

Reversal of Fortune doesn't have any discernible conventional structure. That film was sustained by having a number of small mysteries. You didn't know what was happening with Dershowitz and his girlfriend, you didn't know how the medical case was going to turn out, you didn't know whether von Bulow was lying, you didn't know what was wrong with his relationship with Sonny, you didn't know what really happened. You had all these mysteries, and keeping them alive was like a juggling act. You toss a ball up in the air and the audience wonders when the ball is going to come down. And then one ball comes down, and you throw two more up and they're waiting. There's that feeling that something's up in the air, something's going to *happen*—that's suspense, that's structure.

STYLE

Ideally, you should be able to write a screenplay with virtually no words whatsoever—a sequence of images. I try to tell the reader not only what they see, but how they *feel* about what they see. You can shoot a tree in any way that you want—so that it's frightening or so that it gives you a sense of beauty and you smell the clean air. Or you can shoot the tree so that there's something mysterious and hidden in it. So if you simply say "a tree," as Walter Hill does, he knows what he's going to do with that tree. Being someone who's just begun directing, I don't have the record or clout to just write "a tree" and for people to trust me, so I try to give them the experience of what they are going to feel as they're watching that tree. So I often use "we see," "we feel," to give that sense.

I don't write a lot of description because when I'm reading fiction I don't like to read a lot of description; I get bored and skip it. I don't know why it's there, telling me what color a house is and how the clapboards are this or that—I don't even know what a clapboard is. What I'm interested in is people, what they do, what they love, what they fear, why they laugh.

REVERSAL OF FORTUNE

It was a challenge having somebody around who the movie was actually about. I have a great deal of admiration for Alan Dershowitz. He's very smart and in an interesting way. But I couldn't portray him with license. That was the most difficult aspect of writing this script. If I portrayed him with faults he didn't have, he would say, "My God, you can't do that, I'm not like that." And if I portrayed him with faults that he *did* have, he would say the same thing, out of denial.

He wrote a piece for the *New York Times* before the film opened—they asked him to write about what it's like to be portrayed in a film. He recited two or three things in the film that he would *never* do—he's not really like that, he'd never get angry and smash a phone. Essentially, I think he was hedging his bets in case the film wasn't well received. And he always thought that it was crazy to have Sonny as the narrator—that it was a ridiculous and weird approach and the film would fail on that account. So he was quite pleased when the film did well.

Reversal was about how we all thirst for justice, but we only find it in the arms of God. In other words, Sonny being halfway to God has found justice and knows the truth and so forth. Dershowitz is involved with trying to make the legal process as clean and as just as he possibly can. But it's an impossible task because judges are corrupt, defendants want to get off, and so forth. And

Claus, whatever he did or didn't do, will presumably receive his just reward when he dies, but until then he is legally innocent. And yet there's this nagging feeling that the guy's done *something*—he *smells* guilty. Of what? I suspect he may have stood by and done nothing while Sonny tried to commit suicide . . . or he may have promised her he would let her go ahead with it . . . or he may simply feel that he could have done more to save her, to prevent her from her despair. But whatever that smell of guilt was, it's beyond anything the legal system can touch. He is, technically, "innocent."

I had plenty of work in the preceding three years, but as a result of *Reversal*, suddenly people knew my work who before were unfamiliar—especially other filmmakers, directors, producers, and executives. Not everybody in America saw the film, but most in the film business saw it and liked it and felt that Jeremy Irons deserved his Academy Award.

EXECUTION OF THE VISION

I find work to be completely separate and distinct from the rest of my life, and usually the better it is, the more separate it is. I don't remember my dreams and likewise if I'm working well and it's coming from my unconscious; I don't even *remember* what I'm writing. It's a separate universe, and it only exists in my office. That's what makes it so rewarding when a piece is fulfilled the way you imagined, as it was in *Reversal of Fortune*. And so frustrating when it's not. But you stand in and you receive your criticism regardless of whether it was well done or poorly done. And the horrible thing is you never really know if the fault lies with you or the execution.

The prime benefit of my father being in the profession is that I believed in myself. I graduated from college; I moved to San Francisco and then to Berkeley. I supported myself as a free-lance journalist making very little money—three thousand, five thousand dollars a year. I think one year I made ten thousand dollars, but it was basically subsistence living. I continued to believe in myself and believe that if I kept working, my work would get better and better and eventually I could support myself. That could have been a delusion. As it turns out, it wasn't. The prime benefit of having my father in the profession is that I believed that I could succeed during many years when rational experience would have suggested otherwise.

It's difficult to be judged in terms of somebody who was so

successful, because there is a tendency to think that if you're in the same profession as your father, you were somehow handed your success. Some innate talent has been passed down and doors have been opened and things have been made easy for you. I don't believe there's any innate talent handed down; in fact, quite the reverse. Most of the children of people in the profession don't have talent, and most people who have the benefit of going to the best schools and getting the best presents and having the best vacations don't make the best workers. They feel that life owes them something. I don't believe that. And I've made my own way. So I hate it when people refer to my father, because I project onto myself a whole set of assumptions—stereotypes that I find noxious.

Directing is a lot of fun, but I think of myself primarily as a writer. I think the writer is the more creative position—the person who creates something out of nothing. Everybody else takes something and transmutes it. At their best, they're alchemists—they may take a piece of lead and turn it into gold. If they take a bad scene and make it good, that's great. But they're still taking something and turning it into something else. They're not the original source.

PACING

I frequently have people comment to me, even on scripts that aren't made, what a "fast read!" I have a very fast metabolism. I speak quickly, I'm from New York, I like things to move. Obviously there are times in any drama where you want to slow things down and build tension, but by and large, particularly at a movie, I hate to be bored. I want something to be going on. And I've had trouble with people doing my films whose pace is not my internal pace, especially combined with the natural tendency for actors to milk every moment, as if every scene should be a great scene. Well the truth is that every scene should *not* be a great scene. If every scene has the same emotional weight, then the film will have no variation, no sense of pace . . . you won't get the sense of building to something and then coming down from it.

The problem is that when scenes run long—which they very often do, and they do because the scenes are so good, so rich, so *endless*—the movie runs long. And when that happens, the movie always suffers because something essential (and I say essential because if it weren't essential, it wouldn't be there) has to be cut. And there's a ripple effect: one plot point is cut, so everything leading up to it has to be cut, and everything that follows from it, and suddenly you have massive rhythm problems that you never had before. But there isn't any choice. When a movie is too long or too slow, something *must* go.

I want people to experience in the movie theater what people experience reading the script—that it's moving almost too fast for them—like the moment when you're on a roller coaster, when you start going down and you know you can't stop it. Uh-oh, I'm on this ride and I don't know what's going to happen. One of the exciting things about being able to direct is making sure the film is paced the same way as the material.

AGENTS

I had six agents in six years. The last one has been my agent ever since and hopefully will be for the duration. An agent has to be part psychiatrist, part coach, and obviously a deal maker, but the last and most obvious is the least of it. There are so many bewildering and reprehensible things that happen to writers in the course of almost any project that you need somebody that you can call up and say, "They're telling me *this* or doing *that* to me!" And the agent can say to you, "Just follow your instincts, don't do anything to destroy your material, just make it as good as *you* can make it and if they want more, tell them to fuck off. . . . " In essence, a good agent just reminds you of what you already know, which is you can only be yourself, you can only do the work you do, you have to follow your talent.

The hard thing is finding an agent who shares your sensibility and really responds to your work. What often happens to writers is that they'll write one script that is good and they'll get an agent. Then they'll write another script that is also good but different, and the agent's taste will be more narrow than the writer's talent. I can't say that my agent has liked every single script that I've done—there's one that he really didn't like and there's another that he had some concerns about, and some are better than others. But by and large, to varying degrees, he's liked almost everything that I've done, and so I'm extremely fortunate.

The danger of the big agencies is that you can get lost. No matter who you are as a writer, if you are the most famous and accomplished writer in the profession, your interests are still insignificant to an agency next to the interests of their most important actors or directors, who command fees that are multiples of whatever you can get as the highest paid writer in Hollywood. So inevitably, in the first year or twentieth year, your interests will not coincide with the interests of a more important client, and your interests *will* be sacrificed. That's why I would never go with a big agency. Yes, they can package you. Yes, they can give you certain numbers of jobs. But anybody can make a deal for you, anybody can send your script out. The important thing for me is the personal relationship—someone who will guide me and keep me from going insane.

WRITERS GUILD

I'm glad that there's a Writers Guild. I'm psychologically and temperamentally ready to strike at any time for as long as they want. I love to strike. When we're on strike, I get a lot of work done. I write on spec, as everyone else does when we strike. I'm a writer; I can't help writing. If they told me I couldn't write, I'd have to quit the guild. If you're really a writer, what you *do* is write. They can't make you not write. Anyway, I think that it's good that there's someone looking out for our interests. I think that the health plan and pension plan are good things.

But one problem with the guild is that its the only guild of conscience. All writers—and all dramas—are concerned with moral issues. It's hard to find a movie or TV show that doesn't have some kind of moral question at its core. There's no other profession within this business that is concerned with morality. Obviously, there are writers who are in it simply to make money or to move on to another profession, but even they must deal with morality in their writing.

Therefore, because the writers are involved with moral questions, the Writers Guild is willing to strike over principle. If the companies say to writers, "We're going to have cutbacks," the writers say, "Fuck you, we're going to strike," even if we're not really going to gain anything by it. The other guilds say, "Wait a minute, I have this great part," "Wait a minute, I was on the verge of my big break," wait a minute this or wait a minute that, and they never strike.

Another problem has to do with the fact that the guild embraces everyone so it doesn't accurately reflect working writers. I don't know what would be fair in that regard, but it is unfair to have the decisions of the guild have the greatest impact on those who don't have the greatest say. The Directors Guild has the same problem.

The WGA also oversees arbitrations. I've been involved in two arbitrations, and I've been an arbiter myself twice. I think the process is extremely unfair—an abomination. You're at the whim of people you don't know.

It's unfair to have it be anonymous. Everything about the process should be more open. You should be able to read what the other writers say, and respond to it. And after a decision is made, you should be able to read that decision and appeal it. I know this would create a great deal more animosity between guild members, but these decisions do affect people's careers and therefore their lives—anybody can say anything, can tell any lie, and right now you are powerless to know about it and defend yourself. Also you're given a list of arbiters and you can cross out as many names as you'd like, but the list is three thousand names long; you may forget some person with whom you had a fight five years ago. There may be people on there who are good friends of the other writer or writers involved and you're unaware of that. I didn't cross out my friends; why should they cross out theirs? The two arbitrations I've been involved with, I was never asked whether I was friends with the writers involved, if I knew them.

And the worst thing is that mathematically speaking, there are bound to be decisions that would not reflect the judgment of the guild as a whole because you're picking three people at random. If ninety percent of the guild would rule one way and ten percent would rule the other way, sometimes you're going to get two out of three that are in that ten percent. You're going to get a wrong decision.

There's an inherent paradox in the system—"screen *credit*." Credit implies that you are rewarding quality. You don't give credit for something that's bad. And yet the rules say quality shouldn't enter into it.

But it's absurd not to judge quality, even though quality is subjective. I was arbiter on a film where the first writer wrote a good script. The second writer rewrote it, and it was terrible. The third writer did a good rewrite, and then the second writer was brought in *again*, to write the final draft and fucked it up. So I said—is this screen credit or screen blame? Do these people really want credit? This guy has made this film worse. I want to give credit to the people who did good work, and I want to give the blame to the other people.

The whole process is infuriating. Guild rules favor the first writer, but it's often harder to rewrite a script well than to write the first draft. It's hard to think of an idea, to create something, but it's *really* hard to make it good. You process it, you get your first draft out and it's got some good things in it but still has problems, and then you've got to solve those problems. Solving those problems really takes skill and concentration—you have to know what to keep in and what to leave out.

I think they should have a panel of permanent arbiters made up of distinguished writers who have retired. Each writer on a film would write their statement and then be able to read the other writers' statements and would speak publicly before the panel if they wished. If one writer requests it, then any writer who wants can come and listen to what the other writers say and speak themselves. It would be a public process.

ADVICE

To succeed, you have to move to Los Angeles so that the people who read scripts *meet* you. There are so many people writing scripts, so many scripts. What you always want—whether it's going to the doctor's office when you have a problem or trying to break in as a screenwriter or applying for a job at McDonald's when there are thirty applicants—you want to get whoever is in charge to *notice* you. You don't want to be seen as part of a faceless mob; you want to be somebody special. In this case, you want your script to be read with careful attention, with a sympathetic eye.

Writers write. That's what we do. I wrote maybe ten screenplays before I was able to sell one. I wrote six treatments that were completely worthless; there's no point in doing them. I wrote a lot before anyone every paid any attention—some of it was good and some was mediocre, but I believe the only way you improve is by continuing to do it.

I can't speak for other people. I can only say that if I believe in what I'm doing and I'm excited by it, I'm a pretty good writer. If I don't believe in what I'm doing and I'm not excited by it, I'm a mediocre writer. And I don't see how anyone else can be otherwise.

Trying to please other people is always a problem in life. If you're doing what other people want you to do, you're following their program and not your own. Eventually they will ask you, in one way or another, to betray yourself, and if you follow that long enough, you will never find the way back.

JOE ESZTERHAS

A self-styled lightning rod for controversy, Joe Eszterhas is a two- fisted iconoclast who lives and dies by sales of original screenplays and never compromises his version of any story he wants to tell. He has earned, by the sweat of his brow and pounding of his manual Olivetti, the fattest paycheck ever received by a screenwriter—a cool three million dollars for Basic Instinct—*which bought a colonial-style mansion overlooking the Pacific Ocean north of San Francisco. The tranquil security of this environment is in stark contrast to the furor and firestorm Eszterhas has gloried in from the beginning of his highly successful career. His much-publicized rift with the head of one of the most powerful agencies in the entertainment business is the stuff of which legends are made—he declines to speak of it now other than to say it was a frightening and counterproductive time in his life. But one gets the feeling Joe has always defined himself—in his life and in his work—by a compulsion to stand up for what he feels is right.*

He has already carved a considerable niche in film history with a diverse collection of commercial successes like Flashdance, Jag-

257

ged Edge, The Music Box, Betrayal, *and* Basic Instinct. *For now, what he wants most is to enjoy his two teenage children and the company of his wife in a peaceful environment while continuing to generate undeniable heat with his steady stream of bold—and often controversial—American screenplays.*

I came to America at the age of six after years of repatriation and refugee camps. I didn't know the language and had a thick accent until I was seventeen. I fell in love with reading when I was thirteen, fourteen years old and read incessantly. After a while I thought that maybe I could write. I always loved this country. Early on, I fell in love with baseball and with rock and roll. My parents didn't get it. They tried to influence me to be involved in Hungarian activities, but I always resisted. I was a shy, introspective kid. I ran into a lot of prejudice, a lot of shit, and got called names because of the way I was dressed and the fact that I was an immigrant.

I grew up in Cleveland on Lorain and Forty-first, which is a polyglot kind of ethnic neighborhood, blue-collar and poor. Lots of Appalachians, Puerto Ricans, blacks, Hungarians, Germans.

Two things helped me the most—one was reading and the other was journalism. I was really shy, and journalism forced me into situations. I did street reporting and also did general assignment reporting. Journalism forced me to understand American society on a firsthand basis. I found that considering my ethnic background and shy nature, it was invaluable.

I was never a good student. Partly because I put most of my energy into reading. I read voraciously. I made long lists of things that I read, and one year, I remember, because I would write everything down and take notes on it, I read something like three hundred novels.

There was a paperback bookstore on Lorain and about Thirty-seventh where they sold books for five cents with the cover torn off. The guy who ran it got to like me and he saw this strange kid coming in every day and so he would just give me the books and I'd return them to him. I read indiscriminately. I'd read A. J. Cronin in one day, and the next day I'd read Tennessee Williams. And then I got hooked on writers like O'Hara and Steinbeck and

Robert Penn Warren and started reading everything they had written. I never imagined that I would write screenplays, because my love was really the novel.

My father worked for a Hungarian language newspaper that was run by Franciscan priests whom I loathed. I was always around them because the apartment where we lived was above the printing shop where all the priests worked. They were insensitive, anti-Semitic, and just the coldest people. Seeing these people firsthand, I very quickly rejected religion.

My parents would try to get me involved in things like being an altar boy. My mother was very religious, but I rejected the whole thing. I think I rejected Catholicism certainly by the time I was in my teens.

I was an only child, lonely and inward. When I was about thirteen, fourteen, I loved baseball. I loved playing baseball, and in the beginning I would do it alone. We lived next to the Num-Num Potato Chip factory, and it had a gigantic brick wall. I would throw the ball against the brick wall and it would come back and I'd throw it with my right hand and I'd have a stick and I'd swing at it with my left hand. The ball would go up against the wall and I'd run and catch it. And I'd have the Indians' lineup on a chart on the wall, and I'd say, "Well Bobby Avila's up now." And I'd do this whole commentary to myself. "Al Smith is up—Smith hits a long fly ball. . . . "

And then I started playing ball with the other kids. But I was scrawny. I'd had rickets in the refugee camps. And I wasn't very good. There was an Irish kid who kept making fun of me and calling me "greenhorn" and other names. One day, he was up at bat and I was watching the game and he started pointing to me—"Look at that fucking D.P." When he turned around up at bat, I went behind him with a bat and hit him in the back of the head. He wound up in the hospital for about a week and almost died.

It changed my life. I was there at the hospital. I saw the parents. I realized on some basic level that if I kept living the way I was, nothing was going to come of my life. And that on a human level, I could get hurt or other people could get hurt. It was then that I started making my lists of books and writers. I think I created an artificial fantasy world for myself with my world of books, an escape from Lorain Avenue. Somehow in the course of this, I developed the deepest sort of yearning to be a writer.

I went to an all-boys Catholic high school. Each year they accepted six or so poor kids on scholarships. I was one of them. It was a terrible experience. All the other kids were wealthy. The Brothers who taught were worse than the kids. I remember Brothers saying, "Oh, look, Joe's got a new pair of pants on today," or "Joe got a haircut today, isn't it great?"

The six kids who got in on scholarship ate together for the next four years. Literally. Six poor kids at one table for lunch. You couldn't go off campus. And nobody mixed with you, so you were together with those same kids. So of course you hated each other. You were forced on each other.

In my junior year my parents moved to Youngstown, Ohio, and I went to a coed high school. Simply having girls there had such a humanizing, gentling effect that in some ways, looking back on it now, it was like I'd left the army.

Then in my senior year we moved back to Cleveland. When I went back to the Catholic boys' school it was different because I knew how to handle it. I had seen a different world and I couldn't be picked on and I stopped being hurt. At that point, high school became my conduit to America—my prism besides the streets. And I finally became aware that there were people in this world who were warm and gentle and human.

EARLY CONTROVERSY

My social involvement and activism in journalism started in high school. It was over Tennessee Williams. I wrote a glowing review of *Night of the Iguana* for the Catholic student newspaper. They came down on me and called me into the principal's office, and I'll never forget: I'd gone down to the library and brought in a collection of critical raves calling Tennessee Williams one of the great American writers. I read the reviews to these priests and Brothers. And they just sat there smugly and said, "If you write one more word about Tennessee Williams we're going to throw you out of this school because he's a degenerate."

So about two months later, in the final issue of the paper, I snuck a little box in, in the back, saying that Tennessee Williams's *Glass Menagerie* was playing at Lakewood High School or Rocky River High School on such and such a date.

At Ohio University, I studied journalism. I loved reading the school paper. In my sophomore year, I wrote a feature story and went beserk when the editor of the paper dared to edit it. The editor got so pissed off at my attitude that he took the copy and threw it into the wastebasket. He was a friend of mine and he liked me, but here I was saying, "No, you can't edit this, you can't touch it.'' He picked the person who was going to be the editor of the paper in my junior year. And I couldn't get along with the new editor at all, and so by my junior year, I wouldn't work for the paper. I immersed myself in Faulkner to such a point that I was hardly going to classes. I was living with a girlfriend. They nailed me for it—having women in your room was illegal at that time—so I was on disciplinary probation, and my grades were totally shot.

At the end of my junior year—this was in '65—it came time to select the person who would be the editor of the campus paper the next year, my senior year. You had to have, I think, a 2.5 grade point average and you had to have a clear disciplinary record. Well, I didn't meet either requirement. And I really wanted to be editor of the campus paper. So some friends and I got together, and we got kids to sign petitions saying this lunatic should be allowed to compete to be editor of the school paper because, never mind the other stuff, he wasn't such a bad writer. We got something like eight thousand signatures on the petitions. The school demonstrated its liberalism and allowed me to compete. It was a screening process where you appeared in front of the deans and presented what you wanted to do with the paper. I went in there and said that the paper was shilling for the university and that kids were waking up to the war, the civil rights movement, to music, and that the paper should reflect these things. To my amazement, they gave me the job. Everyone was astounded that this crazy person was now the editor of the campus paper.

I ran a controversial newspaper that was involved in antiwar and civil rights activities, that dared to grade teachers, that explored the relationship between town and gown.

My life in my senior year was the paper. To the point that at the end of my senior year, it looked like I was going to flunk out. I had powerful enemies, because the journalism department was the victim of much of my criticism. I felt that they were training kids to be automatons—not writers, but technicians. And I questioned their own backgrounds and accomplishments. They weren't happy with me.

So here I am, running this unpredictable school paper. I'm flunking out of school. There's no way I'm going to graduate. When suddenly, in late April, out of the blue, I'm informed that I've won the William Randolph Hearst Foundation's award as the outstanding college journalist in America. I'm going to the White House to be given a medal and a thousand dollars by Lyndon Johnson. Great publicity for the university. In fact, I go up to

Washington, to the White House, Lyndon's busy at the ranch that weekend, but Hubert Humphrey is there and he hands me the medal. Someone must have briefed Hubert and told him I was an immigrant, because he treats me like I just came off the boat hours ago. He says things like, "You know Joe, this is a portrait of our own Dolly Madison. . . . "

They still didn't let me graduate, mind you; I never got a degree. We tried to work it out; I had a prof who really loved me. He went all the way to the president of the university and said, "Look what this guy's done, look at this paper." But they wouldn't go for it. Interestingly, a couple of weeks ago I was notified that I'm being considered for an honorary doctorate at Ohio University. I love it. Yogi said it: "It's not over 'til it's over."

POLICE BEAT

I worked at the *Cleveland Plain Dealer* from '67 to '71. I started on the police beat, where I met my wife, Geri. For about six months I did everything there was to do. I won some statewide reporting awards. At the end, I had a column called "The Observer," which was very Jimmy Breslin. I covered the Browns one day, a shootout the next day, political campaigns the next. It was wonderfully existential; you never knew what the hell was going to happen. When you walked in, you had no idea what you were going to do that day. That's where I really learned a lot about people and American society.

While at the *Plain Dealer*, I wrote a book with a friend of mine about Kent State—which I was covering on a day-to-day basis—called *Confrontation at Kent State—Thirteen Seconds*.

ROLLING STONE

I moved to *Rolling Stone* magazine and was there from '71 to early '75. The country was our landscape. Jann Wenner, the editor, had great instincts. He let you follow any story that you thought was compelling.

Rolling Stone was the most exciting place to be. It wasn't just a music publication—Jann was going after *Esquire* and *New York* magazine. There was amazing freedom in the sense that you could write fifteen thousand words about one subject. Ads would be dropped if your piece ran too long.

I saw a five-paragraph wire story about a kid in Missouri who had shot up the town he was in and had killed himself after a struggle with town residents. I took it to Jann and said, "I think there's something here." It was at a time when America was polarized, and the wire story made it seem like this was a confrontation between longhairs and townspeople. And Jann looked at the story and said, "Yeah, go do it." The next morning I was on a plane.

At *Rolling Stone* I never did profiles. The judgmental part of it bothered me. I was nervous about the notion of sitting down with somebody for two or three hours or looking into their lives for a week and making judgments about them as human beings.

I hoped I was moving toward writing novels. I saw myself going from magazines to bigger nonfiction books and then moving into doing novels.

FIRST SCREENPLAY GIG

I got a call one day from an executive at United Artists, and she asked, "Have you ever thought of doing screenplays?" And I really hadn't. We were living in Mill Valley. Jann was about to go to New York, and I didn't want to go to New York because I'd fallen in love with California, with sky and trees and the sea. Geri was pregnant with our son, Steve. I didn't know what I was going to do, and I said, "I really haven't thought of doing screenplays." And she said, "Why don't you come down and let's talk about it?" So I went down and she liked me and she liked my work and she said, "Why don't you go back home and come up with a half dozen things that you think might be original screenplays."

One of them was *F.I.S.T.* It even had that title in the original notes because, accidentally, I'd stumbled on the notion of a truckers' union, and when I named it, it turned out to be F.I.S.T.— Federation of Inter-State Truckers.

Well, she said I had to go back down and talk about it, and when I got there she said, "I think this could be a good movie." I said, "Well, I don't know." They made a deal with me where I think I got eighty thousand dollars for everything—the research, the screenplay—and it took me about six months to research it.

What I did was go across the country and talk to old labor organizers everywhere about what had happened to them and especially what had happened in the thirties when labor unions were forced to go to muscle to protect themselves against banks and bankers.

Now at the end of that process I wrote something that was an eighty-page document, neither a treatment nor a screenplay, somewhere in between fact and fiction. A truly bizarre document. They read this, and they said, "Well, we don't know exactly what this is, it's interesting, we're not sure what it is, but we think it has potential and we'll hook you up with a director."

They brought Bob Rafelson into it, and Bob and I met in L.A. and liked each other and made plans for me to go to Aspen to work with him on the story. The day before I was to leave, Bob called and said, "When are you coming in—I'll meet you at the airport," and I said, "Great." Everything was set up. That night, the executive called from [United Artists] and said, you know, don't go to Aspen because Bob Rafelson is no longer the director on the project. The next day when I'm supposed to land in Aspen I'm still home in Mill Valley, of course, and I get a call from Bob Rafelson who's at the airport and says, "Where the fuck are you?" And I said, "What are you talking about, didn't anybody from U.A. call you?" And he said, "Well, no, why?" And I said, "Well, because they told me you're not the director on the project."

A couple of weeks go by, and U.A. calls to say that Karel Reisz is going to be the director. Same thing happens. I get together with Karel, he comes up to Mill Valley, I make plans to go to London with him. Day before I'm to leave, I get a call saying don't go to London because Karel is no longer the director on the project. This time, I say, "Wait a minute, did you tell him?" And she says, "Not yet, but we're going to."

They bring Norman Jewison in. Okay, so now it's time to get together with Norman, and we meet in Malibu. Then we meet at a little lake outside Toronto; we're meeting all over the place. He's very generous with me, and he's trying to help me with how to shape this thing and what to do with it. And I'm resisting him and saying, "I'm a writer, you're not, and you've done nothing except all these commercial pictures." You know, I don't have the fucking brains at the time to know that I'm getting the kind of help that's going to last me my entire lifetime. So Norman and I go through this thing and we work off and on for almost a year. And he insists on taking me into every production meeting that he has. And I say to him, "Why do I want to meet all these business schmucks?" And he's like, "Kid, just listen to me, will ya, and come into the damn meeting. . . . "

Well, what I learned from him didn't just have to do with the rhythms of the screenplay and with shaping something for the screen; it was much deeper. I learned from him that you can get into fights with studios and you can have differences, and if you're smart enough and feisty enough, you can win. And there is no

reason to simply accept what they tell you, and there is no reason
to compromise unless the compromise is going to help the finished product itself because there are ways around it. Sometimes
there are political ways, sometimes there are direct ways where
you simply say no.

What Norman really gave me was the best kind of graduate
course that you can have in screenwriting and also in terms of
defending your material, because he's a very feisty man and he
doesn't take bad advice well. Good advice, he takes very well. But
bad advice he doesn't take well. I saw him go through this whole
process and learned an awful lot. The man has incredible pa-
tience and generosity. I know: he put up with me.

My first draft on *F.I.S.T.* was roughly three hundred and eighty
pages. And of course I didn't want one word changed. There was
a monologue that went on for five pages. And Norman picked
this thing up, and he said, "Well, kid, this weighs like *War and
Peace* but it doesn't read like it. . . . "

One time, at a lake outside Toronto, he and I had some horrendous disagreement about something in the script. I think it
might have been the monologue, which I was willing to shorten
but not take out of the movie. And he kept saying, "You don't
understand, fuckin' two and a half pages, it's like an oration,
they're going to walk out of the theater." We're going around
and around and I'm being typically difficult and he asks very in-
nocently, "Have you ever been sailing?" And I said, "No, we
didn't have sailboats on Lorain Avenue." And he said, "Let's go
sailing. I've got a little boat out here." So a storm's coming in
and I've never been sailing and he and I go out on this boat and
I'm scared shitless. This thing, this object, this boom or whatever
the fuck it was, is moving around and I've never been in a sailboat
before, the clouds are coming in, the wind is kicking up. Norman
looks over at me and says, "Feeling a little dry-mouthed are you,
kid?" And I say, "Oh, no, I'm okay." And he says, "Well, just
don't disagree with me ever again and I'll never take you sailing
again." He was a terrific person to learn from. He has great integrity. He also taught me to remember never to get too cynical.

JOE VERSUS ROCKY

Stallone got involved after we had sent the screenplay to De
Niro and were really hoping for De Niro and we got no answer.
And Sly had just come off of *Rocky*. Stan Kamen was his agent and
William Morris also represented Norman, and they got it to Sly

and he flipped out and wanted to do it. But he started going around town saying he'd written this new original screenplay called *F.I.S.T.* I went ballistic; I had worked on it for two and a half years. He hadn't written one word of it.

So one day I get a call from an Associated Press feature writer who wants to do this pleasant little story about how happy I must be that the biggest star in the world is in my movie and it's my first screenplay. So I proceeded to say that this man's a thief; he's stealing my script. That I'm Rocky Balboa and he's Apollo Creed. And besides that, I've been in more barroom brawls than he's been in, and he fights like a sissy. And, of course, the feature writer uses that as his lead, and it goes out all across the country.

I was bottled up with this anger, and it just came out. It turns into this big thing, and Sly sets up a punching bag at home that has the name Eszterhas written on it and has himself photographed hitting it. So now it's a very big public thing. *Esquire* winds up doing a long article with a photograph of Sly with the punching bag.

So Norman says, "Listen, Jesus, this is a real problem; you better not come to the set." And Sly at this point starts changing the script. He doesn't want to die, that's the main change, but he can't get his way on that, and the biggest change in the script is that I have Johnny Kovac responsible for directly ordering the murder of his best friend. So Sly's change is that the best friend is killed, but Johnny Kovac had nothing to do with ordering the killing. The friend is killed by the Mafia, and Johnny didn't know about it.

It comes time for the premiere with red carpets and spotlights in the sky. And I go with my wife and my dad, and the studio takes great care to seat us away from the *F.I.S.T.* table. We're down in the boonies. And Stallone is over with Norman. Well, Norman comes over at some point and says, "How you doin', kid?" And I say, "I'm doing fine and I'd really like to meet Sly." And he says, "What do you want to meet him for?" He looks at me suspiciously. I just want to meet him.

So he leads us over, and Sly's got a bunch of bodyguards around his table and my wife is with me and we go up to the table and we start sizing each other up. He gets up, very nicely shakes my hand, and he's about to shake Geri's hand when my wife hauls off and punches him in the gut. Not real hard, but hard enough. So Stallone backs up, grabs his gut, looks at her, and says, "Boy, you throw a mean punch for a girl." I had no idea she was going to do that, but it broke the ice. And ironically, we got to be friends subsequently.

I think part of Sly really thinks of himself as a writer. And I thought *Rocky* was a really good script. Later on, a couple of years go by, and he is directing *Staying Alive*, and I get a call from him, saying, "Listen, come on down here; I want to talk to you." So I go down to the set, and he brings Travolta in, and he says, "Well, Johnny and I are having problems. We're disagreeing on stuff and it needs a rewrite and I thought you'd be the perfect guy to bring into this situation." And I said, "Sly, you fucked me once, now we're friends, why do you want to fuck me again?" And he cracked up and said, "Yeah, you're right."

F.I.S.T. died its first weekend, and it got some of the worst reviews in the world. And I went to my studio executive friend afterward because it was my first script, and she and I were walking around the Warner Brothers lot one day, and I said, "Listen, what's going to happen now? I've written my first screenplay and it comes out and dies; what's going to happen with my career?" And she said, "Nothing. You wrote a wonderful script that everybody in town read, Norman Jewison had made fifteen hit movies, Sly's going to be a gigantic star, nothing's going to happen." I said, "What do you mean, you mean there's no responsibility?" And she laughed and said, "Not in this case."

FLASHDANCE

I knew that I would essentially put the same sort of energy into rewriting *Flashdance* as if I were writing it as an original script. I was going to turn the script upside down and over again before it was done, and that's exactly what happened.

Flashdance in its original form had an old married guy and Hell's Angels. At one point the girl was in the Fashion Institute of Technology and her dream was to be a fashion designer and she was from a prestigious family. But I wanted to write the kind of girl that I knew and loved on Lorain Avenue.

Well, we went to Toronto. I was amazed. For one thing, I didn't know that Toronto had a subculture of strip bars. They would do things like bring a *Penthouse* Pet in for the weekend and put her into a big hall, and they'd have ten thousand people in each night to watch her strip. It was amazing. But there must have been thirty other strip clubs in Toronto, and they were all making big bucks.

So this one particular place was where Tom Hedley—the original writer—had hung out, and Tom found girls who did stripping but did it in sort of an artsy modern dance kind of way, and that's where his notion came from. And of course the other thing he brought to it is the title *Flashdance*, which is a brilliant title.

I was surprised by the success of the film. Although one of the things I never know and I don't think about is what's going to happen commercially to a picture I've written. Everyone thought *F.I.S.T.* was going to be a mega-hit with Stallone in it and Jewison directing, and it went right into the toilet the first weekend. Partly because of the script, I think; I never did get it right. So I came to the conclusion that you simply never know what's going to happen. And I think that a writer shouldn't think too much about what's going to happen at the box office. He should just write it his way and tell the story he wants to tell without considering commercial prospects.

DEFENDING YOUR WORK

I think writers deal with directors differently, depending on the situation. To give you some examples—when Adrian Lyne insisted that Alex be raped by her father at the age of eight, I said I won't do this, I'm sorry. I tried to convince him in a two-hour discussion why this was absurd, and the man wasn't listening to me. I simply walked out. Now that was never done to *Flashdance*, and I'm sure that one of the reasons it never happened was because I threw such a shit fit at the whole notion of it and actually walked out on them.

On *Jagged Edge*, Frank Price and I had a major disagreement on the ending because he felt that Jeff Bridges had to be innocent and that the ending should be a clinch ending with Jeff and Glenn and that the killing be done by the red herring, by the tennis pro. And I said to Frank that if we did that, we had a television movie on our hands, that what made this special was that it was a man who had a sterling-silver front who was capable of doing this this time and he probably wouldn't do it ever again unless he needed to do it again in terms of his career and his life. Frank said if you end this way, you're going to lose thirty million dollars at the box office; you simply can't end this way.

What I did was, I walked out of the office with Marty Ransohoff, who, incidentally, in my case was a terrific producer and supported me one hundred percent. And we walked out of there, and I said to Marty, we can't do this; it'll destroy the whole thing. He agreed, and he had heard through Herb Allen that Frank's days were numbered. So he said to me, why don't you take an endless amount of time to do this script. So I waited and waited and waited and Frank was still there and I kept calling Marty, saying, how long is he gonna be there? He's still there. So, finally they remove Frank, and Guy McElwaine took over the studio. And the very first call Guy made was to call me and say, okay, you got your ending on *Jagged Edge*.

Costa and I had a disagreement on the ending of *Betrayed* because he wanted Debra Winger to come back pregnant with Tom Berenger's child and to go face the townspeople pregnant. And I said, look, you can't do that; it's a can of worms that complicates things so much that it's going to take away from the whole effect of simply confronting the townspeople. He and I had a recurring discussion that went on for three or four days, and finally he saw my point. But it took three or four days.

I'm not saying, incidentally, that you can win in all cases. But I am saying that if you are willing to put your energy and your passion and your brains into defending what you've written, you can win. On *Basic Instinct*, for example, Irwin Winkler and I pulled out of the project because we felt that Paul Verhoeven was going to destroy the script. So we have a public blowout after the very public three-million dollar sale. Paul brings another writer in to try to make the changes. At the end of a five-month process, they discover that the changes won't work and that I was right, and they come back to me. And he comes out publicly in the media and says I didn't understand, I just didn't understand the man's script. He's a rare, gutsy man, incidentally; few directors would have done that. But I'm sure that had I agreed early on, and said, okay, Paul, we've got to get this movie made and you're right, the movie would have been destroyed.

WRITING ON SPEC

If you insist on defending your work, you are going to be perceived as difficult. If you're willing to write scrips on spec, then you can overcome that simply because of the quality of what you write if what you write is good. If you insist on working only on deals, then I think your reputation for being difficult will catch up to you.

I think in my case, the fact that I've had a lot of movies made and that I've had three big hit movies helps. And I've also tackled difficult themes and have written some small-scale movies and that also helps. I certainly didn't always have this kind of strength in terms of defending my material, but some of the defenses that

I've made have really proven to have been good for the finished product.

Working on spec is a source of power, but it's a risk too. You roll the dice. On three of my spec scripts, on "Checking Out," on "Platinum," and on "Magic Man," nobody came. I couldn't sell them. It hurts when you do a publicized auction and nobody comes. The whole town sees what you've written, and the whole town says, "No, thank you." But I think the writer has to understand that's the risk. That if he sits down and writes about something that's close to him instead of trying to set a deal up, then that's the risk and sometimes that happens.

If you view yourself as someone who wants to serve the needs of the director, the studio, etc., it's an inner trap, I think, in terms of your mentality. It's a trap for your work because it's going to hurt you in terms of your self-respect, in terms of your inner dignity. And that's going to be reflected in your work. It also will be reflected, incidentally, in your family life and your friendships and all of that, because it's a kind of spiritual denial and an acceptance of a certain kind of second-class citizenship. If you are a tool to be used by a director and a studio and a producer, then what is it that makes it worthwhile for you to do that? Is it simply the money? And if that's why you're doing it, then you're hooking. You cut past everything; you're just hooking, putting your legs high in the air.

The morality of a character, the morality of a premise, the morality of the message—that has to be the writer's concern. I think it's almost irrelevant whether that's a concern of the studio or not, but it has to be the writer's concern because you are creating something that comes out of your guts, your heart, your brains. No human being is plastic. If you give away parts of your deepest self or if you betray parts of your deepest self, that's going to be reflected in your work and in your life. There will be consequences. There will be damage deep inside you. I think if the writer doesn't protect himself against that kind of damage, it's going to be reflected in his work and his view of himself. He's hurting himself, and no amount of money is worth causing that kind of damage to yourself. Human beings have a self-respect they shouldn't violate, because if they do, there will be tragic consequences.

PROCESS

I use a manual typewriter because I learned to type on two fingers, and I hit the keys so hard that if I use my daughter's electric typewriter or if I use a computer, then everything goes down. And the trouble with it is that they don't make manuals much anymore. Olivetti makes one, but only one, and you can only find it in places like old people's resorts. We spend a lot of time in Florida in the summer, and whenever we go to Saint Pete or Tampa or something, I pick up another manual so I've got five or six Olivettis that aren't old, but are manuals.

I don't like computers; they're too cold. If I get stuck on a script, and it happens to me all the time, then I will retype it from page one. If I'm stuck on page fifty, I'll literally take it and retype all fifty pages. But in the course of doing that, I find where I made a mistake. And I've discovered it's a great editing process to do it that way. Computers make things too easy, I think, and the other thing is, technologically they're just too cold for me. I used to write in longhand until five years ago, and then I would retype, but now I go straight into the typewriter.

When it comes to moving passages around, I would rather rewrite that entire chunk, because it's more fluid and organic that way. I'd rather rewrite, physically retype ten pages, because then the transitions are better.

I work on one thing at a time, and I seem to take two months off afterward—sometimes more. I seem to need the time to refill my well.

I have always been right on the money with my estimates of when I'll be done. If I tell them they'll have it by a certain time, they'll have it by a certain time.

When I write, I write from ten in the morning until four in the afternoon. If I'm really into it, I'll write until about four, and then I'll swim or I'll walk, I'll have dinner, and then I'll go back to it at eight o'clock or nine o'clock at night, and I'll go until two or three o'clock in the morning. It gets very intense sometimes; I mean, *Basic Instinct* I wrote in three weeks because it was so intense. It just came sort of exploding out. *Music Box* took about four months. *Jagged Edge* took about a month. It depends on the script.

When I'm really into it, I can't put it down, including weekends. I get up at four or five in the morning and take notes. If it's really going well, I feel like I'm taking dictation. The characters are talking to me and I almost feel like I don't have much to do with it anymore. Usually at a certain point the characters take over, and I literally don't know from one day to the other what they're going to do next. I have a family relative who is a schizophrenic who hears voices, and this is not far removed from the dialogue process. I hear them talking to me, and I just put it down.

I know the ending, usually, and it depends on the piece whether or not I do an outline. On *Jagged Edge* I did an outline. On *Big Shots* I didn't, on *Checking Out* I didn't, on *Basic Instinct* I didn't. They were just going from one day to another, and I didn't know what they were going to do. On *Music Box* I had a rough outline because of all the courtroom technicalities.

I'm always hooked into a rewrite contractually, but I've been lucky with studios because I've worked with good directors and good producers, and the notes are filtered through them usually. I would rather the producer or the director read their notes, and then we'll talk about it. The rewriting depends. On *Music Box* I did one rewrite, and it had to do with the ending of the picture. The ending that I had on it was completely different. It was a different third act where the ending was the same in the sense that the father was guilty, but a whole series of events happened differently. And Costa's feeling was that if we went with that it would move it into a different kind of direction, and the ending would lose its impact. And I agreed with him. He was right. Thank God he had the brains to see it.

SELF-CENSORSHIP

The reason I suggested changes to *Basic Instinct* didn't have to do with pressure from a political lobby; it had to do with a meeting that I had with a dozen people in San Francisco who were the members of the leadership of the gay community. And what emerged from the meeting as far as I was concerned was they they were wrong about the fact that *Basic Instinct* is homophobic. It's not.

I reserve the right to create a villain who is bisexual, black, white, albino, green, purple, whatever. But what they also pointed to were a half dozen or so of what I would call insensitivities in the script that were mostly verbal in dialogue from certain characters. For example, there was a veteran cop, Gus, who made certain cracks that a certain kind of veteran cop would make. But I felt that if the cracks weren't answered or if they were just allowed to slide, then these cracks in the mouth of a star could be taken as things to emulate by young people. And I felt that you could correct these things by either answering them or by altering them, and at the same time not affecting the plot or the narrative structure or the spine of the piece or the characterization, not hurting the piece at all, and removing the insensitivities. And I felt that since I wrote it and it was my creation, I had the right to suggest changes to it.

In a sense, I was working in a different corner of the same ring that I've worked all these years, because instead of resisting people changing my script, I was arguing for my right to change it since I created it. I wasn't motivated by whatever street protests there were. Incidentally, the street protests that everybody talked about amounted to thirty people waving placards and yelling. The street protests didn't pressure me into making changes—the lucidity and the strength of conviction and the honesty of the people I met with in the same room made me reassess certain things in the script. And I think that if you create the script, if you write an original screenplay and if you then decide that you made some mistakes in the script, since you are the father of the child and since it's your baby, you should be allowed to make those changes.

AUTEUR THEORY

I think that the auteur theory is the result of generations of critics. Two generations at this point. And I am convinced that other generations of critics will look at writers of original screenplays, compare their body of work, and compare the body of work of the director who's done some of those. I think the day will come when a writer's body of work will be judged as a body of work. Because it's a much more honest way to make a judgment.

I have dealt with the same themes in *Jagged Edge* and *Betrayed* and *Music Box* and *Basic Instinct*. The themes are: Do we ever know the people we love? What part of us remains private and inviolate? How do we manipulate each other? Where is deceit in the context of love? Now, okay, those are four pictures. The first was directed by Richard Marquand, the second was directed by Costa-Gavras, the third was directed by Costa, the fourth was directed by Paul Verhoeven. If you look at those movies as a body of work, to whom do those themes belong? Do they belong to the three different directors on those pictures? Or do they belong to the man who wrote all four pictures?

I think the day will come when screenplays are published as literature, and the minute that happens, it's a death knell for the auteur theory. Because when you have a screenplay published in its original form, people can go see the movie, and they can determine whether something was improved or hurt by a studio head or by a director.

I think the writer's name should be right there next to the

director's. I think that if it says a Norman Jewison film and if it's
an original screenplay, then it should say a Joe Eszterhas script.

ON ENTERTAINMENT

I write to entertain. I'm proud of doing that. I think one of the
things that's been forgotten by writers today is their entertainment function. Dickens wrote to entertain—his books ran as se-
rials in newspapers. It has somehow become low-rent to say that
you're an entertainer. I know that I love sitting in a theater, sitting
with the people watching one of my pictures when they're entertained or when they're moved to silence or when they cry. It's
one of the things that I love the most about what I do.

FAMILY

I don't like to fight, but I am willing to do it. People who don't
know me see me as this two-fisted fighter. I don't like to fight,
and I consider myself a gentle person. My kids are very gentle
people.

On a normal day-to-day level, you have no idea what harmony
we live in, our family. I'm very close to my family. They give me
a base that's almost like a fortress. We live in absolute peace with
each other and with the world. But periodically, something hits
the fan. I will say to them, I will sit them down and go over whatever disagreements I may have become embroiled in. I think
that's one of the ways kids really learn. It was never done with
me. My parents were old-style European parents, and there wasn't
a lot of communication. There was very little physical affection.
I've very consciously brought my kids up differently. It's ironic. I
have a two-fisted reputation, but if somebody saw me around this
house for a week—my God, my housekeeper pushes me around.
She does. She's a former sergeant in the Marine Corps. She
pushes me around, and I say, "Thank you."

I've been married twenty-three years. By the time I got to L.A.
I had been through a certain amount of late-sixties, seventies life-
style. I certainly had it together enough by the time that I started
doing screenplays that I knew I wasn't interested in screwing my
marriage up and I was really devoted to my family. Success came
at a good time.

KARL SCHANZER has been a stage and film actor, a private investigator, a non-fiction writer, a motion picture story analyst, a prize-winning documentary and theatrical filmmaker, and a major studio development executive.

At present he is producing a movie based on his experiences as a private detective and developing other film projects involving the FBI and KGB.

He lives in Los Angeles with his wife, Marilyn.

THOMAS LEE WRIGHT has written screenplays for every major studio including *New Jack City* for Warner's. He is the co-writer of Avon Books' *Working in Hollywood* and lives with his wife and family in Seattle, Washington.